PARTNERS in GRIME

Other titles by Neil Anderson

The Lead Goat Veered Off

Forthcoming titles

A Dingo Stole My Shoes
And Other Misadventures in Australia

A Hedgehog Ate My Soap
And Other Misadventures in New Zealand

PARTNERS in GRIME

Escaping the Rat Race

Cycling Across Canada

Neil Anderson

CYCLE LOGIC PRESS
COALMONT BC
www.cyclelogicpress.com

Partners in Grime

Copyright © 2005 Neil Anderson

All rights reserved. No part of this book may be reproduced or transmitted in any form or by any means, electronic or mechanical — except by a reviewer who may quote brief passages in a review to be printed in a magazine, newspaper, or on the Web — without permission in writing from the publisher. For information, please contact: Permissions Cycle Logic Press, Box 2B C8, 432 Campbell Avenue, Coalmont BC V0X1G0 or e-mail permissions@cyclelogicpress.com

The author and publisher have made every effort to ensure the accuracy and completeness of information contained in this book; we assume no responsibility for errors, inaccuracies, omissions, or any inconsistency herein. The author and publisher disclaim any liability in connection with the use of this information. Any slights of people, places, or organizations are unintentional. All editorial and grammar errors are intentional, just to keep you interested.

Cover photo: Sharon "Kissed by God" by Neil Anderson
Cover design: Inspired by Sherry Stinson at cooldesigns.net
Author photo by Sharon Anderson
Interior photos by Sharon and Neil and a tourist from France.
Editors: Paul Carter and Heide Blackmore
Canada map concept: Peter Newman
Maps are not to scale and are for illustrative purposes only.
Some names have been changed.
Special thanks to Lori Thomas for her limitless vivaciousness.

FIRST EDITION 2005

National Library of Canada Cataloguing in Publication
Anderson, Neil.
Partners in grime / Neil Anderson. —
ISBN 0-9686740-1-1
1.Anderson, Neil.—Journeys. 2.Bicycle touring. I.Title.
GV1044.A53 2005 796.6'4'092 C2005-901348-3

ATTENTION CORPORATIONS, UNIVERSITIES, COLLEGES, SCHOOLS, AND PROFESSIONAL ORGANIZATIONS: Quantity discounts are available on bulk purchases of this book for educational, gift purposes, or as premiums for increasing magazine subscriptions or renewals. Special books or book excerpts can also be created to fit specific needs. For information, contact: Special Markets Division, Cycle Logic Press, Box 2B C8, 432 Campbell Avenue, Coalmont BC, V0X1G0; phone 1-866-825-1837 or e-mail specialsales@cyclelogicpress.com

PRINTED IN CANADA
10 9 8 7 6 5 4 3 2 1

Table of Contents

Yukon Territory
Northwest Territories
Nunavut
British Columbia
Alberta
Saskatchewan
Manitoba
Hudson Bay
Ontario
Québec
Labrador
Newfoundland
Gaspé Peninsula
New Brunswick
Nova Scotia
Point Pelee
N
CANADA
© Peter Newman

For
Norman and Kiaira

Sand Castle

Sand castles never just grow

they are pulled up hand by hand

not far from the roaring foam walls

built for a moment when

their maker relaxes and sits back

while the tide pushes forward

till the water crumple-crumbles it

as flat as light brown paper

under a running water film

Castles are not made

for any purpose except

to create inside creation

a kind of sculpted echo

of a medieval time

a mind print

left in the sand

of God's running hour-glass

by
R.Z. Blackmore

Numb

> **"Twenty years from now you will be more disappointed by the things you didn't do than by the ones you did do. So throw off the bowlines. Sail away from the safe harbour. Catch the trade winds in your sails. Explore. Dream. Discover."**
> ~ Mark Twain

Sharon's sister, Faye, allowed us to camp in a spare bedroom. We completed our pre-trip list and were eager to get underway. Or were we? Having totally dismantled our lives we dilly-dallied, clinging to the last vestiges of everyday normality.

Early each morning, Faye would get ready for work. We would dance through what became known as THE GOODBYE ROUTINE. We hugged Faye. She hugged us. She left for work. It began to rain. We would peer out from our cozy confines at a never-ending skyline of grey drizzle. "Hmmm," we'd muse. "Perhaps tomorrow?" It was truly the August of our discontent.

After a week of ritual goodbye hugging, Faye returned home from work one day and found us still camped in her living room. *"Haven't you guys left yet?"* she implored. "I'm tired of saying goodbye!" (Sharon's family began to suspect we would never leave. It had all been a caper — a ludicrous childish ploy for attention.) Were we just hoaxers?

"We have to wait for the right launch window," we assured them. But, truth be known, stepping into the void, the great unknown, frightened us half-silly. It felt like one of those naked-in-public dreams — except we were awake.

The more we contemplated, the worse it became. Doubts assailed us. Had we been a few doughnuts short of a dozen to dream of such a journey? What if the big bad world swallowed us up and we were never heard from again? Or, horrors, what if we returned to discover our job skills outdated and no one would ever hire us again and we had to become bag people, living the rest of our lives on the streets, with nothing but a shopping trolley to hold our possessions?

Alas, Vicky — a friend and cycle touring partner on numerous prior occasions — forced our hand when she arrived to lead us out of Edmonton. She pulled up on her bike one cold overcast Sunday morning. At least it wasn't raining. Yet. After final, final goodbye hugs, we waved so long to Faye. She actually escorted us out the backyard gate — just making sure we really were on our way, I suspect.

We mounted up and wobbled off, trailing Vicky down the alley, through a maze of streets and cycle paths, then out onto the open road ... and into the stiffest headwind we had ever cycled! Sharon and I hunched low, crouched over our handlebars, sheltering behind Vicky like shy children hiding behind their mother's bustle. Part of my problem was I had crawled off to bed at 2 AM. I was paying for my late night movie-watching foolishness. *Who knew we'd be leaving today? Wasn't Sunday supposed to be a day of rest?*

Drooping behind Sharon and Vicky in a quasi-twilight stupor, wondering if my bicycle possessed square wheels, I wanted to know who the wise guy was that had mortared bricks to my eyelids. *Surely,* I thought, struggling to keep up, *someone has dipped my shoes in concrete.* Besides being dog-tired, my load was far heavier than I ever remembered a touring bike could possibly be. (When Vicky hefted my panniers, she had groaned and said she thought it best I leave my rock collection home.)

No rocks, but along with the usual assortment of clothes for every imaginable weather condition (or so I thought), I hauled food and water, stove and fuel, pots and pans, assorted tools and spare parts, tent and sleeping accoutrements. I had also managed to acquire a short-wave radio (requiring a handful of batteries), a flashlight (more batteries), an economy-sized shampoo (such a deal!), two flat-proof tubes, a pair of spare tires — and a sensible long-necked lighter for our pyro stove.

A cyclist passed from the opposite direction — pulling a canoe! Maybe I wasn't that overloaded after all.

Compounding my problems, I hadn't ridden in the past two weeks since our practice run to Medicine Hat and Cypress Hills with friends, Sue and Vicky — running around as I was, trying to complete last minute tasks when one is planning to be out of the country for the next two years.

Feeling about as swift as a glacier, I endured nearly 50 chilly kilometres through rolling, glacial potholed, aspen woodland to Cooking Lake — where we elected not to cook. Instead, we feasted on Vicky's banana bread, and cheered each time old Sol peeked from behind massive cloud cover. The temperature was slow to recover from the previous night's thunderstorm and 50 millimetres of rain.

In Tofield, at 80 kilometres, craving warmth, we straggled into an information centre. A display of birds' nests held me spellbound ... they looked so comfy with all the feathers lining the sides. *Hey, perhaps I should have gotten more sleep?*

"My fingers are numb," Sharon complained. "How about if we go to a café for hot chocolate?"

Vicky and I were quick to agree. I just hoped I could pry my frozen lobster-claw fingers wide enough to grasp a mug.

Cradling hot mugs, sensation seeped back into our extremities. After a second mug, we grudgingly trudged outside. Wind buffeted nearby trees. Leaves, flapping like tiny sheets of green on wispy clotheslines, tore off. Worse, we were about to lose our wind-blocker. If Vicky wanted to make it back to Edmonton before midnight, she had to turn back. We hugged her goodbye. A crabapple lump stuck in my windpipe.

Without a word, Vicky turned and headed back west — with the wind. Her retreating form grew ever smaller on the horizon, eventually becoming a wavery dot suspended above the asphalt that refused to disappear. "That's the trouble with living on the prairie," I said. "If your dog runs away, you can see him go for three days."

Sharon smiled. We were on our own. Putting on brave faces, we hugged one another for luck, and shoved our feet into pedal clips. "I guess this time it's for real," I said, tucking my head, and pedalling off into a roaring easterly wind.

Headwinds: the bane of touring cyclists. Worse than mountains. Like an invisible freighter, it barrels toward us, tiring us, impeding our progress, making a ride seem twice as far. Winds batter us psychologically as well — sometimes, like when we rode across Kansas, for days on end. On the open road — especially the flat prairie — there's no escaping its wicked onslaught.

It fatigues us with its ceaseless chatter, hissing in our ears like an old steam engine. And, unlike mountain passes, there's no feeling of elation upon conquering a summit. No heady freewheel down the other side, gravity working its magic while an altogether different wind playfully tinkles through one's spokes like wind chimes in a caressing summer breeze. Instead, relentless plod; no fun at all. One time, when cycle touring the California coast, we had battled a tempestuous howler. Upon cresting a steep pitch, the windy madness smacked us face-on. We shifted to a lower gear *and* pedalled hard to go *downhill*. Headwinds. Bah!

Two sluggish hours — and a paltry 18 kilometres later — we arrived in Ryley. Underwhelmed by our slow rate of travel, Sharon sputtered, "At this rate, we'll never make it across Canada, let alone around the world."

Suppertime. We plodded into a café to refuel and get out of the wind. The menu praised its nachos. We were off to a healthy start.

The waitress scribbled down our order and returned to the till area. She pulled on a jacket and slipped out the front door. *Huh?* Seated at our window booth, we watched in rapt fascination as she pranced past — more than a little worried she was running out on us! But, she returned in short order, smiling, holding aloft a jar of homemade salsa. We taste-tested the entire jar before giving it two thumbs up.

Bellies full, we rode to Ryley's fairgrounds and selected a camp spot near — but not too near! — wildly swaying poplars. A gale wind raged. Battleship grey clouds scuttled past, seeming in a hurry to get home before dark. Bushed, we voted to hit the sack.

"Oh, aren't we living the life of Ryley!" Sharon said, slipping into her sleeping bag and immediately beginning to snore.

Still light enough to read by, I read my watch: 9:30 PM. For someone who usually toddled off to bed around midnight, it felt incredibly early. But, considering how sapped I was, I had a distinct feeling I was going to need a lot of early nights.

Forgettable Fire

> **"Give a man a fire and he's warm for a day, but set fire to him and he's warm for the rest of his life."**
> ~ Terry Pratchett, *Jingo*

The morning headwind snorted, even more bull-necked. "The sort of breeze that could pin you to a fence post," Sharon said.

Without Vicky to block the wind, we shouldered the full brunt. The daytime high hit a whopping 12 degrees Celsius! Combined with the wind chill, it felt near zero. "Is it possible to snow in August?" Sharon asked. Where was the warm summer weather? Griping, we slogged on.

After 15 kilometres, we stopped to rest our weary bodies. In Holden, attempting to replenish our flagging energy, we bolted spoonfuls of crunchy peanut butter — straight from the jar. "At this temperature," I said, "it has no chance of going rancid."

Fingers and toes like ice cubes, we prodded one another back onto the bikes and pedalled down the road to the community of Bruce, not quite 20 kilometres away. We stopped again and sucked back containers of sickeningly-sweet butterscotch puddings. At least they gave us enough energy to carry on.

Into the freezing headwind, the kilometres ticked by. Slowly. Painfully. Painfully slowly. The only part of my body still warm were my calves — and that was because it felt as if someone was branding them with red-hot pokers.

The exciting prairie scenery didn't help matters. Boredom reached new lows. To pass the time, I counted telephone poles! My sampling indicated an average of 12 per kilometre. (Although I may have missed a couple ... I had my head pulled in as far as I could manage. "Turtles on Tour" Sharon named us.)

Feeling like a couple of frozen cow patties, we shuffled off the roadway and into a picnic shelter a few kilometres shy of Viking. Tired. Cold. Hungry. Those three make a bad combination. Our grand total for the day? Less than 50 kilometres.

"Are you as tired as I am?" Sharon asked.

I groaned.

"As sore?" she pressed.

I moaned, wondering which part of my body ached the worst. "Only hurts when I breathe," I rasped. Pedalling a loaded touring bike without training had its disadvantages.

"This is depressing," Sharon grumbled. I rubbed her clammy hands. We were still doubting ourselves — questioning the sanity of unlocking the shackles to freedom. "A heated office job with a cushy chair is beginning to sound pretty good right about now."

"Yeah," I nodded. "I remember you saying you loved every minute of your sentence there."

Sharon tossed me a thin smile. "Quit trying to cheer me up."

We were alone in the shelter, save for some feathered friends. A mud swallow's nest clung to a rafter. The mother bird heartened us and strengthened our resolve with her endless quests into the bluster to gather mosquitoes for her vociferous brood. Yellow beaks larger than their featherless baby heads, and bellies insatiable: those little tweeters were the epitome of touring cyclists.

Chewing granola bars, we debated calling it a day. The ballot was split. Luckily for me, the weather cast the tie-breaking vote in my favour. It began to rain. Hard. Lightning flashed. An authoritative clap of thunder boomed nearby. Sharon jumped. "I didn't think it was warm enough to thunder," she said.

"Um ... looks like we're staying," I said.

"What about the no camping sign?" Sharon asked, pointing to a CAMPING PROHIBITED notice — so diminutive one could easily have missed it. Really.

"Er, pretend we didn't see it?"

That settled, I ducked out and scratched up an armload of saturated sticks from the nearly depleted woodbox. After several tries, Sharon coaxed a tiny fire to life in the shelter's iron stove. Acrid woodsmoke tormented our eyes, and, unlike the cheery snap and crackle of dry wood, this fire squeaked and sizzled, emitting a feeble orange flicker that constantly threatened to extinguish itself. "Colder than a cast iron commode," Sharon said. We huddled close — palms outstretched, fingers nearly touching the quavering orange flames.

I frowned. "Isn't fire supposed to be hot?"

Hell Broke Loose

"Grow old along with me! The best is yet to be ... "
~ Robert Browning

The day dawned, windier still. "If this keeps up," Sharon muttered, "we'll be blown backwards. In a couple of hours, we'll be back in Edmonton."

"Won't Faye be surprised to see us?"

It felt as if I was pedalling on a windy ice floe: for every three strokes forward, I slipped back two. It took a supremely long time to ride the few kilometres to Viking.

Even though I'm notoriously cheap when it comes to eateries (to Sharon's chagrin), we skittered inside a restaurant — anything to get out of the hellish wind. Studying the map, we searched for an alternate route that would get us away from the relentless easterly that threatened to deafen us.

Leaving the restaurant's comfortable confines, we turned south, out of the direct headwind. "At least it'll give our eardrums a chance to recover."

"What?" Sharon said.

In a short distance, my rear tire deflated. "Man! Not already!" I cried. "I hoped to make it the entire way across Canada without a flat!" Not taking any chances, I installed a new tire, a new flat-proof tube, *and* a Mr Tuffy tire liner. "That should solve my flat problems," I announced confidently.

Killam, Sedgewick, Lougheed, and Hardisty passed by with no flats. On the verge of collapse, we stopped in the hamlet of Amisk and bought groceries for supper. Leaving the shop, the owner, Mary, presented us with a souvenir pen. The store's phone number was emblazoned on its side. "Do you deliver?" I asked. Considering our state of weariness, that may have been a good idea.

At an overgrown ball field on the edge of town, we found a decomposing picnic table. I pulled out our tiny WhisperLite stove, looking forward to mushroom soup and a ham, cheese and tomato sandwich. From a nearby residence, the aroma of barbecue steak lingered in the evening air, stimulating my Pavlovian reflex.

"Maybe I should buy a steak and introduce myself," I said. Distracted by the mouth-watering essence, I overflowed the stove's fuel cup. With a *whoosh,* the picnic table was alight. Dull yellow flames danced three feet higher than our heads. "Do you think the fire department will hose us down?" I joked, silently complimenting myself on having had the good sense to purchase an extra-long lighter.

"That'd be great," Sharon smiled. "I haven't had a shower in three days."

Four minutes later, I plunged a cinnamon-apple tea bag into a litre of bubbling water. That little blowtorch was amazing.

Before I took my first sip, a young fellow, accompanied by a slightly older woman, approached us. Mark and Jeannette introduced themselves. Mark lived next door to the ballpark with his mom, Luella; Jeannette lived down the road a ways in an old farmhouse. They had done some bike touring in the past.

"We biked to Cypress Hills two years ago," Jeannette said. "It was scorching!" I rubbed my hands together briskly, hoping her comments would bring back a flood of warm memories.

"I'd like to ride to Winnipeg next," she said.

"That's the direction we're headed," I said. "Why don't you come along?" I had a nasty habit of making flippant invitations. I wondered if I would ever learn the lesson of thinking first?

But before Jeannette answered, Mark shivered and asked, "Would you like to come over for a hot chocolate?" In a flash, we accepted his kind offer.

Mark's mom, Luella, wasn't home. She had driven a neighbour lady to Edmonton for the woman's weekly chemo treatment.

Mark was going into his third year of mechanics at Vermilion College. He drove a Volkswagen Beetle with a special tailpipe. "Does that stinger give you any extra oomph?" I asked, interested since I owned two underpowered VW's myself.

"Oh, yeah!" Mark said. "One night, at a stoplight in downtown Provost, a tricked-out Camaro pulled alongside me. The Camaro driver gave me a sideways stare and revved his engine a couple of times. Rrrmmm! Rrrrrmmm! I gunned my Volksie. Poor old Betsy backfired so hard flame shot out her stinger six feet! I looked over at the muscle-car guy. He was slunk so far down in his seat I could barely see him." Mark laughed. "The dude was beat before the race began."

After a second mug of steaming hot chocolate, sensation began creeping back into my fingertips. At 10 PM, fully thawed, we said good night to our new friends (we were past exhausted and Mark had to work in the morning). We wandered back to the ball field and erected our tent. Not taking any chances, I chained our bikes to the picnic table. Satisfied with my handiwork, I crawled inside the tent, ready for a good night's sleep.

"Aren't you going to zip the vestibule?"

"Naw," I said. "I'm going to watch the stars for a while."

"It's overcast," Sharon said, glancing at the heavens. "There are no stars."

Okay, she had me there. The real reason I didn't close the vestibule was that I wanted to have a clear view of our bikes in case anyone tried to steal them. Totally irrational — Amisk was tiny; our bikes were padlocked to a picnic table; and a six-foot chain-link fence surrounded us. Overwhelming fatigue did weird things to one's brain.

"You're paranoid," Sharon smirked, guessing my real reason.

"There's 300 people here," I countered.

"Exactly!" she hooted.

At midnight all hell broke loose. Not anyone intent on absconding a pair of unwieldy, loaded touring bikes, mind you. Instead, bright bursts of lightning and corking cracks of thunder detonated in the heavens. The thunder was loud enough to cause the dead to sit bolt-upright. But not me. I barely stirred. After two more hair-raising explosions, one on top of the other, it began to pour. Torrentially.

Rain spattered my face.

Sharon wearily rose on one elbow and closed *her* half of the vestibule. "Now you wish you hadn't left it open?" she asked, lying back down. I was still too groggy to close my side. It gaped open like a yawning funnel. Rain continued to splatter my face. Maybe I should have broken out the shampoo?

Not long after that, I remembered the ground sheet. Normally the vestibule covered it. But with only half the vestibule closed, the fabric channelled a runnel of water onto the ground sheet, and then beneath the tent. Before I was conscious, a sizable pool had collected inside the tent — luckily most of it was on Sharon's side. Still half asleep, she sat up and muttered something exclamatory. Using one of her bandannas, she set to work sopping up the puddle. "A hundred and one uses," she mumbled.

"Quack, quack," I said, watching her paddling motions through half-closed lids. "Weather fit for a duck."

"You're the one who's quacked," she spluttered, zippering shut my half of the vestibule.

Send Off

"Friends have all things in common."
~ Plato, Dialogues, *Phaedrus*

Fumbling with our stove the next morning (trying to not light the picnic table on fire again — a skill taking more time to master than one might first expect), a woman hurried over. Perhaps she had heard of the previous evening's near call to the fire department?

"Hi!" she called from her side of the fence. "Mark told me about you two before he left for work this morning. I'm his mother, Luella. I'll bet a hot chocolate would taste pretty good right about now, eh?"

Having no feeling in my fingers again, I found it difficult not to agree wholeheartedly.

"Come on over," she invited. "The kettle's on."

Sharon and I packed our sopping tent, our sopping fly, our sopping....

I wrung my socks with gusto. *Why does it always rain on me?* I wondered while securing the sodden mess beneath equally sodden bungees. Humming, we pushed our bikes over to the neighbour's. Free as birds, we were content to let our days unfold as they may — even if they weren't all sunny blue skies.

Inside Luella's warm home, the hot chocolate transformed into toast and jam, as well. We tucked in while Luella busied herself at the kitchen counter buttering more toast.

"Would you like some pancakes?" she suddenly asked. Sharon and I exchanged glances, not quite believing our good luck. We waffled too long, however; Luella interpreted our slow response as meaning we didn't think it a good idea. "Oh, dear, no," she said. "That would be too heavy for the road, wouldn't it?"

Before we could protest that it would not be too heavy at all, she waltzed over with another golden tower of buttered toast, accompanied by peanut butter and gooseberry jam.

"Ah, this is the life!" I said, toppling the leaning tower. Already forgetting the pancakes, I imagined the only thing better might be a hot shower.

Luella read my mind. "I'll bet a hot shower would feel good right about now," she bubbled.

We scarcely believed our ears, but this time we were quick to accept. We didn't intend to let the offer slip away like the flapjacks. While Sharon enjoyed a second mug of hot chocolate, Luella steered me toward fresh towels.

Emerging a short time later, I felt (and smelt) like a new man. Even the sensation in my toes had returned!

Sharon floated off to her own few minutes of bliss.

"Forget the 15 minutes of fame," she sighed upon her return. "Just give me an equal allotment of hot water."

Jeannette arrived for morning coffee. After rehashing more cycling tales, we exchanged addresses. "I can hardly wait for you guys to finish your trip so we can share your adventures," Jeannette said. She even offered addresses for family members in Ontario. "But I don't have their phone numbers with me," she said. "We'll have to go to my place to get them."

Sharon and I jumped into Luella's little car with Jeannette and we roared off down the country lane like Mario Andretti.

We arrived in short order at Jeannette's renovated farmhouse. Plenty of warm wood and sparkling glass greeted us along with the smell of just-baked cookies.

Jeannette gave us a quick tour. Every nook and cranny held a surprise from a bygone era. But my favourite room was a snug library loft, chockablock with all manners of just-begging-to-be-read books — a superb place to curl up for a month or two.

Sharon's favourite was a sunroom resplendent in old glass. "I love old, paned glass," she said.

"Looks like a pain to wash," I muttered.

After polishing off half a dozen cookies, we headed back to Luella's, and arrived just in time for lunch. "I'll bet some homemade vegetable soup would taste pretty good right about now," Luella said, continuing her winning ways.

After more good food and conversation, we said goodbye to our new friends. How were we ever going to cycle around the world if we couldn't even get out of our own home province?

"I'll bet it would be fun to ride with you a ways," Luella said. We paraded out to the front yard at the same moment Luella's eldest son, Philip, arrived from Calgary for a visit. Hey, no problem; Phil would join us as well. Luella liberated three clunkers from her shed.

We all set off down the road. Pedalling along, laughing and joking, like kids without a care in the world, we felt as if we were old friends who had known each other for years. After ten easy kilometres, our new old friends decided it was time they headed back. Goodbye hugs all around. They turned their bikes and pedalled off, wobbling and laughing and shouting and waving.

Sharon flashed a wide smile. "That's the reason I wanted to leave from our back door," she said. "I didn't want to travel around the world without getting to know a bit of our own country first."

Maybe we didn't have to journey to far off corners of the globe to find caring and generous folks. They existed right in our own backyards — if only we took the time to look.

Ice Cube

> **"There are three easy ways of losing money— racing is the quickest, women the most pleasant, and farming the most certain."**
> ~ Lord Amherst

Past Provost, we skimmed across the Alberta border and into Saskatchewan. This prairie province didn't even have rolling hummocks. The only protuberances bumping above the skyline were faded grain elevators – some looming five stories tall (and seen from an equal number of kilometres). Few trees obstructed the view. Pancake flat prairie, filled with waving grain fields, swept past the horizon, as far as the eye could see ... practically into tomorrow.

"Too bad there's no herds of wild buffalo left roaming the prairies," I said. "At least it'd give us something to look at." I found it hard to believe that of the estimated 30 million bison that had teemed across the great plains of North America before the arrival of the white man, the large animals had been slaughtered to decimation – by 1900 as few as 1500 wild buffalo remained.

A park in Unity, Saskatchewan, provided lunch. A kids' summer program was in the midst of a barbecue. A fellow employed by Parks and Recreation trotted over and introduced himself. Keith chatted for a couple of minutes, then waved to the chefs, "Make sure these two get a hot dog!" I liked prairie hospitality!

After lunch, we visited my friend Tim's mom and dad. Hard, old Saskatchewan farmers (only the tough survive the prairies' bone chilling winters and searing summer heat), Tony and Helen had retired to Unity.

Tall Tough Tony had farmed numerous years in the nearby community of Reward. (I suspect his only reward for tilling the unproductive quarters was that he hadn't gone bankrupt.)

Along the way, they managed to raise several wonderful children – most of whom had moved away. Tony joked that he had heard Saskatchewan was the best place in Canada to be from – at least that's what I suspected his son Tim always said when he called from Vancouver. But, kidding aside, it was easy to see why he and Helen loved the dusty province. The absolute grandeur of an unbroken cobalt skyline stretching to infinity; the vastness of acres upon acres of grain rippling in the wind like waves on a rolling golden ocean; and, at night, an overhead panorama of crisp celestial bodies set in the blackest of black velvet tapestries.

After catching up on news, we got ready to depart. Of course, Tony and Helen wouldn't let us leave without stuffing our panniers with fresh produce from their expansive backyard garden.

"Once a farmer, always a farmer ...," I said, wobbling away.

Early evening, 30 kilometres down the road, we coasted into the town of Wilkie, seeking the municipal pool. On a tree-lined residential street, an older couple raked grass in their front yard. We stopped and asked directions.

The Kellers didn't intend to just provide us the information and send us on our way. Oh, no, they had to get the entire low-down on our trip, asking all sorts of cycle touring questions. Once that avenue had been thoroughly explored, they turned to careers, and then to what our parents did. "My mom and dad are farmers," Sharon told them.

Mr Keller chuckled. "I'm a poor farmer, too!" he said. "What'd the farmer say when he won the lotto and they asked him what he was going to do? 'Guess I'll just keep on farming till it's all gone.'"

The Kellers had ten kids (beating Sharon's mom and dad by one — those farmers sure are into producing!). They recited where each offspring resided, and what each did for a living.

We eventually got directions to the pool and said goodbye to the Kellers — them bidding us a safe journey, and Sharon and I wishing them a bountiful harvest. (Seeing the late hour, we should have asked to camp on their lawn.)

The Kellers were good with their directions. We located the pool, immersed ourselves in the showers, then struck off, squeaky clean and happy, for the farming community of Landis, 32 kilometres distant.

But before anywhere near Landis, darkness overtook us. We had spent too long in the shower.

All we needed was a patch of ground for eight hours or so. With empty land stretching in all directions, how difficult could it be to find a spot for our little tent? We were about to find out.

A grain elevator hulked in the near distance. On the prairies, we never seemed farther than a stone's throw from one (the number of elevators in western Canada peaked in the late 1930s at over 5,000). We headed for the faded-green structure. "No one will mind if we spend the night beside it," I said.

A police car zipped up behind us. Braking hard, it slowed to our rate of travel — 20 kilometres per hour.

"He must be wondering where we're off to at such a late hour."

"Keep pedalling, Sherlock," Sharon replied.

A bit worrisome, the cop stayed on our tails, pacing us for two long kilometres. I kept glancing furtively in my mirror, expecting to see lights flashing, pulling us over.

A mud-puddled gravel road appeared on our right, heading toward the grain elevator. We signalled, and turned off the main highway. My rear-view mirror reported the cop had turned off behind us. *Oh, great,* I thought. The music from *Jaws* played loudly through my head. *Now what?* I wondered. *For sure we're going to have a lot of explaining about why we're out at dusk riding bicycles with no lights.*

"Do you think we'll be arrested?" Sharon asked.

"Beats me," I shrugged. "At least that'll solve the problem of where we're spending the night."

A rambling farmhouse stood on the corner. On its sprawling front yard, a family tossed a football back and forth. They eyed us warily. Sharon and I stopped and gave them big waves. The cop car stopped a few feet behind us. The football-throwing family returned our greeting with smiles and big waves of their own. We were getting ready to be interrogated by the Mountie when we heard the patrol car's radio crackle to life. We couldn't make out what the dispatcher said, but the officer suddenly swung his cruiser around, and sped off, back in the direction of Wilkie. Maybe it was coffee time?

When the police car was out of sight, it was Sharon's turn to shrug. "How about that?" she said. "All that worrying for nothing."

"Must be our lucky day," I said, and waved again to the still-staring family on the lawn. Shoving my foot back in my toeclip, I began pedalling merrily toward the grain elevator, Sharon hot on my little tail. But, as Lady Luck would have it, we weren't quite home free yet.

Within spitting distance of the grain elevator, a battered and rusted two-tone blue Ford F150 pickup, wet gravel scrunching beneath its bald tires, splashed alongside me. A corpulent woman, occupying the passenger seat, flopped her head out the window and barked, "Where are you going?"

"Québec," I replied, smiling.

"Why did you turn back there then?" she growled in a voice so husky it could have pulled a dog sled. Maybe everyone in Canada wasn't as friendly as I had come to believe? Maybe she thought we were a pair of Bonnie and Clyde cyclists on the lam from the law? Maybe she figured I had a poor sense of direction?

"You mean I'm lost again?" I grinned, wondering when the poor woman had last smiled. A distasteful frown drooped the corners of her bulldog mouth; flinty eyes narrowed, pug nose wrinkled — as if getting a whiff of poo. Not the slightest trace of humour betrayed her canine features. My heart leapt; I felt like a postman being targeted by a doberman.

"*You* should'a stayed back in Wilkie," she snarled.

Before I could agree with her latest revelation, and ask her: 'What has four legs and an arm?' (a happy pit bull), her husband piped up, "Would you folks like to camp in our yard for the night?"

"Sure!" I accepted. "That'd be great!"

My eager response didn't improve his wife's disposition one smidgen. Her forehead creased in displeasure; she glowered at me. But, hey, a deal's a deal. We swung our bikes around and followed the truck back down the puddled lane to — you guessed it — the house on the corner where the folks had waved so friendly-like only minutes before.

The man parked alongside the garage. His wife bolted from the pickup without so much as a glance our way (I would have hated to have been a fly in that truck's cab on the drive home). She stormed inside the house like a spinster who had just received an unwelcome amorous advance, screen door slapping behind her.

Her husband ambled over and asked a few polite questions ... but his heart clearly wasn't in it. After a couple of minutes, he pointed to a mown patch near the garage where he said we could set up our tent, then slouched off to do chores. (I had a feeling he spent a considerable amount of his time outdoors.)

A rooster announced the dawn. I scratched a quick thank you note, and tucked it between the farmhouse's screen door.

We headed down the drive, and spotted the good farmer's wife staring out a streaked bathroom window at us; dark and brooding, the ever-present scowl etched plainly on her unvarnished features. Apparently, a good night's sleep hadn't softened her demeanour any.

"She really ought to give her face a rest," Sharon muttered. "How *does* one get such a sour puss?"

"Vinegar douche?" I replied crudely with a tight little grin, and waved to our reluctant good Samaritan.

If

"Hindsight is 50/50."
~ Scott Anderson

An hour later, we arrived in the community of Landis. The early ride had piqued our appetite. "How about if we treat ourselves this morning?" Sharon asked, stopping across from the Landis Hotel. As if in response, before I could protest, an unshaven fellow threw open the Hotel's creaky screen door and yelled to us, "Come on in! The coffee's on."

"Our invitation," I said.

We leaned our bikes against the building's aging clapboard side and sauntered inside.

Old farmers, furrows lining their craggy faces, sat at a window table, slurping black coffee. We nodded 'morning' on our way past, and eased ourselves into a couple of ratty chairs at a table near the back.

Farmers' gravelly voices wafted in the restaurant's still air. Like farmers everywhere, they complained non-stop about gas prices, grain prices, farm equipment prices, and, last, but not least, their favourite whipping boy, the uncooperative weather.

"It's a farmer's prerogative," Sharon whispered. "When your living depends on the weather, you're allowed to complain about anything and everything."

"Yeah," I agreed. "Probably about cyclists, too." (My urban paranoia was showing ... after last night's hostile treatment from the farm wife I wasn't expecting the best from rural folks.)

A train rumbled past — so close the building shivered like a 4.5 tremor on the Richter scale. One old-timer turned in his chair and looked our way. "Twenty trains a day," he shouted above the din. The building quit shaking, the rumbling faded, and the farmers resumed their complaining. "Can you believe those grain prices?" one muttered. "Lower per bushel than during the depression."

A pockmarked waiter, looking as though he'd had a rough night (not his first by any means), brought glasses of water. He plunked them down, looked us over, scratched his knobby chin, then read our thoughts. "I asked them why they farm then," he said. "They told me, 'Only thing we know how to do.' Complain, I figure, is what they meant. Don't pay no mind — they're like this every day." He shook his head. "I figure someone must be making money though ... all those trainloads of grain going east and west day and night eight days a week."

He disappeared into the back. The fellow who invited us in came over and introduced himself. He was Don, the establishment's fine owner.

"Happy to see you folks this morning," he drawled. "You should'a been here last night though. Didn't ya know we give free rooms to cyclists?"

Sharon and I shook our heads. So close, and yet so far.... We had to learn to ask locals more questions about accommodations.

"Where did you stay last night?"

"Oh, a little B&B down the way," Sharon said. (Bitter and Bummed-out, I thought was what she imagined the initials to stand for.)

Don looked momentarily confused. "Hey," he said, brightening. "A girl stayed here last Tuesday — she was cycling on her own. Did you pass her anywhere on the road?"

"Nope," I answered. "If we had, we would have stayed here last night."

"Ya," Don continued, ignoring my comment, "she's a little bit of a thing. I tell everyone who comes in here, so they can keep an eye out for her."

Someone worried about cyclists? Comforting to know people watched out for us. Maybe rural folks weren't so bad after all.

"So," Don said, "what can I do for you this fine morning?"

A low growl discharged from Sharon's stomach. "Can we order breakfast?"

"Well," Don answered, "my cook's not in yet." He rubbed his grizzled chin and looked doubtful. "I guess if you pick something not too hard, I can make it for you. He handed us a pair of tattered menus off an adjacent table.

"Pancakes?" Sharon ventured.

"Nope. Too hard."

"How about an omelette?"

Don mulled it over a full minute. I thought we had entered a time warp where the fourth dimension had ground to a halt.

"Okay," he mused. "I can do an omelette."

Half an hour later, the hard-day's night man slapped two white plates in front of us. The accompanying slimy omelettes skittered around our plates, gliding like champion figure skaters. I stabbed mine just before it slid off the rink's edge.

"Maybe you should have waited for the cook," the server said. He gave us a misty, little half-grin and departed.

Canned mushrooms, so slippery they could have been brown-headed eels, slithered beneath a gooey raft of liquified, processed, simulated cheese slices. "Fresh from their cellophane wrapper," I remarked as the pallid orange scum floated across my plate. Looking at the slop, I seriously considered digging a package of oatmeal from the bottom of my pannier and firing up our trusty stove.

"I'm starved," Sharon said. She hoisted her fork and ventured a bite. I waited in anticipation for her proclamation. "This is the *most* disgusting omelette I've ever tasted," she said, and nearly retched.

Since she put it like that, I had to try the stuff. "Sounds like a challenge," I said, loading up a quivering forkful and choking it down. "Goose poop," I winced. "Just out."

"Scraped from the bottom of someone's boots," Sharon added. "The regular cook doesn't have anything to worry about." She grimaced and forced another quivering glob of orangey-yellow detritus into her gullet. "Talk about job security."

"Never trust a skinny chef," I said.

Don sashayed over. "How do you like it?" he asked, smiling. "I made it myself." Don may have been short on culinary skills, but he was long on friendliness.

"I've never tasted anything quite like it," Sharon said, diplomatically.

"Don't quit your night job," I said, somewhat less tactfully. Honesty was always the best policy, right?

Back outside, I discovered my rear tire had suffered a nasty deflating episode. "Will you look at that?" I said, pointing to its airless condition. "That's one flat 'no-flat' tube."

While I lifted the back of my bike so I didn't have to remove my rear rack's contents, Sharon extricated the wheel from the chain and rear derailleur. I laid my bike over, located the offending hole and got out the patch kit.

"Do you think a patch will hold on a 'no-flat' tube?" Sharon asked.

"Oh, sure," I responded. "It says right on the box: PATCHES LIKE A REGULAR TUBE."

I rubbed a patch on, reinstalled the wheel, and departed Landis, heading eastward with a brisk tailwind.

We coasted along, enjoying the lack of scenery. Then, with usual fickleness, the wind turned on us — with a vengeance. The next half-hour consisted of our heads tucked, staring at our shoelaces. Maybe I should have splurged on fluorescent ones?

On the outskirts of Biggar, we raised our heads long enough to read a sign: NEW YORK IS BIG, BUT THIS IS BIGGAR. Chuckling at the inhabitants' sense of humour, we struggled 32 kilometres to Purdue, the wind hitting us obliquely off our left shoulders.

Stopping at a gas station, we flopped onto a bench. I had just finished inhaling my last swallows of chocolate milk when a whistling sound — reminiscent of a fat porker's final exhale — pierced my tympanic membrane.

I gaped repugnantly as the rear of my bike sagged like a boxer who had taken one punch to the head too many. The Landis patch had failed.

"How about that?" I said in dismay. "Maybe those 'no-flat' tubes should be named 'no-patch.'"

"That's the problem with those," Sharon concurred. "Once they're punctured, they're tossers."

Not one to be deterred, I bonded a larger patch right over top of the old one. "Let's see how long this sucker lasts!"

By the time we got underway, the wind hit us square in the face. We crept along. *Can't get any worse,* I thought.

Of course it could.

It began to rain. Sharon pulled off and scrambled about, grabbing laundry from beneath bungees and stowing the still damp articles inside panniers. (We washed our few articles of clothing wherever we could, and "hung" them on our bicycles, giving us a gypsy caravan appearance. I joked about buying clothes pegs and fastening my garb to my flag pole where they would dry quicker and obtain a daisy fresh airing.)

Laundry secured in drier confines, we struck off. Before long, the heavens really opened. Through a grey torrential downpour, I spied a garage. And the door was up!

We hustled off the road and scurried into someone's driveway. I ran to the house's door and banged on it. A balding, chin-whiskered fellow, well into middle-age, opened the door. His potbelly protruded, hanging out beneath a moth-eaten T-shirt with the words FEAR THIS nearly worn off.

"Can we wait out the storm in your garage?" I stammered.

"Certainly," he replied, gawking out at our loaded bikes. "I'll even join you!"

The next half-hour was spent with Wendell the Hilarious. His good humour and earthy philosophy infected us. Soon, we were splitting a gut at everything he uttered.

"*If* is a very big word," he said. "*If* may have only two letters, but it is a much bigger word. Like my Daddy told me: "*If* the dog hadn't stopped to take a shit, it would have caught the rabbit.'"

We nodded solemnly. Ah, there had to be a nugget of wisdom there somewhere, didn't there? Not finding one, I shrugged. At least we were dry.

"*If* don't change nothin'," Wendell continued with his philosophizing. "Couldn't have happened any other way. Meant to be. Just the way it is. No ifs, ands, or buts about it."

Our dampened, emotional states lifted as the storm passed to the west. Sharon and I waved so long to Wendell. *If* it hadn't been for the storm, we never would have met him.

He had fed our spirits and given us invaluable advice: "Worrying is wasted energy."

Ball Diamond

> **"When the One Great Scorer comes to write against your name, He marks, not that you won or lost, but how you played the game."**
> ~ Grantland Rice

"Camp anywhere," the folks at a store in Asquith offered. "No one will mind."

Maybe people understood about touring cyclists after all? It's not as if we can just hop on our bikes and pedal another hundred kilometres down the road to the nearest campground.

The next day, after 160 kilometres, we arrived in Esk — an insignificant hiccup of a prairie town. No gas stations. No restaurants. No grocery stores. Town proper consisted of a cluster of squalid hovels.

I asked a passing chap: "Do you think anyone would mind if we camped in that field?" I pointed to an unkempt parcel yonder, yellowed grass thigh-high.

"Ball diamond," he corrected.

Whatever. We camped at the 'ball diamond' — somewhere beyond shortstop I suspect — six feet from several gopher holes, twenty feet from a derelict railway track. The tent had been set up and our gear unloaded for less than ten minutes when I heard a train whistle.

"It can't possibly be coming by on *that* track," I stated.

But, sure enough, a couple of minutes later an engineer waved to us as he chugged past, the ground chuddering beneath our feet. I waved back — thoughts of a peaceful slumber derailed.

"Free vibrating beds," I said.

"Pass the ear plugs," Sharon grumbled.

During the night, two freight trains rumbled past. When the first passed, the ground shook so violently I clung to the side of my ground pad in fear of falling off. When the second passed, I nearly jumped out of my skin. I dreamt I was *on* the track!

From 3 AM on, we laid awake, waiting for a nonexistent third train. We arose a couple of hours later, frazzled. *We're never camping near train tracks again,* Sharon's bloodshot eyes conveyed.

Sunday morning greeted us — the sky such a brilliant blue it hurt our eyes. Blinking, we pedalled into Jansen. If Esk had been a hiccup, then Jansen was a burp.

"At least it has stores," Sharon pointed out.

"Yes," I replied, "but none are open."

Perhaps the sleepy little town snoozed late on Sundays? We wheeled around town, looking for anything showing signs of life. The back door of a restaurant swung open. I ventured over. They weren't open for customers yet a helpful woman told me, but she sold us two litres of milk.

We sat at a picnic table and ate a gigantic pancake breakfast in what was once-upon-a-time a school yard ... or it may have been a ball diamond.

Back on the road, I noticed we weren't the only ones looking for lunch. Lazy raptors squatted on fence posts — waiting for roadkill. We swam past Big Quill Lake — the first real lake we had seen in Saskatchewan. Other so-called 'lakes' were sloughs, populated with fuzzy cattails and herons pacing amongst lily pads and scummy green algae. Saskatchewan didn't appear the best place to buy lake front property.

In a forsaken settlement with dirt streets, we entered a Chinese café. Dusty floral curtains and outdated gold and red embossed wallpaper spoke of prosperous days' past. We ordered a round of egg rolls. "There's little in these time-forgotten prairie towns," I said, "but there's usually a Chinese café on main street."

I shoveled in a mouthful of egg roll and gazed out the window. "How do you know you're in small town Saskatchewan?" I asked, snickering. A New Holland combine had arrived and was parallel parking in front of the café. (Across the street, at a tavern, more tractors than cars occupied the parking spaces.) "Yep, no mistaking it," I said, snatching another bite of egg roll. "We're in Saskabush." Chortling, I nearly choked on the minced vegetables.

"When you're bad-mouthing farmers," Sharon chastised, "at least have the courtesy not to do it with your mouth full."

We departed the coffee shop. Dust swirled down main street. We continued into the wind, dodging tumbleweeds as they bounced across the grassy plains and cut in front of us. Past flowing oceans of golden grain rolling in the wind, we passed the farming community of Mozart where the hamlet's streets are named for the classical composers Schubert, Haydn, Wagner, Gounod, and Liszt. "Look at that," Sharon said, pointing. "Even the street signs have little musical notes on them."

Foam Lake (Saskatchewan's answer to real lakes?) was our next spot of interest with its 6,500 acre marsh. A real gem as far as prairie marshes go — its ideal environment is practically a factory when it comes to breeding ducks. And, every autumn, it turns into a bird watchers' paradise when thousands of geese, ducks, swans, and cranes all congregate for their southern migration.

We continued to Sheho (Cree for prairie chicken). We didn't see any grouse, but we did spot our all-time shortest train. The entire string consisted of two locomotives. "Do you have a feeling," I asked, "that someone at the yard yelled at the engineer as he left? 'Bud! Hey Bud! Wait!'"

Devil Got Your Tongue

> **"We are what we think. All that we are arises with our thoughts. With our thoughts, we make the world."**
> ~ Buddha

On empty stomachs, we rode 70 kilometres into a stiff headwind. Progress was slow. "We'd make lousy gamblers," Sharon said. "Our luck is so terrible! We can't even get a tailwind across the Prairies!"

In Yorkton, Saskatchewan, we hit an all-you-can-eat restaurant and filled up on "brupper" — breakfast, lunch, and supper. (When we arrived I had the shakes from not eating for so long; Sharon figured I was trembling from looking at all the food.)

We were famished, and, I dare say, got good value for our money. After cleaning out the fruit section, we moved on to main course, cleared that department, then headed for dessert. Sharon gasped for breath, laughing uncontrollably, when she tried to rise for a fifth helping and could not. "The next time they see cyclists coming," she said, "they'll lock the doors before the poor devils can get in."

Riding after Yorkton was painful in more ways than one. Not only were our bellies hitting our handlebars, but we hit another cyclists' nemesis, as well: road construction. The surface was rough ("newly pebbled," someone said) and cracked. Adding to our discomfort was the heat. "Hang the environmental concerns," I complained, mopping my brow. "The next bike I get is going to have air conditioning."

We cycled past bulky construction workers playing with hot tar. Low slung pants revealed more cracks than the road. Malodorous fumes and clangorous machinery engulfed us, assaulting our ears, eyes, and noses. For two hours the stony surface jarred loose our fillings, swelled our hindquarters, and agitated our stomach contents. The hot miles dragged by. Road grime stuck to our sweaty legs as if we were giant Venus dust traps.

On a corner marked with a WROXTON sign, we slithered our sorry carcasses off the sticky tarmac and into a gas station to buy cold treats. Biting Popsicles, we relaxed on a strategically located bench and watched the world go by.

The gas station owner and a customer looked at our loaded bikes and debated how long they reckoned it'd take to ride "a blooming bicycle" to Winnipeg.

"Well, I've never done it," the owner confessed.

"Hell, we don't even ride bicycles," the customer confided.

After some questionable math, whilst swatting several bothersome flies, they settled on four days.

"That's probably accurate," Sharon said, calculating the distance to be about 400 kilometres.

"If we want to be there in four days, we better get a move on." We finished our icy treats and hauled our aching bods back onto our blooming bicycles to tackle the remaining stretch of destruction.

Fortunately, we soon struck pavement. The miles slipped by. Save for a few scrub trees and fields of radiant yellow canola there was nothing as far as the eye could see.

"Can you believe this?" I said, staring at the immense open space surrounding us. "There's miles between houses."

"When each farm averages over a thousand acres," Sharon said, "there's no such thing as close neighbours."

Pedalling along, deliberating the merits of irrigation systems versus living with seasonal rain vagaries, we crested a lip of land. There lay a verdant valley and silky-smooth lake; its surface reflecting the first hill we had seen in ages.

"Guess what?" Sharon shouted. "We just survived cycling across Saskatchewan! The flat prairies are behind us!" she spouted jubilantly. "Better days ahead!"

Compared to our previous snail's rate progress, we zoomed down the hill, and surged across a bridge spanning Lake of the Prairies. "Woo-hoo!" I yelled. "Remember this?"

Then, abruptly, we found ourselves grinding up the other side. "Ughh," I groaned, getting a dose of reality while attempting to use muscles that hadn't been tested in a long while. "I had forgotten about this. What am I ever going to do in the Pyrenees?"

In a few kilometres, we hit Roblin, our first Manitoban town. A congregation milled about a church parking lot after a mass exodus. I was about to experience an unwelcome welcome to the province that boasts the slogan: FRIENDLY MANITOBA.

Two elderly parishioners strolled the sidewalk. "Hi!" I called. "Could you give me directions to a grocery store?" They stared back, looking me over. Without a word, they stepped around me and continued on their way. *Huh?* What could possibly have gone wrong? "They still speak English in Manitoba, don't they?" I asked Sharon. "Maybe they were deaf?"

"They must have used up all their goodness in church," Sharon concluded. "That 'Friendly Manitoba' motto does have an 'r' in it, doesn't it?"

Two more elderly women hobbled toward me. *Do I dare ask them?* When they arrived, I was still standing there wondering whether the devil had their tongues too. I chanced it. They turned out to be regular, friendly Manitobans. Not only did they direct us to the nearest convenience store, but they also threw in (at no extra charge) directions to a free campground.

We found the campground easy enough and chose a choice spot — a vantage point overlooking tiny Goose Lake. "I guess that's why it's singular," Sharon mused, surveying the pittance of water. "Not enough room for two."

The campground was indeed free. Even better, so were the showers. "And they're open 24 hours," a youthful employee at the information booth noted. She must know cyclists!

A petite, white-haired woman, all of four and a half feet tall, stood next to the counter. She was the information worker's aunt, and had come to chat. Another woman arrived (the worker's mother). The two older women spitfired questions at Sharon and me about bicycle touring.

When they had exhausted the usual questions, the aunt asked, "Don't you get scared? Out there on your bicycles, all by yourselves?"

"No," I replied. "We don't watch TV." I figure most people harbour a distorted view on personal — indeed world — safety due to 'news' on the nightly boob tube. Lots of fear mongering. Lots of violence. The more blood splattering the living room floor, or bedroom carpet, the better the ratings. Great stuff to watch before going to sleep.

The majority of people who inhabit our old world are decent human beings ... or at least harmless. Everyday good deeds (such as these women's wonderful hospitality), don't sell newspapers. And rarely have I seen a good deed by common folk make the nightly news' top billing.

The women listened to my rant politely, then the aunt said, "I like to watch the news."

The mother nodded. "Me too."

"In colour, too, I'll bet," I said.

Rain Harder

> **"The rain fell alike upon the just and upon the unjust, and for nothing was there a why and a wherefore."**
> ~ W. Somerset Maugham

At 5 PM an insatiable nacho craving struck Sharon. Unfortunately for her, exactly zero of Roblin's five restaurants had gone Mexican.

More to my liking (I often left restaurants hungry and feeling ripped off), we hoofed it to a grocery store and bought all the requirements for a super-sized nacho oink-fest.

By the time we returned to the campground with our fixings, a boisterous bluster was threatening in the east. Concrete grey clouds, pregnant with rain, looked ready to deliver the mother of all storms. We secured our bikes under a picnic shelter's roof and got down to business — making a serious dent in our nacho ingredients. (Like our friend Rebecca says, "Eat fast! It only takes 20 minutes for your stomach to know you're full.")

By 9 PM — freshly showered, laundered, and attired — we were cocooned in our sleeping bags, enjoying the evening's serenity and waiting for sleep to overtake us.

"Can you believe it?" I yawned. "Free showers."

"And open 24 hours," Sharon reminded me. "Nothing like the option to shower at 2 AM, eh?"

"This is great," I sighed, listening to gentle rain patter the tent roof.

At 9:30 PM, nearly asleep, our bliss ended. Four pre-school kids with a barking dog arrived. I peered out the tent door and watched a haggard male straggle far behind the shouting boys. The little darlings, accompanied by their overzealous furry friend, traipsed through the trees beside our tent, gathering firewood. The father lit a smoky fire and they all attempted to roast marshmallows. Or at least the dad gave it a valiant effort.

The youngsters, meanwhile, ran about yelling, chasing one another, yelling, throwing sticks for the dog, yelling, hurling rocks into the lake, and yelling. The father hollered at them non-stop to be quiet and behave themselves. His false threat: "Stop that or we'll go home right this instant!" wasn't impelling to the boys. They didn't stop. And they didn't go home right that instant. Undeterred, they continued running around and yelling at the top of their voices. My eardrums were in danger of imploding.

Sharon pulled her sleeping bag over her head. "Rain harder," she muttered over and over like a personal mantra.

Forest Phone

> **"Miracles are natural; when they do not occur, something has gone wrong."**
> ~ Helen Schulman

The sky dawned pewter grey. A miserable east wind howled. But at least the screaming kids were gone.

"How about a rest day?" I suggested, looking out at the dreary conditions. "What better place than Roblin? Free accommodation; free showers." Sharon agreed. We bundled ourselves in rain gear and hiked downtown to sample Roblin's restaurants.

"Now here's a town that's thinking," Sharon said between mouthfuls, over her second breakfast in as many restaurants. "They make the campground free ... travellers stay and spend money in a place they may not even have stopped otherwise. That's what I call smart marketing!"

"Amazing more towns haven't discovered it," I said. "The free campground is like a built-in gold mine for local businesses."

The next morning, gale abated, we elected to hit the dusty trail for Moon Lake campground in Riding Mountain National Park before the four winds regrouped. But first we had to make a pit stop at Roblin's bakery. Not that we needed incentive, but the info centre had provided coupons for free cinnamon knots.

We picked up our sugar fix. I was greedily stuffing the package of gooey buns into my pannier for later consumption when the bakery door popped open. The counter-girl hurried over.

"Do you have room for these?" she asked with a smile while holding forth two rotund brown bags. I peeked inside. The first contained still-warm doughnuts; the second, laden with calorie-rich chocolate eclairs, tickled my nostrils with mouth-watering deliciousness.

"Always room for doughnuts!" I assured her, flashing my pearly whites as I accepted her gifts.

"We never refuse food," Sharon laughed. (Except, perhaps, cheese omelettes.)

"Who needs this many clothes, anyway?" I asked rhetorically, pulling shirts and shorts from my pannier and strapping the bundles to my rear rack to make room for fresh baked goodies.

Sheryl introduced herself. "My boyfriend's a cyclist," she confided, "so I know what it's like." She gave a broad smile. "He's always hungry."

"A true cyclist," I grinned in return.

We spoke with Sheryl for a few minutes, then she excused herself "before they fire me." Sharon and I bid her goodbye, and pedalled off, all smiles.

"Just another example of what won't appear on Channel Eleven news tonight," Sharon said.

The slender route to Dauphin wiggled and waggled, corner after corner. Compared to Saskatchewan's kilometre upon kilometre of identical straight flatness, anticipation of what laid around the next bend, or over the next rise, spurred us on.

I checked my watch and noticed the date: August 17. "It's Mom and Dad's anniversary," I said. "Keep a lookout for a phone. I want to call and wish them our best."

Near Dauphin, rambunctious vehicles reminded us once again that cyclists occupy the lowest rung on the traffic food chain. On a straight stretch, two tractor-trailer units — one overtaking the other — thundered toward us at 100-plus kilometres per hour, taking *all* the narrow two-lane road.

"There's no room!" I screamed in a falsetto voice.

At the last second, metres before impending impact, we bailed onto the gravel shoulder, skinny bicycle tires squeamish on the unaccustomed surface, threatening to dismount us. "Elbows in!" I bellowed, cold sweat beading my brow. The semis bombed past in a firestorm of rubber and violent wind, tires mere feet from our bobbing heads.

"Whew!" I sighed. "That was *wheelie* close!"

"Omigosh!" Sharon breathed as we cowered on the road shoulder. "They have *no* idea...."

The rigs were an omen. From that point on, traffic became a nightmare. Nothing but aggressive mule skinners "shared" the road with us. Even when the opposite lane was traffic-free, vehicles brushed past so close we could smell whether the occupants had used arm deodorant that morning or not.

"I think going into Dauphin to find a phone is too risky," I said, still shaking after our 36 wheel close encounter of the worst kind. "Better to abandon my phone search in favour of staying alive to call another day," I said.

"Don't worry," Sharon said. "We'll find a phone."

We swung wide around Dauphin and headed south toward the park. The parkland, forming part of the Manitoba Escarpment, rises like an island out of a sea of surrounding agricultural land. (Apparently, cyclists weren't the only persecuted animals: Riding Mountain National Park holds the distinct notoriety of the largest-known black bear in North America being killed by a poacher.)

Fortunately, once in the park, we left behind madcap double clutchers and brain-dead, road hoggers. Unfortunately, thigh-burning hills replaced them.

The scenery improved though. And an added bonus: instead of clenching my teeth and willing my bike to maintain an unwavering line in order to avoid being clobbered from behind, I could actually look around and enjoy the ride.

We pulled into Agassiz Lookout — a four-story platform rising above expansive timberland — and gaped clear across the treetops to the prairies' very origin. "See any phones?" I kidded.

We followed the park road — really just a swath cut amongst tamarack, Jack pine, balsam fir, and stands of tall white and black spruce. A breeze sashayed through the boreal forest; whispering boughs swayed like waltzing waves of rippling, green silk. Rabid traffic left behind, we pedalled in the middle of a forest ... all seemed right with the world.

On a straight section, with nothing but acres of evergreens in every direction, I came upon it. Not even a parking spot. But there it was. I braked to a stop and stood staring. Strangest place for a phone booth I ever did see.

"It's for you," Sharon teased, pulling to a stop behind me.

I didn't pass up the opportunity. I dialed mom and dad and wished them a happy anniversary.

"Sometimes the cosmos works in a truly strange manner," I muttered, hanging up the phone. "Weird how things we need turn up in the most unusual circumstances." I pedalled off, whistling, wondering if the universe was laughing behind my back.

One Tree Hill

> **"If you think Alberta is flat, just wait till you see Saskatchewan and Manitoba!"**
> ~ Mark Kile

A good distance from the forest phone, we arrived at Moon Lake campground. There were no phones.

We set up on a *wonderful* 'no service' site — crushed rock, packed as hard as concrete. "I think I need a sledgehammer to get these tent stakes in," I said. Unfortunately, we were fresh out of sledgehammers. The vestibule fluttered over the door. I zipped it, and hoped we weren't going to awake to water beds.

At 3:30 AM a major bombardment from the heavens began. Thunder resonated like sonic booms. Lightning zigged in dazzling white brilliance. Like peacefully sleeping troops, we hadn't suspected a thing. When we retired, harsh orange moonlight had illuminated the area like an arc-sodium street lamp. In contrast, with the barrage underway, I couldn't see my hand in front of my face — except when flashes of lightning lit the tent, and my fingers, with the power of million-watt strobe lights.

The morning sun shone weakly. The temperature hovered in single digits. It had rained hard — mud lay splattered a foot up the tent walls. "The day's off to a stellar start," Sharon remarked, flapping her hands so vigorously I thought she was trying to shake off her extremities. "It's so cold my fingers are tingling."

We packed up and pushed our bikes down a forest path looking for a breakfast spot in the sun. Fog swirled amongst a labyrinth of tangled thicket; sun filtered through gauzy mist, splaying light like a movie projector in a smoke-filled room.

In a quarter of a kilometre, we arrived at a large picnic shelter. "Here's where we should have set up last night," Sharon decided, surveying the interior's capacious and dry confines.

While eating pancakes smothered in butter-flavoured real imitation maple syrup, the sun burned off the ground clouds. After running out of batter, we gathered enough courage to venture forth. The forest still dripped from the liquid shelling.

Our route rambled through a sun-dappled forest. Light rays streaked through evergreen boughs like shafts of glittery diamonds. The magical scene and sparse traffic buoyed our spirits. We putted along — never quite fast enough to fully warm up — feeling as though we were traversing our own private bike path. In too short a time we arrived at Clear Lake and the village of Wasagaming, which we promptly renamed Walkamileinmymoccasins. (Like they say: Never criticize a man until you've walked a mile in his moccasins. Good advice. That way, you're a mile away, and you have his shoes.)

Vacationers toodled around town on balloon-tired cruiser bikes. Bathing suit clad families swam along the beach, searching for shade. Sunscreened youngsters paddled about on air mattresses. And there we were, shivering, swaddled in long pants and fleece pullovers.

Caught in a cobweb-like sunbeam, we lolled on a park's grass, rallying our body temperatures while quaffing litre containers of warm fruit juice. A couple strolled over. Joanne and Lance, from Winnipeg, were touring cyclists on a car vacation.

"We tried cycling to Halifax last summer," Lance said, his face strained. "But our trip ended when I injured my Achilles tendon. All the cold rain did it in."

Joanne's eyes were big and bright. "Our next trip is going to be to Vancouver."

They inspected our bikes and accompanying mountain of gear. "We have a Trek tandem," Lance said. "And we love it ... but we can't carry anywhere near the amount of stuff you two have." He hoisted my bike barely an inch off the ground. "Your loads are astonishing!"

"Yeah," I agreed. "We're the Winnebagos of cycle tourists. Funny thing is, we're actually pared down quite well compared to previous trips. You should have seen what we carried when we cycled across the States! We're practically tent trailers compared to then."

Joanne and Lance exhorted our accomplishment. Their cheerfulness and enthusiasm warmed our hearts. Leaving them to plan their next excursion, we pressed on, and rode out of Riding Mountain National Park. Like stepping through an exit after a wondrous Disney ride, we left our magical surrounds and were deposited back onto bald prairie. No trees. No corners. No hills. Except one. The road jogged, tumbled over a small bump next to a lone tree, then resumed, flat and straight as an arrow.

"Just because it was there?" I asked, gaping back at the insignificant rise.

"Good to see road engineers have a sense of imagination," Sharon laughed.

A blue sign indicated picnic tables ahead. We left the pavement and cycled a muddy path half a kilometre without tripping across the promised tables. A half-kilometre farther, I spotted an outhouse. I dropped my bike onto the mucky earth and rushed to the biffy.

Pushing the door open, a two-foot high charred mess greeted me. Someone had enjoyed a roaring campfire — right in the middle of the privy. With the amount of ash and blackened remains it was amazing the entire structure hadn't burnt down.

"Interesting picnic area," Sharon said upon my return. "There's not one table."

"They burned 'em in the toilet."

I forayed into the bush — the outhouse was unusable, after all — and glimpsed a table, hidden in a clump of trees. "Hey!" I called. "I found one the vandals missed."

We squelched through bog and knee-high wet grass, over broken glass and heaps of trash, to reach the coveted table. Our reward? Hordes of bloodsucking mosquitoes!

"Let's get out of here!" Sharon screeched, flapping her arms like an overzealous bat as the little vampires attacked her. Abandoning any thoughts of eating, we beat a hasty retreat — or at least as quick as the mud allowed.

"Maybe we should get mountain bikes?" I puffed, sliding off the slippery path.

Back on Highway 10 traffic became ugly. Visions of rejoining route 16, the Yellowhead Highway, with its smooth and wide shoulder was all that kept us going. After almost getting plastered head-on for the umpteenth time by careless drivers passing the vehicle in front of them, I shouted, "Folks on the way to the park sure are in a hurry to get there!"

"Yep!" Sharon snorted. "So they can start relaxing!"

Streams of traffic hurtled past — slowing neither one iota, nor moving over one fraction.

A car stormed past, narrowly missing us. Sharon raged. "If they have to slow down two seconds — forget it! They don't care whether they kill us or not!"

Her words hanging in the air like noxious exhaust, a honkin' Ford Thunderbird swerved into our lane, intent on overtaking another sedan. The driver careened straight toward us. Feeling like a rodent being dive-bombed by an eagle, I flipped the oncoming road hog the bird. Nothing like one final act of defiance.

"Hit the ditch!" Sharon screamed.

Hearts in our mouths, we veered onto the gravel shoulder, missing becoming dead meat by scant metres.

"They really ought to take away some licenses!" Sharon fumed, wobbling back onto the road edge.

"Or at least charge more for the box of cereal they got them out of," I sputtered.

Blood pressure rocketing skyward, we intersected the Yellowhead. A major highway, it boasted a wide paved shoulder that allowed us to keep a tolerable distance from the obnoxious speeding metal behemoths. I glanced over my shoulder and sneered. We had survived Highway 10.

I shouldn't have been so hasty. In a few kilometres we hit the cyclists' dreaded road condition: construction. Our paved shoulder disintegrated beneath a layer of loose gravel. Compounding our misery, a headwind bucked into us, blowing dust from every passing vehicle into our watering and stinging eyes.

A sign warned: SLOW DOWN. SAVE YOUR WINDSHIELD. Autos roared past. Peppermint-sized pebbles spit from beneath their tires like machine gun fire. We tucked our heads. Gravel bounced off our headgear. *Windshield, hell,* I thought. *What about my glasses?*

"Another use for helmets!" I yelled to Sharon.

"I need a break!" she called back.

Black olive thunderclouds, draped in beetle-browed satanic faces, blotted out the sun. Shivering and famished — exhausted from battling the headwind and drained from dodging pea-brained drivers — we pulled into a Minnedosa gas station. *Just how much more of this fun can we take?* I wondered.

Crack the Sky

> **"The weather-cock on the church spire, though made of iron, would soon be broken by the storm-wind if it ... did not understand the noble art of turning to every wind."**
> ~ Heinrich Heine

I entered the gas station and asked the traffic advisory expert behind the till about our upcoming route. Freight trucks, buses, and, worst of all, holiday traffic — plied Highway 16 non-stop. (How 80-year-old drivers qualify to operate 40-foot Winnebagos towing a sport-utility vehicle *and* a motorboat is beyond my wildest imagination.)

"Ya know," the expert drawled, screwing his lips. "I've driven it countless times ... but I can't say for sure whether it has a paved shoulder or not."

I reckoned that meant not. Our dream route atomized in a puff of dusty smoke.

Despondent, I exited. The convoluted afternoon sky had grown dark — so dark that streetlights flickered feebly, attempting to illuminate the baleful gloom. I stared heavenward. An uneasiness gripped me.

Anvil-shaped thunderheads had closed within hammering distance. Funnel clouds dangled wispy tendrils earthward.

"It's headed straight this way," Sharon said, calculating the wind direction. She pointed to a restaurant across the road. "I vote for waiting it out."

Being the ever optimist (tailwind!), I taunted her. "It'll pass."

Sharon regarded the sky's sinister features. The wind shrieked like a banshee, rebuking me for even daring to think about challenging its menacing supremacy. "An all-out drenching is assured," Sharon said, and prepared to launch into a full-scale difference of opinion. But before she could, a fellow hopped out of a cow-patty brown aging Buick. Engine running, headlights glimmering, windshield wipers flapping, he ducked under the roof's overhang alongside us.

"Hi," he said with a big smile. He reached out and grasped my cold fingers in a warm and hearty handshake. "My name's Jerry," he introduced himself. "I ride a bike, too."

As the wind gathered intensity, Jerry asked us questions. "I've seen a lot of cyclists go by," he said. "And I've always wondered what you guys carry in all those bags."

While presenting Jerry with a list of essentials we lugged in those burgeoning packs, fat raindrops began splattering the parking lot. Like an overweight tap dancer on a trampoline, pear-shaped globes bounced off the tarmac and leaped against our shins. "Not good biking weather," Jerry judged.

"It'll pass," I said.

The rain turned to hail. Ice particles shot from a pistol-grey sky, ricocheting off the blacktop like wayward bullets at a Serbian wedding celebration. "That would have caused some bruises," I winced. The wind twisted, whirled, writhed, corkscrewed. Hail turned back into rain. Hydrous globules slobbered our bare legs like some over-friendly St Bernard.

"I think your riding is done for the day," Jerry surmised. I nodded. "Can I buy you folks a coffee?" he asked. "My lady works across the road at the coffee bar."

I accepted his kind offer. It sounded a rather salubrious way to spend the next, oh, 24 hours or so. I didn't even have to consult Sharon. Call it male intuition.

We dashed across the road in record time. Carl Lewis would have been proud. I held the door of the Prairie Pantry as Sharon stepped through. "See?" I whispered. "It's passing."

"Yeah," Sharon nodded. "Like a kidney stone. And a good thing about raindrops that size? We can dodge 'em."

As Jerry guided us toward a booth I was thinking that something we had come to term as the 'kindness principle' was in effect. The first time we noticed the rule was on our cycle trip across the States. Whenever we became dispirited — from rainy weather; a bike breakdown; or just from being on the road too long, far from family and friends — someone (or something) happened along to rally our spirits. It occurred repeatedly ... so often that we began to wonder if a series of occurrences weren't merely coincidences at all. Perhaps a patron saint really did look after wayward travellers?

Jerry's wife, Ruth, hustled over. While exchanging introductions, pleasantries, and weather forecasts, Ruth offered to buy. "Tips have been good today," she smiled. What a province! Regardless of the weather, that Manitoba hospitality persevered.

Jerry peered out at the fury still swirling in the heavens. The storm had turned, taking another run. "Looks like this cloudburst isn't over yet," he remarked. I'd say his appraisal held water. Ruth brought hot chocolates. Jerry turned to his wife. "How about if we ask these folks if they'd like to spend the night at our place?"

Ruth agreed to Jerry's good idea. "I have to work till 8 PM," she said. "We'll have a late supper." She brought more hot chocolates. We slurped appreciatively, savouring the rich goodness, feeling the warmth flood down into the very depths of our beings.

An hour later, the rain eased to a drizzle. Jerry led us back across the road. While we grabbed our bikes, Jerry hopped into his car (still idling, headlights dim, windshield wipers slapping).

At a stop sign three blocks later, we pulled alongside two mud-spattered mountain bikers. Sharon and I chatted with them, waiting for traffic to clear. In a brief opening, Jerry zipped out. Pedalling at 40 kilometres per hour, Sharon and I glued ourselves to Jerry's bumper. The mountain bikers sprinted behind, trying to catch up. Just when they were about to close the gap, Jerry picked up the pace. Sharon and I, tucked in the big Buick's slipstream, smiled and shifted onto our large 52-tooth chainrings. That was the last we saw of those pretty mountain-biker-dudes-clad-in-sleek-cycling-duds.

"Well at least they look fast," Sharon laughed, glancing at their rapidly diminishing forms in her mirror.

"Bring your bikes through here," Jerry said when we arrived at his place a few minutes later. We pushed our loaded bikes through a backyard gate. There, parked on the grass, was a much-chromed and gold-plated Harley. I laughed. So that's what Jerry meant when he had said, 'I ride a bike, too.'

"Great bike!" I said, admiring the gleaming machine.

"Yeah, I like it," Jerry responded. "Over the winter, I park it in the living room." (And to think, I had felt remiss about working on my bicycle in our *basement.*) "Come on in," he invited. "I'll introduce you to the kids. Well, only one — our daughter, Sabrina, is away at Turtle Mountain bible camp." Like a proud, but nervous papa, he added, "She's 13 and drop-dead gorgeous."

We met Jerry's 11-year-old son, Jerry Jr. Or, as Jerry referred to him: "Little Jerry."

We also met Jerry's dog, Sabo — an intimidating hulk of Doberman-Shepherd. "Good Sabo," I muttered. "Good doggy."

"Just stand still until he gets a sniff of you," Jerry advised. "He's only bitten three people." He paused, and squinted, as if remembering something unpleasant. "Oh, yeah, and mauled one guy."

Comforting.

Sabo smelt us. He liked us. At least he didn't bite us. I wondered if the mauled guy counted as one of the three?

"I'll show you his training," Jerry said. *"Sabo! Watch 'em!"* The big dog's ears perked. Sabo glared at us and growled. I gulped. A guttural laugh broke from Jerry. "At ease, Sabo." The big dog relaxed. "That's a lot of fun when the sister-in-law comes over," Jerry said. "Your bikes will be safe here tonight."

"No kidding!" (I didn't even bother to lock our bikes that night. I thought it'd be kind of fun, in a sick sort of way, to watch a thief *try* to steal them ... but a bike wouldn't be much good to someone without legs, would it?)

Jerry glanced at his watch. "I have to get ready for work," he said. "I'm a plant engineer in Neepawa. Actually, it's pretty much a Homer Simpson job," he joked. "I watch dials to make sure the plant keeps cool. It's a pretty good job. Lots of time for doing what I like ... and getting paid for it. I've taken a ton of courses," he said. "Sometimes I play computer chess. In the summer, I spend a lot of time polishing my bike. As long as I keep those dials in the right place I can do anything I want...."

"That's the job I'm looking for!" I said.

"Of course," Jerry said slowly, "if an ammonia line ruptures, you're dead."

Hmmm. Always a downside.

Jerry left. Ruth wasn't home yet. Sharon headed off to shower. I was left alone to entertain Little Jerry.

I took the opportunity to show him some of our biking gear. "This is one cool stove," I said, pulling out our WhisperLite mini flame-thrower.

"How does it work?" Little Jerry queried.

"I'm so glad you asked." Little Jerry was about to receive one brilliant stove demonstration. One he'd still be talking about when he graduated — from university. I assembled the miniature blowtorch on the kitchen table and began pumping the plunger with long and steady strokes, pressurizing the metal fuel canister. "You guys have fire insurance, right?"

Slightly after 8 PM, Ruth arrived home on her mountain bike. Somewhat of a miracle, the house was still standing. Nothing a little ceiling paint wouldn't fix.

"No fender," I said, observing the telltale mud skunk-stripe decorating her backside.

She shrugged. "Yep, hardly ever rains around here. You guys hungry?" As usual, we were.

Ruth set to work frying chicken, boiling baby potatoes, and stirring a big pot of beans. Sharon and I tossed together a cucumber and tomato salad. While waiting, Little Jerry shared a box of chocolate-covered almonds with Sharon and me.

When Little Jerry departed to rent an Arnie video, his mom said, "Those are his favourite! He must really like you guys."

"Yeah," I grunted. "We've bonded." I didn't mention the fab stove demo.

Mysterious Ways

"To see a World in a Grain of Sand,
And a Heaven in a Wild Flower,
Hold Infinity in the palm of your hand,
And Eternity in an hour."
~ William Blake

Jerry returned from his 12-hour work stint before Sharon or I stirred the following morning.

Upon arising, we lingered over breakfast, chatting with our hosts.

"Yeah," Jerry began, "Ruth and I have done some bike touring, too. On my Harley, that is. One summer, we rode through the States." He paused, reflecting. "In Tennessee we pretty much ran out of money. We were down to our last two dollars. It came to a choice of eating or buying a couple of bucks of gas. I figured I could earn a tank of gas by throwing bales for a farmer, so we decided to eat.

"At a McDonald's I ordered a burger for me and a salad for Ruth. 'How come I only get a salad, and you get a burger?' she asked. 'Well,' I told her, 'all you have to do is sit and watch the bike while I throw bales.'

"While we're sitting there eating, a guy comes over and asks me if that's my bike outside. 'It's the best I've ever seen!' he says.

"At that point I began networking. I explained we were out of cash and asked him if he knew any farmers in the area that needed a hand for a day or two.

"'I have an even better idea,' the guy says. He walks out the door, then comes back in a couple of minutes later. 'My wife says it's okay," he says. 'You can come over to our place.'

"We stayed with Tom and his wife for three days," Jerry said. "When we left, Tom handed me $40 to buy gas so we could get home. Ruth and Tom's wife have been pen pals ever since."

I hoped we never ran so short of cash we'd have to rely on complete strangers for handouts.

"When I saw you guys at the gas station and that storm brewing to be a doozy," Jerry said, "it brought back memories. Kinda like payback time, I figured, for all the times people have done good deeds for us."

Maybe we already were relying on complete strangers?

"Another time," Jerry said, "I was at a bike rally in the States. Big, fat, hairy, American bikers were razzing us Canadians as usual. 'Wussy riders,' they called us.

"At the time, I was working as a guard at Stony Mountain penitentiary and doing a few hours of weight lifting everyday. I guess you could say I was in pretty good shape.

"I waited until the biggest fat-assed biker dude got onto his bike to do a beer run. I snuck up behind him, and lifted the fat bastard and his hog a couple of inches off the ground!

"Fatty put it in gear ... but he didn't budge one inch. He revved his motor, but he still didn't move. He couldn't figure out what was going on. When he turned around, and saw me holding up both him *and* his bike, I tell ya, Fat Bastard looked surprised. I let go of his bike. He wobbled a little ways in the sand and fell over.

"I figured he was going to kill me anyway, so I said, 'I thought you were telling us what a good rider you were!' Fat Bastard's friends looked at him sprawled ass-over-teakettle in the sand, and they started laughing real hard, falling all over themselves. Finally, Fatty started to laugh, too."

After more reminiscing — and lunch — Sharon and I departed our new friends' home. We felt fortunate to have met and shared time with them — another instance where someone came along at precisely the right moment. (When accepting invitations, we tempered our enthusiasm by following our intuition. If either of us felt uncomfortable, we declined the offer.) Odd as it may seem, whenever we were down, someone invariably appeared and raised our flagging spirits.

Spuds

"Cogito ergo spud. I think, therefore I yam."
~ *Graffito*, reported by Herb Caen, *San Francisco Chronicle*

We left Minnedosa and passed an oxbow lake. Horses and colts, secure behind wired fence, cantered over to the fenceline to gape at our mounts. Perhaps they thought our bicycles were cayuses that had broke loose from the herd?

We tossed a few apples their way, then galloped south on Highway 10, abandoning the under-construction Yellowhead route (Jerry confirmed it had no shoulder). After my sneering, I guess the road had had the last laugh.

At Brandon, we turned east, and, devoid of good sense, cycled on the four lane, but no paved shoulder, Trans Canada Highway. Yikes! And I had thought the Yellowhead traffic was bad. Hugging the right-most strip of asphalt, we timorously surveyed our mirrors as vehicles buzzed past.

After two hours, we were more than ready to flee the hornet-like traffic. "We have to get off this road!" Sharon yelled. "This isn't what I call bicycle touring. It's more like a demolition derby!"

Fleeing onto rural Highway 351, we left the swarm behind. In Carberry, the town's fairgrounds provided a spot for overnight camping. Sharon silently watched our pasta boil. Suddenly she blurted: "I know this sounds crazy, but I have a sudden craving for baked potatoes."

I grinned. "I'll keep an eye out."

Leaving Carberry the next morning, the cosmos continued its beguiling ways. We hadn't gone more than a kilometre when we spied an oblong object lying on the gravel shoulder. It looked like ... no ... it couldn't be!

We pedalled closer, still not believing. But, sure enough, a huge potato, caked in earth, lay on the road's edge, just waiting for some wishful person to come along. Chuckling at the absurdity, I stopped and picked it up (I'm sure it winked at me). I held it high for Sharon to see. "You should be careful what you wish for," I kidded her. "Now we have to figure out a way to bake it."

For the next few kilometers we traced a trail of taters strewn along the roadside. My pannier was overflowing by the time we began passing field after field of hilled potatoes. Carberry's nickname? We learned later it was 'Spud City.' Who knew?

Cinnamon Buns

> **"God could not be everywhere and therefore he made mothers."**
> ~ Jewish Proverb

It was late afternoon when we arrived in Swan Lake. The only place open for miles around was a drive-in. But before Sharon would eat there she had me check the washrooms. Luckily, they were spotless (I wasn't in the mood for baking potatoes). I reported my findings to the waiting outside Sharon. She ventured in and we sat at an old-fashioned booth.

After inhaling a couple of delicious gooey pizzas, I sauntered to the till and paid. "Do you suppose we could camp behind your restaurant for the night?" I casually inquired. "We're on bikes; we're really quiet, and we'll leave early in the morning."

"Sure," the fellow answered. "Plenty of room." He extended a big hand, and with a hearty handshake introduced himself as Mr Van Cauwenberghe.

"Adeline," he called. "Come here a moment. I have someone for you to meet."

Mrs Van Cauwenberghe was even more hospitable than her husband. "Would you like a shower?" she immediately asked.

I snapped up her fine offer.

She showed us around back. Opening a door to her son Mike's living quarters, she toured us to the bathroom. "Use as much of the soap and shampoo as you like!"

Much later, our skin scrubbed shining pink, Sharon and I sat at a picnic table behind the restaurant writing postcards. Feeling homesick for family back home, we were missing them as much as we imagined them missing us. Adeline appeared, breaking our melancholy. "Come in for a bedtime snack," she invited warmly.

We entered the restaurant. Adeline motioned us to a table marked RESERVED. She brought over tall glasses of cold milk. Mr Van Cauwenberghe set two plates of steaming cinnamon buns in front of us.

I was shocked. It wasn't like me to miss something like that. "I — I didn't see cinnamon buns on the menu," I stammered.

"Oh, they're not," Adeline said, smiling. "We make them once a week, special for family."

How about that? Sharon and I grinned. Warmness spread through our beings. A couple of hours earlier we had merely been anonymous smelly strangers. Now these kind folks had adopted us as part of their family. Savouring the sticky treats, we realized even though we were a thousand miles from home, no one was ever truly far from home when mothers were around.

Baba

> **"Kind words can be short and easy to speak, but their echoes are truly endless."**
> ~ Mother Teresa

Cool air and coppery hills rolled together for a memorable morning ride. The sun playfully peeked through cloud cover. Sunbeams pierced clouds and hop-skipped their way with us, scampering across the tan plains.

It was a Sunday. And on Sundays, in small prairie towns, everything was closed more tightly than a two-year-old's fist clenching a handful of Smarties. Having left Swan Lake before our hosts were up, we passed through Somerset, Deerwood, Miami, Rosebank, Jordan, Roland, Myrtle, Kane, and Lowe Farm. Not a single place stirred.

Sparse traffic continued from Morris to La Rochelle. Then, T-boning Highway 59 we had to make a choice. Head north and reconnect with the Trans Canada Highway — the route east into Ontario — and try to carve out some elbow room alongside motorhomes, freight trucks, and Greyhound buses? Or, head south to the Canada-US border and meander along gentle trafficked rural routes through Minnesota? Gee. Let me think.

We chose the southern route. "Besides," Sharon said, "if we head north, we'll hit Winnipeg traffic. South will be quieter."

"And safer," I added, shuddering from our previous Trans Canada Highway misadventure.

Our southerly route turned out to be as treacherous as the Clan Campbell. A weekend ball tournament hosted in Saint Malo had recently concluded and a line of scrappy traffic returning to Winnipeg snorted toward us. Impetuous lead-footed apes gambled on any conceivable break in traffic to leapfrog ahead of their neighbour. Sharon and I kissed the dust several times.

Near Saint Malo, three oncoming heavy-footed chimps, trailing each other by scant car lengths, pulled out simultaneously to overtake a fluffy footer in front of them who was "only" doing a hundred kilometres per hour.

"Bail!" I shouted between swears. We hit the gravel, narrowly avoiding being smushed like lowly worms. "I wish more people rode bikes," I lamented, dusting myself off, "so they'd know what it's like to see a two-ton Chevy barrelling straight between their eyeballs."

We arrived in Rosa, shaken. "How about calling it a day?" Sharon asked. She headed over to a new community hall to inspect the grounds for camping possibilities as a car pulled into the driveway next to us. I walked over and asked the fella if he thought anyone would mind if we camped outside the community hall overnight.

Larry said, "I have an even better idea. You can stay right here in my mom's yard." He shook my hand. "I've just driven down from Winnipeg for my weekly visit. Traffic's frightful, eh?"

"I'd say!" I was in the midst of telling about our near-miss by Malo when Sharon joined us. Larry's elderly mother, hearing the commotion, appeared from around a corner of the house. An aged woman clung to her arm. Larry introduced us to his smiling mom, Theresa. "She's known locally as Mother Teresa," he said. Her grey eyes twinkled as she patted his arm.

Larry introduced the other woman as his Aunt Ann. Aunt Ann appeared a trifle eccentric. A wind-blown leaf peeked from a tussle of blue hair. Larry kindly plucked it free. I pulled a twisted little half-smile, imagining a bird's nest (and a happy wren or two) cached away in there somewhere, too. Aunt Ann smiled, and patted Larry's hand.

Larry invited Sharon and me in for tea and cake. "That's one good thing about Ukrainian families," he joked. "No visitor has ever left hungry."

After our snack, Larry bundled us into his sports car and we shot off to visit his sister Elsie, and her husband, Steve. They turned out to be kind and generous folks as well, feeding us tomatoes and cucumbers, freshly harvested from their garden.

The topic turned to travelling. When Steve and Elsie heard the list of places Sharon and I planned on cycling, they confessed a lifelong dream: to visit their homeland in the Ukraine. We encouraged them to realize their dream and not be like the countless people who had told us, "I wish we had done that."

It was dark by the time Larry shuttled us back to his mom's (headlights sure are handy). Back in his mom's kitchen, we talked and talked. Larry noticed the time. "Whoops!" he abruptly exclaimed. "Time for me to get back to Winnipeg. I have to work in the morning."

Shaking my hand goodbye, he shoved a $20 bill into my shirt pocket. "A small contribution to your trip. Maybe you can send us a postcard if you get a chance?"

With Larry's kind words and good wishes warm in our hearts, we got ready to set up our tent. Theresa (or Baba, as she insisted we call her) offered us the use of beds, but we didn't want her to go through the trouble of making up beds, then having to launder sheets and pillowcases. We stuck to our guns and maintained we would be fine in our tent. Baba eventually agreed (it was well past her bedtime, too). But, before doing so, she made us promise we'd return for extra blankets if we grew even slightly chilly.

Dead tired, we wandered out to Baba's front yard. I hadn't noticed before, but on the other side of her fence was a graveyard. Under creamy moonlight we pitched our tent. It resembled a giant headstone. We crawled into our coffin-like sleeping bags, and buried ourselves six-feet deep.

"I've never had a Baba before," Sharon murmured as she prowled off to netherworlds with a rest-in-peace smile.

In the morning — the moment we stirred — Baba called out, and invited us in to shower. While we availed ourselves to plentiful hot water, she busied herself in the kitchen making mountains of toast and buckets of tea.

While consuming my fourth slice, a cat strutted past. I chuckled, wondering if I strapped a piece of buttered-side up toast on the cat's back and dropped it off the table, whether the opposing forces of nature would cause the cat to hover.

At 9 AM the phone rang. "It's for you," Baba sang sweetly, handing me the receiver.

"How did you sleep last night?" Larry asked.

"Like a dead man!" I replied. "And no one from the graveyard ripped off our bikes for a midnight ride."

An hour later, Sharon and I waved goodbye to Baba. We met many fine folks on our travels, but Larry and his family's caring attitude elevated the definition of hospitality to a whole new level. Baba's euphonious golden warble lives within us still.

Big Hill ?

"I've got to get to the top of the hill ... "
~ Last words of John Pierpont Morgan

In Piney, it appeared someone's summer job was to paint the town. Not red, mind you, but industrial green — a shade so hideous it made me think someone had gotten a very good deal on a bulk quantity.

We located the town's fairgrounds and were burning our lunch, as usual, with our pyro WhisperLite stove. (I had discovered 'simmer' was about a foot off the burner and a bit to the right.) As we swatted out the flames a dusty pickup pulled up. A young fellow jumped out and charged over to our table. Perhaps the three-foot flame jumping off the burner had fired his curiosity?

He stood beside us, not saying a word. Neither did we.

He settled himself down on the other side of the picnic table — on the end farthest from us. After a couple of disquieting silent minutes, it turned into a virtual staring contest. With his unblinking eyes riveted on us, Sharon began to squirm. I thought perhaps he was mute? Perhaps he thought the same about the two of us?

Still not saying a thing, he rose from his seat (lunch break over?) and trotted back to his pickup. Sharon and I gave each other questioning glances. Maybe the dude was a loony and had gone to get his gun?

He returned holding forth two white ball caps — PINEY emblazoned in navy blue across their peaks.

"Thanks," we said, as we accepted his gifts. The ice broken, we spoke nonchalantly with him for a few minutes. He told us he was a Grade 12 student who had been hired to paint the town. They had given him a box of caps to hand out to tourists. "But you're the first I've seen. And I almost forgot I had them in the truck." Ready to be on his way, he asked, "Do you guys need anything?"

"Anywhere I can get water?" I asked.

"Sure," he said, and motioned to his truck. "Hop in."

I gave Sharon a shrug. "Be right back," I said.

We drove to a church. "It's another place I'm painting," he explained. From a huge ring of keys, he unlocked the door and led me to the kitchen. With all those keys he was a handy guy to have around. After filling our water bottles he drove me back to the fairgrounds. Sharon and I held up our new baseball caps and waved goodbye as he drove off to paint another building.

Sharon grinned at me. "It sure is neat how just being on bicycles brings out people's generosity."

I led the way to Sprague. A beardown wind made the distance feel twice as far as usual. The terrain was nearly dead flat, but the temperature equalled the 30 kilometre per hour headwind that impeded our progress. We endured a long, hot, slog. But we made it.

Knocking back ice-cold lemony drinks outside a store, five kids rode up on old BMX bikes. Straddling their top tubes they stared at our bulging loads, and asked questions about bicycle touring.

Conversing with them I learned that the definition of a hill was a relative thing.

"Where did you ride from today?" one boy asked.

"Rosa," I answered, and glanced at my odometer. "About 116 kilometres from here."

"Whew!" they breathed, impressed. But they had never heard of Rosa. I rattled off the names of a couple of other towns en route. Still blank looks.

"Piney?" I tried. Their eyes lit up.

"Did you have to push up that big hill?"

I narrowed my eyes, thinking back.

But I still couldn't recollect any 'big hill' the entire way from Piney to Sprague. Just that horrendous headwind. "Huh?" I said. "What big hill?"

"You know," one answered in an annoyed tone, thinking I was teasing them, "the one right after you leave Piney."

I paused, thinking hard, and finally recalled what, to us, had been nothing more than an insignificant bump!

"Nope," I answered. "We pedalled it."

"All the way!?"

"Yep," I nodded gravely.

"No way!" one exploded, shaking his tousled head. "*No one* can ride a bike up *that* hill!"

"Especially on those things," another sputtered.

"You must have had to push."

Grand Central Station

"As soon as you feel too old to do a thing, do it!"
~ Margaret Deland

Sharon, exhausted from the brawny prairie wind (or was it that big hill out of Piney?), was ready for a good night's rest. Constant headwinds, combined with flat unchanging 'scenery,' and lack of amenities in small prairie towns had worn her down. Calling it an early night we cinched down our flapping tent fly in an impenetrable spot behind the local bingo parlour.

At 3:30 AM, booming cracks of thunder roused me. Wind gusts animated our tent like a German Shepherd shaking a rat. Rain splattered the tent fly. Claps of thunder rocked the bingo hall. Sharon didn't twitch a muscle. Who needed sleeping pills? Cycling a loaded touring bike into a headwind all day was a sublime insomnia buster.

In the morning, I discovered my shoe was more akin to a drinking vessel than it was to footwear. I had left it outside the tent in a *perfect* spot to catch water draining off the fly. I dumped the water out, and gingerly inserted my foot. My wonderfully warm and dry sock absorbed leftover rainwater. "Oh, man," I grimaced, "what a terrific way to begin the day!"

Everything was soaked — from bicycle seats to panniers. Even my cycling gloves, left in an upside-down helmet, were sodden hunks of curled leather. And the plastic sheet we had covered our bikes with to protect them from inclement weather? It had flown the coop (no wonder I hadn't heard it flapping). I searched the area and found it some distance away, cloaked around bushes in a hearty hug, clucking gently in the morning breeze.

Sharon wrung out apparel that had been strapped to her rear carrier to dry. We left the tent set up, hoping it would dry a bit (packed wet, it added considerable weight — and in our current physical and emotional slump extra weight wasn't what we needed). I strapped my still-dripping helmet under my chin and rode to a store to buy breakfast.

I didn't have much luck. When I returned from my scavenging foray, Sharon peered into the bag. The carrots were soft and withered; Bugs Bunny would surely have rejected them. Tiny rock-hard plums would have made superb slingshot ammo. But as food they were nothing but dental bills. Oranges — so blemished and of such a despicable blue hue — more rightfully should have been called 'three-day old corpse.'

"This stuff is garbage!" Sharon lashed out, none too happy about having to suffer the dual indignities of being wet *and* having nothing to eat but horrid tasting grindage.

I picked through the morass and ate the less putrid bits.

"I'm hungry," Sharon complained when I had finished.

We rolled up our limp rag of a tent, hopped on our bikes, and descended upon the nearest restaurant to ravage their breakfast special. When I had licked my plate clean for the second time, we were both in better spirits.

With a spring in our step we exited and retrieved our bikes from the parking area. A youth strolled over. "I'm in my last year of high school," he told us before asking the three usual cycle touring questions: Where are you from? Where are you going? How many miles a day do you do? He listened intently, then floored us. "When I was younger," he said, "I thought of riding my bike long distance." A nostalgic look appeared on his face. "But now I'm too old," he lamented. "I'm seventeen. I'm over the hill."

Huh? Sharon and I looked at each other — startled — our eyebrows arched in wonder. But, before we could protest, the school bus pulled in and the driver honked. Leaving us dumbstruck, our old-before-his-time, young friend departed.

"Jeez," Sharon said. "What age does he think we are?"

"Less than seventeen, apparently."

Feeling like two kids, we cycled to the Canada-US border near Middlebro, Manitoba, and crossed at Longworth into the state of Minnesota.

"Where are you headed?" a border guard asked.

"Rainy River," we answered (a town in Ontario about 80 kilometres away).

"Have a good ride," he said, waving us through with a chuckle. "Hope it doesn't rain."

Skirting Muskeg Bay, a pleasant portion of Lake of the Woods, we found something different between Canada and the States that only cyclists might notice: American canines took a much greater interest in us than their Canadian brethren. In Canada, it had been a rare treat when a dog chased us (I had thought of carrying dog biscuits to toss to them for encouragement). But in the States, the chase-after-cyclists affair dogged us all along our route.

"Another item to add to our list of tribulations!" Sharon yelled, sprinting past another junkyard mongrel. So intent on welcoming us to the States it had even dropped the bone it was gnawing on to give chase. Compounding our dilemma was the fact that most American houses were closer to the road than houses had been in Canada. It gave the American dogs an unfair advantage — kind of like jumping the gun in a hundred-metre dash.

And the American pooches were less friendly than their Canadian cousins, too. "Definitely not as laid back," Sharon yelped as a mongrel snapped at her heels. The canines pursued us, in ones, twos, and packs of three and more, yipping and yapping, snapping and snarping. It was all quite unsettling. As a smaller mutt made a run at my ankle I had the inclination to kick at it. America's first drive-by booting? But I thought better of it. As we raced past another unleashed crossbreed, a silly little doggerel ran through my head: 'Who, who, who let the dogs out?'

Having momentarily left the dogs behind, a van pulled alongside. The passenger window rolled down. I wondered if the woman behind it intended to hold out her lap dog so it could bark at us too. "We want to take your picture!" the woman yelled. "You look so cute with your little helmets!"

Gosh, golly, and gee whiz. We were tourist attractions! And cute ones at that. We complied. Smiling shyly, of course.

Highway 11's wild flowers and paved shoulder swept us (and our cute helmets), into Baudette, population reportedly 1,300. I thought the population sign was missing a zero. The amount of traffic plying the streets astounded us.

"All 1,300 citizens must have jumped in their cars for a joy ride around town at the same time," Sharon surmised.

Traffic wasn't the only thing in the little town that was big. The Ralph and Randy's food store was humongous. There was even a Pizza Hut.

"Welcome to civilization," I grinned. (When we had cycled across America, Sharon and I fell in love with the big people and their friendly all-you-can-eat buffets strung from one end of the country to the other.)

"Americans know how to eat!" I stated with relish, enjoying my 'America is superior' attitude. After all the mom and pop backwater grocery stores we had the misfortune to come across in the Canadian prairies, Ralph and Randy's looked like Grand Central Station.

The ripe fruit was immaculate. I scored a package of Nutter-butter cookies (my favourite, and not available in any of the prairie stores we had frequented). There was even *two*-quart chocolate milk. "What a country!" I said.

We retreated with our spoils and found a seat beneath a shady oak, near Baudette's giant 40-foot walleye fish statue, and ate until we couldn't eat any more. I laid back, patted my stomach, and watched splendid Rainy River tumble past, sneaking through pools and spilling over rocks as it made its way downstream. Late in the afternoon, the low-pressure system that had been building since morning increased. "I don't think I've felt it this muggy since cycling in Kentucky," I griped, and pushed a button on our short-wave radio to check the weather forecast. But the radio wouldn't turn on. Moisture from all the humidity messing with the circuits?

"I don't need a weather report to tell me the humidity is 98 percent," Sharon said. "Let's find a shower!" Feeling as sticky as two candy canes leftover from last Christmas, we set off.

Luck was on our side. Or was it? We located a public swimming pool. Only one problem: It was closed. We continued on, shirts sticking to our backsides like flypaper, and came across a football field. Sharon spotted a spigot. She threw her bike down and charged the faucet in slow motion like a haggard explorer who had just crossed the Sahara.

Sombre clouds the colour of old inner tubes bunched overhead as we splashed cool water over our bods. After throwing on clean clothes we hightailed it to a park and set up our tent. Once plastic bags had been securely fastened over our bicycle seats, we entered the tent — but not before one final check to ensure our shoes were high and dry.

Dave? Is That You?

> **"There is only one difference between a madman and me. The madman thinks he is sane. I know I am mad."**
> ~ Salvador Dali

Back in Canada, after our 80 kilometre US detour, we traipsed into a Rainy River grocery store and discovered it stocked with bits of second-rate fruit (not to mention the extortionist prices the little store was asking).

"What did you expect?" I scoffed when Sharon complained. "Ralph and Randy's?"

"You just like the US better," Sharon shot back, "because you're an extrovert and Canadians are introverted."

"Huh?" I said. "I just like to eat real fruit." I held aloft a banana as green as spring grass. "What's this?" I questioned. "An edible wood product?"

In downtown Rainy River, we stopped at a park. Even though garbage receptacles reared their silver heads every few feet, the place was strewn with garbage from one end to the other. The mess of cans, papers, and bottles didn't make a favourable first impression for folks entering from the States.

A cracked and bumpy highway led us along chocolate brown Rainy River, past ripe hay fields, and autumn leaves of multihued reds and oranges. All the signs were there for a perfect fall day. But it didn't feel that way — the temperature reached a sticky 30 degrees Celsius.

Overheated, we plodded through towns with names like Sleeman, Pinewood, Stratton, Barwick, and Emo. By midafternoon — shirts adhered to our sweaty backs like they'd been crazy-glued there, hair plastered against our foreheads — we arrived in Fort Francis and headed straight for the public pool, dreaming of wallowing in the refreshing showers. There, a detestable sign confronted us: OUT OF ORDER.

"Just our luck," I groaned.

"Dirty luck," Sharon frowned. "Maybe we can break in? I'm beginning to feel like we're partners in grime, anyway."

We stood there, forlorn, staring at the perturbing sign, sweat trickling down our temples, wondering if it was possible to feel more grubby than we already did.

A woman approached and interrupted our clouds of dark thoughts. "You won't make it to Thunder Bay tonight," she said.

Sharon nodded. "You're right about that. Thunder Bay is about 400 kilometres away."

"Not exactly what I'd call an after supper romp," I affirmed, and brought the subject around to more pressing matters. "Do you know where we might find a place to shower around here?"

"Pither's Point has a public beach," the woman said. "Maybe the showers are open."

We thanked her and headed for the Point. Following the woman's directions, we found it without any problems. "Maybe our luck is changing," I said.

"Maybe even for the better," Sharon added.

She dropped her bike and tried a shower door. It was unlocked!

"Woo-hoo!" I whooped. "The god of cleanliness is on our side, after all!"

I decided to experiment with an all-in-one shower and clothes wash, and entered the shower fully clothed (except for my shoes and socks — I hate wet socks!). Perhaps the humidity had addled my brain circuitry?

After a good sudsing, I emerged dripping wet, looking like a scraggly alley cat who had inadvertently slipped into a washtub. Even my billfold was drenched. I held it up. "I don't understand all the fuss over laundering money."

"You're a nutter," Sharon said with the barest winkle of humour. She eyed my sopping state and shook her head. "So this is what happens to people when they're on the road too long."

"Hey, you've heard of 'wash-and-wear'?" I retorted. "Well, this is 'wear-and-wash!'"

"Brings a whole new meaning to drip-dry," Sharon said. "And I'm emphasizing *'drip,'*" she said. "You know, someday we're both going to look back on this, laugh nervously and change the subject."

"Let's ride," I declared. "I need to blow dry."

The only route heading east was the infamous bicycle-eating Trans Canada Highway. And since we wouldn't make Thunder Bay by nightfall anyway, we decided not to take the bicycle-munching route and headed south to the US border instead.

By the time we crossed into Minnesota at International Falls, population 8,300, I was mostly dry. We rolled up to a tourist information centre. The only sign greeting us upon our arrival read a terse one word: CLOSED. "Why don't tourist information places leave a couple of maps outside for late-arriving travellers?" I whined.

"Oh, that'd be too easy," Sharon replied.

A grounds custodian noticed us and strode over with a brimming smile. "Need anything?" he asked.

He unlocked the door. Reaching inside he fished forth a map. He even threw in some tourist trivia. "The Boise Cascade Kraft paper plant in International Falls is the largest in the country," he stated proudly. I had noticed giant pipes spanning the river between Canada and the States and had wondered what they were for. Trees were cut on the Canadian side, pulped, then pumped across the river to be made into paper products. (And, no doubt, sold back to us for double.)

"Have a great time in the States," the groundskeeper said.

He was one of the friendliest people we met working at a welcome centre.

I heartily shook his hand. "I think you missed your calling," I told him.

We rode into town and watched families promenade down sidewalks, enjoying their first breath of cool air since sunrise. Darkness suddenly fell. "Where are we going to spend the night?" Sharon asked. We cycled the streets slowly, on the lookout for an unobtrusive spot to pitch our little tent.

"There's an ideal spot," I said, pointing to a ball field.

"Yeah," Sharon agreed. "Only one problem ... it's in use."

Sure enough. A ball game was in progress — complete with stadium-bright banks of floodlights.

We leaned our bikes against the bleachers and sat down to wait. "It can't last much longer," I said. "It's a weeknight and they have to work in the morning, right?"

We watched inning after inning. The game finally wrapped up at 10:30 PM. They were getting good use out of the megawattage lights. "About time," I said, anticipating the teams departing our campground posthaste. But, to my surprise (and dismay), the teams switched places on the field and another game began!

"A double-header," I groaned. "Don't these people work?"

The aroma of fresh popcorn drifted through the air. I followed my nose and located the vendor to buy a bag of buttery goodness.

Much later, popcorn long gone, we were still sitting in the stands (wondering why they're called 'stands'?). Mercifully, the second game ended. I glanced at my watch: midnight. The stadium lights winked off and players trundled for home — except for three fellows in the parking lot. Leaning against a Camaro, they rehashed the game over a couple of brewskis. "Why don't these people get jobs?" Sharon muttered.

We slipped out of the stands, and under cover of darkness, pushed our bikes to an adjacent covered shelter. Our plan was to set up our tent inside the shelter once the stragglers departed.

Fifteen minutes later, beers finished, last cat hung, they tossed their empties, hopped into their vehicles, and, horns tooting, bass thumping, drove off into the night. Sharon and I high-fived one another. Our patience had finally paid off. Or so we thought.

I yanked the tent bag from my rack and froze. Someone had ridden up on a bike and stopped near the stands. Even in the blackness, I could tell he was staring straight at us.

"What's going on over there?" he called. We didn't respond. He called out again. "I said: 'What's going on over there?'" We still didn't answer, hoping that Mr Nosy would tire of our lack of communication and be on his way.

But after a couple of long minutes, it became clear: Mr Nosy wasn't leaving. At least not anytime soon.

"Jeez," Sharon whispered. "Do you suppose he sleeps here?"

"Oh, man," I moaned. "Just our luck."

"Let's get out of here," Sharon hissed.

We eased our bikes out of the rear of the shelter and melted into the shadows. Riding down the street, away from our late night interrogator, I glanced back. Mr Nosy was slinking into our shelter.

A few blocks away, we came across an abandoned lot. I went off in exploration and discovered a flat spot hidden neatly behind a clump of trees. "Looks like home to me," I said.

Sharon's shoes crunched on broken glass. "Oh, oh," she muttered. "Looks like a party spot."

"Hah!" I scoffed at her detective reasoning. "That glass has probably been there for two years," I said. "Besides, it's after midnight on a Wednesday for crying out loud."

More than tired we quickly pitched our tent and crawled in. Within a few breaths, we were both sawing logs like a pair of lumberjacks.

Around 2 AM my trusty chainsaw backfired, sputtered, and quit. I opened one eye. Had I heard voices?

"Hey, Dave!" someone shouted lushly from afar. "Is that you, Dave? Who's over there? Dave?"

Terrific. Sharon was right. It *was* a boozing spot. And no trifling matter of being a weekday night was about to keep our intrepid hero from his favourite beverage and spot of choice.

"Dave?" he called again. "Is that you?" I felt as if I were in the middle of a Cheech and Chong comedy skit. Only not as funny.

I propped myself on one elbow and squinted through the tent's mesh. Mortified, I observed a drunk's haphazard approach. He came to the tent door and knelt beside it. Pressing his big schnozz against the screen, he almost touched mine.

Flicking a Bic, he shoved the flame roughly against the screen. The stark glare lit up his face — a kisser so harsh the guy had the unmistakable characteristics of someone who had been living on the street and drinking booze for an extended period of time.

"Hey! Watch it!" I cried, worried he might accidentally torch our tent. "I don't think this thing's fireproof!"

At my outburst he recoiled, then closed in again. Smooshing his nose flat against the mesh, he gaped in like some bad-breathed monkey searching for a dropped peanut.

"You're not Dave," he puffed, exhaling a heady combination of stale tobacco and Jack Daniel's directly into my nostrils. "Who are you?" he asked.

I told him, and, guessing which questions were coming next, I followed up with where we were from and where we were going. The information seemed to satisfy him. In fact, he was most impressed. "Cool, Dude!" he spouted. "Awesome! You guys are cool!"

Voices hollered from afar. Some of his soused elbow-bender buddies across the field had tracked him down and were summoning him. "Gotta go!" he said. He stood. He wobbled. He reached out and grabbed ahold of the tent. *Steady there, boy. Those poles are only aluminum.* "Sorry to bother you!" he apologized, and lurched away into the night.

Fearing a possible repeat performance, we didn't sleep all that well after that. Even the rhythmic thump and grind of the paper plant couldn't lull us back into dreamland.

Sabotage!

> **"Everything is funny as long as it is happening to someone else."**
> ~ Will Rogers

I was cotton-pickin' sabotaged in Cotton! Leaving our bikes out front at a gas station without a second thought, we went in to buy some energy food (that's what I call junk food while on tour). Back outside, we spotted lounge chairs on a lawn across the way.

Relaxing in back-supported comfort, we savoured our calorie-laden purchases. The only problem: an ice machine blocked my line of sight to our bikes. But no worries — I imagined Cotton to be a typical crime-free small place. I believed I could have left my bike for a week and found it right where I had left it.

Finished our snacks, we traipsed across the sunburnt grass and collected our bikes from the exact spot we had leaned them an hour prior.

Back on the road, we hadn't gone more than a hundred metres when I clacked over a gaping frost crack in the road surface. A disturbing *clank* emanated from my rear rim. "Flat!" I yelled, and pulled on my brakes.

Sharon stopped beside me. "Yep," she acknowledged, frowning. "Both of them."

Huh? *Dang!* She was right. Both tires were flatter than month-old roadkill. How had that happened? My tires had been holding air just fine before we stopped. I suspected foul play. Had someone at the gas station played a mean trick on me? With that hulking ice machine blocking our view, was it possible some wily character had surreptitiously liberated the air from my tires?

I grabbed my Zefal pump and flailed away, jacking the plunger up and down like some delirious one-armed wanker with a new issue of *Hustler*. But air was releasing faster than I could pump it in. Conceding defeat, I ripped out the inner tubes. Two holes, side-by-side, looking like a rattler's fang strike, accentuated both lifeless bulges — even the "flat-proof" tube in my rear tire sported a matching pair of snake bites.

"Well, I guess that's a wake-up call," I mused, fingering the holes. "If someone had enough time to let the air out of *both* of my tires, they could just as easily have stolen my bike. From now on, no matter how small the place, I'm going to lock them."

"Good idea," Sharon said. She had been trying to persuade me to lock our bikes for the past month.

Fresh tubes installed, we lit off down the highway as if we were a couple of rabbits being chased by hunting dogs. In a few kilometres, my rear tire suffered another inexplicable debilitating lack of confidence.

Bumping to a halt on the road's edge for the second time in less than an hour, I fumed, "Rear flats are the worse!"

"Yep," Sharon agreed. "And, because most of your weight is on the rear, that's where you're most likely to get them. Look at the bright side, though," she said, "at least it's not raining."

The sun's naked glare reflected off my spokes as I laid my bike over in the gravel. I removed everything from my rack, including my panniers, then fiddled with the rear derailleur to slide the chain past the gear cluster and extricate the wheel. Only slightly greasy, I repaired the tube, reinstalled the wheel, reassembled my load, wiped my hands, and jumped back on my bike, still steamed from my bout of bad luck. Hoping to burn off some frustration I cranked up our touring speed a couple of notches.

Our effort paid off. We reeled off a hundred kilometres in just over three hours. Sharon calculated the average. "Pretty good for fully loaded touring," she said, smiling widely.

"The roses were really whipping by there for a while!"

To celebrate lessons learned about not leaving our rides unattended, we locked the bikes to a chain-link fence and loped into a pizza joint in the middle of nowhere. Inside the deserted diner I requested a window booth so I could keep an eye on our bikes. "Never can be too careful," I smiled.

By the time our bellies were full, darkness had descended. Unlocking our bikes, we pedalled down the road until we came to a rest stop. Behind a dense copse of alder and hickory we set up our tent. I hoped we didn't have any of the other type of cops as nighttime visitors.

My worry, as usual, was for naught; our only disturbance was a nursery of fat ring-eyed raccoons. The sow and her cubs showed up around eleven, and helped themselves to our leftover deep dish pizza.

Awakened by the raccoons' atrocious table manners, Sharon mumbled, "Some things are nearly impossible to defend against."

Kind Strangers

"Let us be of good cheer, remembering that the misfortunes hardest to bear are those which never happen."
~ James Russell Lowell

Our day was filled with kindness from strangers. It began early, the morning air already muggy, as we pedalled toward Duluth. A van with dark tinted windows, slowed, then paced alongside Sharon at our mere twenty kilometres per hour. I found it a trifle unsettling. The passenger window rolled down. I got ready to duck.

"Do you need anything?" a woman asked Sharon.

"No," Sharon stammered. "But thank you for asking."

The woman smiled, thrust a camera out the window (those cute helmets), snapped a shot, and off they zoomed.

"Ah, next time," I drawled, "see if they have any iced Coke."

The wind growled and snorted with the smell of thunderstorm on its breath. Heads down, we humped a strong headwind until we smacked into a bridge spanning St Louis River. Our road, linking Minnesota to Wisconsin, suddenly became Interstate 535. Not unlike a pair of tykes who had spotted a Dickie Lee ice cream truck but were forbidden to cross the street, we stopped, and stared longingly at the river's far side.

"Think we should go for it?" I wondered aloud. Traffic, rumbling cheek to jowl, threatened that any attempt to bicycle across the bridge would be met with a short and unhappy end to our illustrious cycling careers.

"I don't like the looks of this," Sharon muttered, wagging her head, and glancing behind at the solid stream of traffic. "I'd bet we have about as much chance of making it across as we do of winning the lottery with a bus ticket."

"Maybe we should flag down a bus," I suggested.

But before we could, our very own fairy godmother (disguised as a state trooper), zipped in behind us. His cruiser's rooftop lights flashing like colourful gum balls, the highway patrolman vaulted out of his vehicle and strode jauntily toward us.

"You can't go on the Interstate," he advised, shaking his head like a protective Mama bear. "Follow me," he offered. "I'll show you where there's a pedestrian walkway."

Headlights and rooftop lights winking, he grandly escorted us to an exit. As we rode up the off-ramp, the man in blue gave us a cheery salute, gunned his screaming gasser, and roared off down the freeway to attend to more pressing matters than tourist escort duty. Where was that nearest Krispy Kreme doughnut shop?

On the bridge walkway we were met with a strong, fast-moving cold front. It yowled in our ears like an air raid siren, ripping unfettered across expansive Lake Superior. I was positive that my helmet was the only thing preventing my hair from blowing off. "Welcome to Wisconsin!" I shouted.

Within minutes, the previous agreeable temperature plummeted to a miserly 15 degrees Celsius. Coal-black clouds, sooty and brooding, tunneled into the area. Low growls of distant thunder warned of an imminent and monumental storm. Just as a few spatters of rain began to fall, we spied a Welcome Centre and ducked inside to warm ourselves and keep our tail feathers dry. We were about to experience another round of kindness from strangers.

"I've never seen it blow from that direction before!" a grandmotherly woman behind the welcoming counter exclaimed. A shotgun-like blast of thunder, as if punctuating her statement, rattled the Centre. Gazing out the large windows (with eyes almost as wide), we watched as purple-tongued lightning forked across a lampblack sky. Suddenly, torrential rain writhed forth from the smutty cloud banks. Wind gusts slammed wave after wave of the deluge into the Centre's picture windows. Streams, the thickness of my thumb, wriggled like snakes down the panes.

"You folks bring your bikes in here, right now!"

Quick as two bunnies, we retrieved our wet bikes from the entryway, and leaned them, muddy and dripping, against the nearest wall. "Do you have a mop?" I asked the woman, eyeing the growing puddle with concern.

"It's no problem," she assured me. "Relax. Make yourself at home. I think we have some hot chocolate around here somewhere." She slipped into the back.

Our matron reappeared holding forth two mugfuls of steaming cocoa. "Looks like a doozy of a storm," she said. "It's a good thing you made it here when you did." We nodded and accepted her offering. The toasty mug felt delicious against my numb fingers. For a long while, we just cradled the mugs, silent, enjoying the tingly sensation creeping back into our extremities while watching mauve-coloured lightning flick across an ebony sky.

Two motorcyclists clomped in, a watery muddy trail accompanying each footstep. They unfastened their helmets, revealing flattened hair. "Helmets are hell on hairdos, eh?" Sharon quipped to the burly motorcycle mama. The strapping female shot Sharon a less than amused look.

"Hail up the highway smashed out some windows," her male counterpart stated. *Ouch,* I thought. *That would'a left bruises.* "A weather warning is for winds up to 80 miles per hour."

"That's calm in Newfoundland," Sharon said, pressing her luck. That statement pretty much killed any chance of conversation with the bikers. They headed for the washrooms and that was the last we saw of them.

Half an hour later, our hot chocolate mugs empty, the storm had passed. At least the most severe clouds had diverged toward other locales. We thanked our Welcome Centre host and went to haul our muddy steeds back outside.

"Promise you'll send a postcard!" the information centre's matriarch said, and handed us a business card with the address. As we departed, she set to work with a mop, swabbing up our not-so-small mucky puddle.

In a short distance, I spotted a sign for a Lake Superior Circle Tour, and turned to follow it. Dairy cows, comfortable in their fields, complemented the rolling Wisconsin countryside.

Zinging down a steep hill as if I had been shot out of a cannon I ignored a 15 mile-per-hour SHARP CORNER warning sign. Then, just before the bend, sensing I was not going to make it around at my speed I hit the brakes — hard. Skidding, I released the death grip on my brake levers. Leaning like a motorcycle racer, I swooped around the 90-degree corner at twice the recommended speed. *Whee!* Luck was with me. There was no gravel on the roadway!

Not unpredictably, after our screaming descent, a stiff climb smacked us in the face. I grunted and shifted onto my smallest chainring. At a barely perceptible four kilometre per hour ascent, I concentrated on ignoring the *whish-whish-whish* emanating from somewhere rearward. *Probably my fender,* I thought. *No big deal.*

Whish-whish-BOOM! My rear tire exploded in an ear-splitting blowout. Like a discombobulated rickshaw driver, I wobbled onto the gravel shoulder. I gaped down. The blast had blown the tire right off the rim! The inner tube hung off to one side like a stricken black mamba. The dangers of not properly maintaining one's ride became crystal clear (one of these days I may even change my evil ways). I thanked my lucky stars it hadn't happened on the downhill.

When Sharon caught up to me, I explained (with much waving of arms and cool sound effects) what had happened. She looked at my brakes. Apparently they weren't adjusted properly (now there's a surprise!). When I applied them for the corner, they rubbed the tire's sidewall ... and then hadn't released completely.

"From now on," Sharon advised, "if you hear something rubbing, please stop and investigate!"

"To maintain or not to maintain," I said. "That is the question."

"Yeah," Sharon retorted, "if you don't maintain this thing you may not be around next time to ask the question."

Hmmm. She had a point. I dropped my bike and installed a new tube and a new tire. I even tweaked the brakes a little.

At dusk we arrived in Port Wing, a small Lake Superior fishing settlement. Storm clouds, plum-coloured like a two day old bruise, threatened. We found a park and, under cover of a picnic table roof, assembled sub sandwiches.

A cottony mist settled in, cloaking us and our surroundings in wet gauze. I watched, fascinated, as water drops condensed on fine wisps of hair framing Sharon's face. I was still marvelling when the skies opened. Bitter cold, dime-sized raindrops, driven sideways by wind gusting from its very heels, popped against our Gore-Tex jacketed backs.

We were about to abandon our soggy picnic when four touring cyclists materialized out of the foggy dinginess like ships coming into port. Three swept past silently, giving mandatory waves. The fourth fellow stopped. His bike sported the most immense front light I had ever seen on a bicycle.

"I'll bet that lights up the roadway pretty good," I said, and wondered what size batteries the thing ate.

"Oh, yeah!" he replied. "Car drivers flash their high beams at me! We really need the big lights though. We're riding across America, but we only have a month off work, so we ride a lot at night."

I nodded. *Sure glad we're not forced to ride in the fog or the dark.* That magnificent Michigan Upper Peninsula scenery they had missed! How could they appreciate that in pitch blackness? (I could understand riding across Kansas at night ... just the thought that one *might* be missing something would make it more exciting.) For us, bike touring was about slowing down and enjoying a more peaceful pace than the headlong frantic race we endured at our workplaces. We consciously tried to not let goal setting become the focus. And, having no jobs to hurry back to, we had the luxury of setting a more relaxed pace.

"Where are you going tonight?" Sharon asked.

"Oh, still down the road a ways," he answered. "We're headed for my aunt's place in Duluth (60 kilometres away). She's got hot showers and steaks waiting."

"We'd better not hold you any longer then."

With thoughts of hot showers and barbecued steaks ruminating in our heads, we watched him push off, his light illuminating the morose gloom.

We stowed our bikes under a plastic sheet, pitched our tent, and, just as a serious deluge struck, dove inside. Snug as two bugs in our sleeping bags, we listened as the wind snapped the fly in an upbeat tempo, while chubby raindrops drummed down like tom-toms.

"Those poor guys," Sharon said, imagining our four intrepid comrades battling the inclement conditions. "I'm glad we're not out there."

"Barbecued steak sure sounded good, though!"

South African Rest

When a soul is motionless
something powerful comes
to our world from somewhere
Like freezing water
or solar wind
or grass shoots
that split concrete
or asphalt in a parking lot
or breezes around leaves
on a South African night
Something before
which this world
must wait and watch
maybe even God

by
R.Z. Blackmore

Tacking!

"A ship in a harbor is safe, but it is useless."
~ Anonymous

We awoke refreshed, but feeling half-starved. Out of provisions, craving food, we packed and hit the road in search of sustenance. Stately red maple lined the thoroughfare like a giant arbour; their branches arched over the roadway, leaves ablaze in a canopy of fiery crimson. The picturesque route, a feast to the senses, helped us to forget — at least momentarily — about our hunger.

I let out a little half-chuckle as we passed through the town of Cornucopia — hunger gnawing my belly. Not a single place was open. Talk about false advertising.

Farther along, following the shore of Lake Superior, Apostle Islands in the distance, a sign caused me to do a double take. "Hey! Get a load of that," I said, motioning in the sign's direction. In bold letters, it proclaimed: LAKE SUPERIOR.

"Just in case you were wondering," Sharon laughed.

In Bayfield, we found an open store and went crazy buying heaps of bananas, peaches, yogourt, and Grape-nut cereal. Well provisioned, we headed for the beach, on the lookout for the most scenic breakfast spot.

A huge red oak, surrounded by sculpted boulders and driftwood, looked the perfect spot. Secluded, we settled in, enjoying the parade of passing boats, sails flapping in the forceful wind. It looked as if most sailors were on the losing end of a gangplank to nowhere.

In a futile attempt to soften the rock-hard Grape-nuts, I soaked them in yogourt (nothing like breaking a tooth on one's breakfast cereal). A handsome fellow on a single speed rode up.

"Hi," he said. Vince introduced himself, then asked the three usual questions: "Where are you from? Where are you going? How many miles a day do you do?" (I had heard the questions so many times I was thinking of having a T-shirt printed and just point to the answers when people asked.) "I'd like to cycle in Ireland," Vince said. "After I sail there."

Now that was something we hadn't heard before!

"Do you sail?" came Sharon's immediate question. Indeed he did! Vince was a member of a Saint Paul crew that raced sailboats. And, he informed us, they planned on going out that morning.

"Would you like to come along?" he invited.

"Wow! Sounds great!" we chorused.

He pointed across the water to a harbour. "We're the one with the tallest mast. Come on over if you'd like to go."

Like to go?! Vince pedalled off, and we hurriedly crunched our Grape-nuts (who cared if one lost a filling when racing sailboats awaited?). We skipped over to the harbour like two kids promised a visit to a candy store.

"Hi!" Vince greeted us. "I'm glad you decided to come. Just to let you know: I'll have to get the official approval from the captain when he gets here — wouldn't want to upset protocol."

Sharon and I, two landlubbers from landlocked Alberta, waited in front of the tall-masted boat. I felt like a kid before a fully decked tree Christmas morning. We had never been on a sailboat in our lives, let alone a 42-foot schooner with a 60-foot main mast. To our untrained eyes the thing looked immense! We stood, nervously shifting from foot to foot, waiting for Chet — the boat's owner — to arrive.

Another crew member, Jeff, arrived with Chet. Then, quickly on their heels, Mike — the fourth and final crew member — appeared. Vince hustled over to Chet and, waving in our direction, popped the question. "Yep," we overheard Chet say. We were relieved to receive the informal formal okay. Chet ambled over and introduced himself with a hearty handshake. "Looks like we could use some extra ballast today," he said, the robust wind whipping his curly grey locks.

Leanne, Vince's girlfriend, arrived — she had been invited along as ballast, as well. Leanne was from Omaha. When I kidded her that she must work for Mutual of Omaha then, she said, "No, I work for 3M in Mexico. In a week," she added, visibly excited, "I'm off to work in South Africa for six months." Whew. It sounded a long way from where we were at present.

One final requirement before we got underway: the marine weather forecast. The radio broadcast a gale warning with 45 knot winds. *A bit disconcerting for one's first ride,* I thought. *Wouldn't want it to be my first and last.*

Sharon must have been having the same concerns. "Wh — What do you do if it's too windy?" she stammered.

"Put out more sail," Jeff replied tartly.

I noticed boats that had been out during breakfast had returned to the safety of harbour and were being securely moored. A lone charter sailboat, on its way out, puttered past. But then, still within the protection of the harbour, it thought better of the gusty action just beyond, and turned around. *No gust, no glory,* I thought.

A tug-like craft passed us, loaded to the gills with wetsuit clad divers. A heavyset fellow sat propped on the prow, scowling. Missing only his trident, the grey-whiskered chap struck an uncanny resemblance to Neptune himself.

We climbed aboard the schooner. Even getting out of the berth was no easy feat. The boat was so large there was no clearance to swing her around; after a series of short back and forth maneuvers we were free.

We motored to open water, choppy waves hitting us on all sides. Mike, an owner of two sailboats, unfurled the main sail. The wind caught it in a huge snort. The boat jumped sideways like a skittish colt and suddenly we were skimming across the whitecapped waves. *Whee!*

Jeff manned the tiller; Vince operated computers; Chet and Mike worked sails — Chet on mainsail, Mike on jib. Dacron made up the mainsheet's construction with Kevlar stitched into the stress areas. The smaller jib consisted entirely of Kevlar. Chet told us the jib alone cost over five grand and "doesn't last very long when used for racing." It was far too windy to even think about putting out the billowy spinnaker. *Drats! I was beginning to like this speed.*

Zipping across the waves, I yelled to the tillerman, "We could pull a water skier!"

"We're in Lake Ontario," Jeff shouted, kidding me about how far we'd gone. "There's Toronto over there."

Vince watched computer displays, reading everything from wind speed and direction to the lake's depth. One monitor even showed the lake's bottom. I was relieved. I didn't notice any sailboats down there!

Leanne, Sharon, and I, locked our arms around the boat's rear railing, near Tillerman Jeff. With the tenacity of octopi, we clung for dear life. Our job (besides ballast), we were told, was twofold. "One: Don't fall off. Two: Stay out of the way." Accomplishing both at the same time proved not as easy as one might first think. I learned the hard way there wasn't a whole lot of excess room on a racing sailboat. Whenever Jeff reefed the tiller, it solidly smacked my thigh. I would have a few bruises as mementos to my first sailboat ride.

Clipping across waves was exciting. But tacking was exhilarating! Our high and dry perch suddenly became the side sweeping the water's surface. The mainsail swung around. Leanne, Sharon, and I, like three about-to-be-drowned rats, scurried to the opposite side (keeping the racing sailor's time honored rhyme in mind: Keep low and never let go!). The one time Sharon lost her grip, she nearly toppled overboard. No one wore life jackets. "If you fall in," Jeff said, only half kidding, "the water is so cold it'll kill you before the coast guard can pick you up."

With that comforting thought in mind, my fingers practically embedded themselves into the metal railing. After all, if I fell in, they couldn't exactly just swing around and pick me up. The most they could do was radio the coast guard. I could hear it now: "The last we saw Neil, he was wearing a neon-green ball cap, bobbing at 47-degrees North and 90-degrees West."

An occasional rogue wave sent up a smashing spray, soaking our faces. "*Yahoo!* Refreshing!" I yelled. The sun even made an appearance to see what all the commotion was about. But, even with Old Sol, racing across the waves proved to be chilly business. Luckily, before we set out, Sharon persuaded me to don long pants. Leanne, not so lucky, clad only in a T-shirt and cut-offs, shivered non-stop, her slender legs blue and covered in goosebumps.

Three hours later, we were safely back in harbour. (We heard on the radio later that due to the high winds the coast guard had had their busiest 36 hours in their history.)

"That's as good as it gets!" Chet announced with a meaty grin as we berthed. "That's the most wind I've ever been out in."

"Me, too," I replied.

Atomic Sunset

> "**You got to have a dream. If you don't have a dream, how you gonna have a dream come true?**"
> ~ Bloody Mary, movie *South Pacific*

A howling wind pushed us out of Bayfield. I called to Sharon, "Maybe I should raise a sail!"

We made spectacular time to Ashland. "It's going to be dark soon," Sharon hollered from behind. "I'm tired of dodging motorhomes." (Last chance holiday traffic crammed the roads.) "Let's pack it in for the day and get an early start tomorrow."

"Aw, let's keep going!" I wailed, still high from our sailing adventure, and revelling in our strongest tailwind in weeks. We pushed through Ashland. On its outskirts, the wonderful paved shoulder we had been cruising so merrily, petered out. Cracked pavement jolted my tires; motorhomes brushed past my elbow. Suddenly I was a lot less enthusiastic about continuing.

"How about we call it a day, honey?" I said.

"Good idea," Sharon called back.

We spotted an industrial plant with a picnic table near a back door. An acre of aspen, across from the plant's parking lot, had a large sign posted: No Trespassing. Perfect.

We wheeled in and leaned our bikes against the picnic table. While Sharon rustled up dinner, I stepped over to the parking lot to talk with a trucker walking around his rig. He turned out to be from Oklahoma City and said he was waiting for morning when the plant reopened so he could unload (actually his language was a little more colourful about the plant being closed).

I asked him, "Do you think anyone will mind if we set our tent over in the trees for the night?"

"I doubt it," he answered. "The folks around here are hard-headed — like there's some in the plant right now, but they won't unload me — other than that, they seem all right. Can't say they'll mind. Besides, all they can do is tell you to leave ... and by then it'll be morning." He gave me a pleased look. Maybe that line about "misery loves company" wasn't far wrong.

The trucker and I stood silently, arms folded across our chests, watching an atomic blood-red sun set over Chequamegon Bay, enjoying the fine art of male conversation where neither says a word ... and both are comfortable with it.

The sun sank below the horizon. I returned to Sharon and relayed the trucker's comments about no one minding if we stayed there.

"Oh yeah?" Sharon retorted. "While you were over there shooting the breeze, a watchman came out. 'You're not planning on staying around here are you?' he said, and not very pleasant-like either. 'We try to discourage it,'" he said.

"Hmmm," I drawled. "Hasn't he heard Wisconsin's tourism motto: 'YOU'RE AMONG FRIENDS'?"

"Well apparently his friends stay in motels," Sharon said.

After a truncated meal, we decided not to trifle with the guard. We packed up, and headed away from the plant, down a darkened dead-end road. Maybe we could ask a family for permission to camp on their lawn? But, at the end of the road, we hadn't passed any houses. The street ended. The night was as black as a witch's cat. Now what?

Being lifetime members of the 'no-plan travel club' may be an exciting way to travel, but our unscheduled style sometimes caught us unprepared. And it's not as if we can just jump back in our auto, turn on the headlights, hit the gas pedal and tootle another 100 kilometres or so down the road. (At times we debated whether or not to ask permission. When darkness fell, it sometimes seemed better not to ask — and deal with the consequences if someone discovered us — rather than be told no, and then what would we do? However, that approach led to some sleepless nights battling guilty consciences while waiting for the police to show up.)

"I think we should set up in the back of the park," I said. "We'll leave early," I added.

"I don't know...," Sharon was hesitant, clearly not keen on the idea. "The guard might come looking."

A small laugh burst spontaneously from me. Considering we couldn't see our hands six inches in front of our faces, I doubted the guard would present much of a problem.

I persuaded Sharon to sneak off into the trees with me. Not wanting to risk our flashlight beam being seen, we set up the tent by feel, then tossed in our sleeping bags, and faded off to slumberland with an uneasy feeling lining our guts.

Sometime later, Sharon nudged me.

I opened one eye. The inside of the tent was as black as a coal mine. "Is it time to pack up yet?" she whispered. I fumbled for the light button on my digital watch. (Sharon had deemed it unnecessary to wear a watch while on vacation. *Why then,* I wondered, *is she forever asking me the time?*) I read the numbers in the light's tiny glow: 12:30. It was half past midnight! "Uh, we still have at least another hour of shut eye," I assured her. I set my watch's alarm for the absurd hour of 5 AM — an hour I had previously considered fictional — then closed my eye.

I fell face first into the Land of Nod. Down, down, down an endless spiral tunnel and into a very peculiar dream. In my dream, at *precisely* 5 AM, my alarm went off and all the plant workers simultaneously arrived in the parking lot. In my dream they exuberantly slammed their car doors, and ran (yes, *ran*) to the park where our tent was set up, to partake in an early-morning gymnastics and calisthenics program. In my dream two athletic women vaulted on top of our tent like Olympic gymnasts, collapsing it. They then blithely continued their jumping and stretching exercises on top of our flattened tent (and us). After a rousing hour of exercises, a bell rang. Everyone stopped, picked up a white towel, and bounded off, joyously, for work. Except for one man with a handlebar moustache. He approached us. "Just because you are a cyclist," he castigated me, a raspy French-Canadian accent tinting his voice, "you think you can do anything you please!"

I was about to assure monsieur that was not the case, when the real life squeal of tires roused me from my dream. I rose wearily on one elbow (all that exercise) and squinted through the mesh. Brake lights streaked a reddish glow through the night. The vehicle screeched to a stop in the parking lot, then wheeled onto a side street and sped away.

Still peering through the mesh, I watched in fascination as a string of vehicles streamed into the parking lot, headlights illuminating the woods in front of our tent. Smoky light cast unearthly shadows like some alien scene in an *X-Files* episode. *Oh no!* I thought, still in a quasi-dream-waking state. *They're here for their morning calisthenics!*

I roused my soundly snoozing partner. "We've gotta get out of here," I blabbered. "The plant workers are here!" In blackness we stumbled about in our half-asleep fog, packing wildly. In our mad scramble, I had forgotten our tent fly and left it laying on the ground. It blended in without a trace. Fortunately, luck was on my side — I tripped over it. (Stooping to retrieve the fly reminded me of a forest campground bulletin board notice I had seen: 'Lost in the woods. One camouflage wallet.')

As I secured the tent to my rear rack, my watch alarm beeped: 5 AM. In darkness, we pedalled away, following a service road paralleling the main highway. In a short distance, the service road dead ended.

Still too dark to dare venturing onto the main route, we sat on a concrete barricade, shivering in the pre-dawn, eating crunchy Kraft peanut butter straight from the jar like a pair of homeless people.

"This is too weird," Sharon said, sitting in darkness and digging in for another spoonful.

"This is nothing," I said. "Wait till you get a load of the dream I had...."

Burning Amber

"You can't be lost if you don't care where you are."
~ Dutch Caribbean Proverb

The morning dawned raw. I slipped on a pair of Nashbar full-fingered 'storm-shelter' neoprene gloves. It was only the end of August, but autumn's colder temperatures were already on the way.

When it was light enough to ride, we discovered only a short stretch of road had no shoulder. Before long we were riding on a three-foot-wide road edge of smooth pavement. It was a very good thing. Traffic wasn't light. But, instead of our gale-force tailwind like the previous day, we had to contend with a brutish headwind. In the cool morning air my sluggish legs felt like they had ran a marathon during the night. *Has my bike put on weight?* I wondered, lamenting my lack of sleep.

We left Wisconsin, fighting a fugacious headwind into Michigan's Upper Peninsula. Approaching Ironwood, the wind died and the sun finally peeped out — a welcome sight indeed. We pulled into a Michigan Welcome Centre to obtain a road map. The not too-welcoming attendant tossed one our way. Perhaps mornings weren't his forte either?

"Maybe he thinks he's working at a Michigan Unwelcome Centre," Sharon said once we were back outside.

An info centre plaque provided us with insight into ironwood. WOOD AS HEAVY AS IRON, it read. What grabbed my attention was the bit stating, 'Boats built from ironwood will not float.' "Hey!" I declared. "That's probably what Farley Mowat's boat was made of!"

Pleased that I had solved Farley's perplexing little conundrum of *The Boat That Wouldn't Float,* we sat at a picnic table to eat brunch — the sun feeling especially good. I was tired. So tired, in fact, I felt like indulging in a siesta (I already knew I was going to like Spain!). But, instead of napping, Sharon somehow coaxed me into patching three tubes.

The sun disappeared, replaced by slate grey clouds dribbling rain. "At least it's not snow," Sharon grimaced as we departed the frosty Welcome Centre.

I smiled. "You always look for the bright side."

In downtown Ironwood, the spatters of rain turned into a full-scale assault. For the better part of an hour we huddled under the overhang of a grocery store. "No sense riding in the rain when shelter is so close by," I said.

"Remember when we used to ride in all weather conditions?" Sharon asked. (One time, along the coast of Oregon down Highway 101, we had ridden in rain for twenty-one straight days). "We were rugged. Now we're such wimps."

"I prefer to think of it as older and wiser," I sniffed.

While debating the merits of waiting it out or hitting the road, a TOMBSTONE PIZZA truck rolled up. Sharon chuckled. "I wonder if their motto is 'PIZZA TO DIE FOR'?" The sombre clouds broke. We rose like the dead and pedalled out of Ironwood.

I spotted a sign: SUPERIOR CIRCLE TOUR. *Sounds good,* I thought. Abandoning plans to follow busy Highway 28, I made a quick left onto the unplanned detour. The roadway was ultra-smooth. *Perfect,* I thought. *This 'Superior Circle Tour' will connect us with a route that follows the shore of Lake Superior all along Michigan's Upper Peninsula. We'll just follow it east and head back into Canada at Sault Ste Marie.*

Traffic was practically non-existent. "Michigan is great!" I raved. "The roads are so quiet."

"Perhaps too quiet," Sharon mused.

Somewhere, way back in one of my mind's dusty recesses, I heard a small tinkling bell. But, instead of listening to that cautionary note, I blithely carried on, sweeping down oak-treed lanes awash with leaves of burning amber. Superior!

Michigan enchanted us. "This reminds me of Washington state's backroads," Sharon said.

"All it needs are a few crystal clear brooks," I responded.

But we didn't pass any crystalline creeks — or even names that inspired such thoughts. One waterway — clogged with rustling brown reeds — was named Montreal Mud Creek. Dead snags reflected in the stagnant water. Another waterway was named Black River. *Rather dark,* I thought.

We cruised, enjoying the traffic-free environment ... mainly downhill with the wind (more clues!). Perhaps lack of sleep, or maybe just wishing to have a good ride, allowed us to ignore the warning signs that something was not right.

Sharon eventually concluded something was seriously amiss (besides the tailwind). She flagged me to a stop. "Either the sun is in the wrong place," she said, "or we're headed in the wrong direction."

"Who cares?" I said, squinting, and following her gaze skyward. "With this road and tailwind, I could pedal forever."

"Yeah," she agreed, "but we're headed back in the direction we came from this morning. Hand me the map, Tonto." Whimsical, spontaneous route setting is not without its downside. Progress, in the conventional sense, is not always made. Like Joe Kurmaskie says: "All who wander are not lost ... but many of us are skimping on our medication." On the plus side, we did get some excellent riding in that helped us remember that when cycle touring, it's the journey, and not the destination that is most important.

Even without a GPS, Sharon was able to pinpoint our location. We were on our way to Little Girl's Point. It was nowhere near where we wanted to be headed. We had cycled 20 kilometres in the wrong direction. Sharon scrutinized the map. "The road loops around not far from here. We may as well continue to Little Girl's Point."

Legend has it that the point's name comes from a many moons ago event. A hunting party, returning from an expedition, rounded the point in their canoes. They glimpsed what they took as a small girl standing in the mist. Thinking her lost they beached their canoes to rescue the little one. But after scrambling up the steep beach, and even though they conducted a thorough search of the point and surrounding forest, they could find no one. When the men arrived home they learned one of the hunter's little girls had gone missing in the nearby forest that day. She was never found. And since that day ...

Little Girl's Point jutted into Lake Superior like a broken anklebone. We limped around the turn and pedalled back toward Ironwood.

"Must be some magnet in that ironwood," I said. "At least we sure seem to be attracted to it."

On our second attempt we broke free from Ironwood's magnetic pull. A short nineteen kilometres down the road a municipal campground in Wakefield reeled us in. The cheap showers helped lure us. They cost one thin dime.

We staked a claim on a hillside overlooking the sultry lake. On a hot day it would have made a great spot for a dip. But the day was cool; we wanted warmer water. Sharon wasted no time rustling out her towel and scavenging a few dimes from the bottom of her handlebar bag before hustling off.

She returned a half-hour later, a broad grin across her face. "A superior end to our circle tour!" she declared.

Dead tired, we called it a day. By 8 PM we were dozing, snug in our sleeping bags. Rain pattered the fly. We slipped off to dreamland, listening to the happy sound of singing raindrops.

Ducky

> **"Slow down! Take a deep breath and just take a moment for yourself."**
> ~ Sibyl McLendon

We awoke to the unhappy sound of pounding rain. "Rest day!" Sharon announced mirthfully. Maybe she was getting the hang of the 'older and wiser' school of cycle touring? She searched my handlebar bag and scrounged up a handful of dimes. Heading forth into the downpour jovially, she spent a joyous two hours at the shower. Maybe she had some strange notion she could stockpile cleanliness?

"How long do you think this can keep up?" Sharon asked, clambering back into the tent.

"No more than 40 days," I assured her. "Maybe we should start building an ark? Or do you think this thing floats?"

"I don't want to find out," Sharon said. "Certainly looks like monsoon season has arrived."

Evening came and still the rain hammered down. Tired of the tent's tiny confines (and out of dimes), we wrestled on rain gear, double-bagged our shoes in old grocery bags, and trudged to a covered picnic table down by the lakeside. On our watery excursion, I very nearly stepped on a family of sodden ducks seeking refuge in the long grass. Apparently even they thought the weather too wretched to be out in. But they didn't appear to be getting in a big flap over it though.

Partway through our washed-out dinner, a fellow in a bright yellow slicker — looking remarkably like Big Bird — hopped over to collect our camping fees. "Since the weather's so lousy," he said, rain dripping off his beak, "I'm only going to charge you for one day." He carefully wrote a receipt — not an easy feat considering the paper wasn't waterproof. Handing me the limp bill, he asked, "Is there anything you folks need?"

"More dimes!" Sharon exclaimed.

Pasties

> **"This life is yours. Take the power to choose what you want to do and do it well. Take the power to love what you want in life and love it honestly. Take the power to walk in the forest and be a part of nature. Take the power to control your own life."**
> ~ Susan Polis Schutz

We swept out of Wakefield through a whispering forest. In nearby Covington our calm route joined a busy highway — trucks, campers, and car traffic inundated us from all directions. But it wasn't the metal behemoths scraping past our churning legs that drew our attention. No, rather, it was the numerous roadside signs advertising FRESH PASTIES.

"What the heck are 'pasties'?" Sharon wondered aloud after we had passed what seemed like our tenth sign in as many kilometres.

"Maybe that's how they spell 'pastries' in these parts?"

At the next roadside joint shouting PASTIES in red six-foot-high vertical lettering, we pulled in to find out exactly what pasties were. They turned out to be a locality specialty: meat pies. Hot, scrumptious, filled with mystery meat and diced vittles. After inhaling three pies each we felt like a pair of leopards — those meat pies hit the spot.

A local informed us that pasties originated in Cornwall, England, and were a favoured food of workers there. Cornwall miners even hauled pasties into the underground tin mines for their lunches. "A good thing about pasties," he told us, "is that they travel well and can be eaten with dirty fingers." (I looked at my hands and immediately ordered two more.) When folks from Cornwall came to work in Michigan's Upper Peninsula's iron and copper mines, they brought pasties with them (they really do travel well!). The peninsula mines have long since closed, but the pasty tradition lives on.

The meat pies must have been high-octane fuel — they powered us down the road for over a hundred and fifty kilometres. When we arrived at the tiny Lake Michigamme rest area it was dusk. The water, blanketed in a thick mist, appeared ready for bed.

In the deserted picnic area we downed a couple more meat pies before bushwhacking along an overgrown lakeside trail, searching for a spot to spend the night. At a grove of juvenile curly maple we found an opening just large enough to wedge our two-person tent into.

"Ah," Sharon sighed as we settled in to admire the swirling fog. "This is the good life."

"I have to agree," I said, patting my stomach. "Do you think the meat pies in New Zealand are going to be as good?"

Happy Anniversary

"For it was not into my ear you whispered, but into my heart. It was not my lips you kissed, but my soul."
~ Judy Garland

It was September 1st — our tenth wedding anniversary. "Happy Anniversary!" I sang upon awakening, and leaned over to give Sharon a syrupy smooch (it must have been those maples we were camped under).

"Mmmm," she replied, giving me a big smacker in return. "Maybe we should stay in bed all day?"

I smiled. "Good idea. How about if we treat ourselves to a motel room tonight ... steak dinner ... Jacuzzi?"

Sharon must have thought it a fine idea. We had one of our fastest getaways ever.

Past Lake Michigamme, we swung off the busy main highway and onto a sinuous county road near Ishpeming and Negaunee.

Folks warned us, "Steep hills ahead!" But any hills we came across turned out to be more down than up. For awhile we even traipsed along a spectacular flower-lined bike path with a perfect view of Lake Superior. An anniversary gift from the scenic cycling gods?

In Marquette, we splurged on a motel room. Being inside somewhere warm and dry, the temptation proved too great — we hauled our bikes inside, unloaded our panniers, and spread out our damp gear. "Is that moss growing on the tent?" Sharon joshed. Our space looked like a Camper's Village bargain basement.

While I enjoyed a luxurious steamy shower, Sharon ransacked a nearby grocery store. She bought steaks, all the trimmings, an assortment of snacks, and even a watermelon.

"Want to relax in the Jacuzzi before supper?" I asked her upon her return.

That was a mistake. After the Jacuzzi's hot hydrotherapy massage, our legs felt as heavy as oak trees with all the sap drained from them. "It's a good thing we don't have to cycle anywhere," Sharon murmured, sleepily.

Too fatigued to cook steak, we munched a few snacks and called it an early night. Warm and content in the soft bed, we fell asleep, wrapped in each other's arms.

Pictured Rocks

"On the shores of Gitche Gumee,
Westward by the Big-Sea-Water,
Came unto the rocky headlands,
To the Pictured Rocks of sandstone."
~ W.W. Longfellow, *Song of Hiawatha*

We slept in, getting good value for our money. When we finally got underway, our panniers bulged with food — we were lugging at least a three day supply. "I may have gotten a little carried away on our anniversary splurge," Sharon allowed.

We followed a bike trail along Lake Superior, coasting along in silence, enjoying the expansive view and lack of traffic.

Before long, Sharon complained that with all the food she was toting she felt like an Overwaitea grocery store. (I figured she was more like a small Trading Post.) We stopped, and she rifled through her panniers. We consumed the watermelon, but otherwise made little dent in her cache.

Underway again, our silent mode of travel allowed us to glide right up to a huge bald eagle. Hunched in a ditch, he was ripping into lunch, engrossed in tearing apart some meaty road-kill. When we were scant feet away, the great bird of Jove finally spied us. Startled, he sprang sideways. His four-foot wingspan pounded the air, thudding like a chopper on takeoff; sinewy legs braced like steel rods; sharp, hooked talons flexing; brown eyes piercing with a baneful glint.

Down the road, Christmas came early — we had arrived in the town of Christmas. It didn't snow, although it felt chilly enough. "Appropriate name," Sharon sniffed. "My nose is frozen."

"Feeling a tad Rudolphish with that red schnozz?" I kidded.

We hit Munising's Park Centre for information about the condition of a gravel road leading into Pictured Rocks National Lakeshore. With all the rain in the past few days we thought it might be a tad mucky.

The ranger didn't go out of his way to reassure us. "Maybe mountain bikes could make it through," he mulled. "But I wouldn't recommend tackling it on touring bikes." He shook his head. He looked at his watch. "And, at the moment," he added, attempting to put a final nail in the coffin, "there's strictly no camping in the park."

With that information and the "no camping" warning ringing in our ears, we took a vote, decided to ignore his professional advice, and struck out for Pictured Rocks.

On the muddy road, littered with puddles and potholes deep enough to swallow a Volkswagen, a ranger flagged us to a halt.

"You know there's *absolutely* no camping in the park?"
"Yep," Sharon replied, nodding vigorously.
"We're camping outside the park," I assured him.

At Pictured Rocks two-hundred-foot high cliffs rose dramatically out of Lake Superior. Mottled browns, tans, and greens, from iron, manganese, copper, and limonite oxides, coloured the sheer banks in a dizzying array that ran together in an abstract painting. The name 'Pictured Rocks' comes from the supposed images that appear amidst the multicolored sandstone and mineral stains. But one has to cross his eyes and look really hard.

I squinted. "Looks like a television tuned to a test pattern."

"Maybe the pictures are only available during the tourist season?" Sharon mused.

We climbed a viewing platform and had better luck spying Miners Castle, a fortress-shaped outcropping of Cambrian sandstone. Over the past 500 million years, wind, ice, and water — relentlessly scraping like sandpaper — had carved numerous caves, arches, and castle-shaped formations. Dirt clumps, resembling giant flower pots, surrounded individual alders and hemlocks.

"Those are the largest bonsai I've ever seen," I kidded.

"At least you wouldn't have to water them," Sharon said.

Our tittering died as a ranger approached. "No camping in the park," he said. I had heard the line so many times, I almost beat him to the punch.

To ensure we made it out of the park before darkness swallowed us, we abandoned plans to cook our steak at the well-appointed picnic tables. Under the ranger's watchful eyes, we indulged in a high-fibre snack of cake doughnuts, instead. "We serious athletes have to watch our diets," Sharon joked, washing it all down with slugs of chocolate milk straight from the container (touring brings out the best in one's table manners).

We abandoned Pictured Rocks to the rangers and more imaginative minds. As darkness fell, we were still on the road, red VistaLites blinking. Chilled to the bone, we cheered each time we got to a hill.

An hour later — night having descended around our slender shoulders like a black cape — we reached the edge of the park. Quietly schlepping our bikes off the road, we slipped into Hiawatha National Forest, and set up our inconsequential tent.

Half-Star

"The flush toilet is the basis of Western civilization."
~ Alan Coult

In the morning, Sharon 'raced' slow motion to the nearest rest stop in Shingleton – ten torturous kilometres. Her morning constitution was often inopportune. Reaching a restroom was sometimes a challenging ordeal. A hardship of touring by bicycle is the distance between facilities: rest stops are spaced for car travellers. And what takes an hour for them, takes us a day.

We pulled into the roadside rest stop as an old gent exited the outdoor biffy – holding his nose. Not a good sign.

"Better use the motorhome," he advised his frail-looking wife. "It's pretty stinky."

Not having the luxury of a motorhome washroom alternative, Sharon plugged her nose and bolted inside. Moments later, she staggered out. "Definitely half-star," she choked. (We had devised a five star rating system for washrooms. Never before had one attained the lowly status of half a star!) "What I'd like to know," Sharon shuddered, "is how someone can sling crap four feet up the bloody walls!? For crying out loud, it looks like someone took a dump in there while swinging from a fan."

"Gives a whole new understanding to 'the shit's gonna hit the fan,'" I said, not especially eager to take my turn. Outhouses were a definite downside to biking and camping. The brown stuff may make great roses, but it sure doesn't smell like roses.

The old man's assessment turned out to be unanimous. On a 1 to 10 smelliness scale, I rated it a generous 11. Talk about extreme sports!

And, being the only rest stop for miles around, it procured a steady stream of 'customers.' The weekend was just beginning, but already the outhouse's toilet paper had run its course. Thankfully we carried our own. We sat at a nearby (but not too near!) picnic table to watch the fun. A big stocky fellow entered. *"Oh, my!"* he exclaimed in a high voice. What fun!

"Reminds me of the old man who lived by the sewer," I said. "One day he was found dead. Some thought it was murder ... but it was actually sewercide."

As we ate breakfast – upwind – a retired couple pulled in with a beautiful motorhome (the older I get, the better motorhomes look). They spotted our Canadian flags and beelined over to chat. From British Columbia, they were tired of the travel life and were headed back home. "Travelling for two months has plain tuckered us out," the old gent sighed.

"My goodness," his wife put in, "we were nearly shaken to bits near Sault Ste Marie. You aren't going to dare ride that on pedal bikes, are you?"

That particular stretch of Trans Canada highway is infamous for eating bicycles (and cyclists) — both bike tourers and car drivers had tabled a smorgasbord of horror stories: narrow ... abysmal surface ... nonexistent shoulders ... heavy truck traffic ... countless motorhomes ... high-speed drivers in a hurry to run cyclists off the road. The combination made for a deadly cycling experience. (A friend of ours had cycled solo all the way across Canada with no problems till he hit that section. After being run off the road three times in one day, he turned his little bicycle around and headed back west. When Cross-Canada tour groups ride that segment they begin at dawn. A support van, hazard lights flashing, herds everyone down the road in one unit.)

Since we weren't with a Cross-Canada tour group — and wishing to live long and healthy lives — our plan was to head south to Port Huron, Seney, Manistique Lake.... Rather than jousting with freight trucks and motorhome mirrors, we would enjoy a tranquil ride on peaceful country roads. Or at least that was the plan.

Sweet Buns

> **"Come along inside ... We'll see if tea and buns can make the world a better place."**
> ~ Kenneth Grahame

Near Gould City, on Highway 2, a roadside restaurant sign boasted: WORLD'S LARGEST CINNAMON BUNS. The sweet sign lured me in like a two-year-old spotting a candy store.

We each ordered one. *Ha,* I thought, *I could probably eat both myself.* When the buns arrived, their size shocked me. The suckers were a full eight inches square and an astounding six inches tall! Sharon and I shared one, still warm and oozing, laden with high-calorie brown sugary and cinnamon goodness. It filled us. Holding my stomach, I wandered back outside and, like a squirrel storing nuts for the winter, cached the leftover *undisputed* World's Largest Cinnamon Bun inside my pannier for later.

The extra-large calories propelled us along Lake Michigan's lakeshore. In the dark, near Mackinac Island, we were in serious tourist country. Labor Day long weekend had increased the usual hordes of city-evacuees. Non-stop traffic plied the roads in both directions. Making matters worse, it was the weekend of the annual Mackinac Bridge walk. Throngs of 'weekend warriors' filled camping grounds past capacity.

Since finding a vacant campground was out of the question, we kept our eyes peeled for a likely-looking spot. Passing through Lake

Superior State Forest, Sharon spied a faint track disappearing off into the woods. We waited for a rare break in traffic, then rushed our bikes into the concealing forest.

Once we were in 50 feet and behind a few trees, it was near impossible for anyone to see us. And, when we sat down, we couldn't even see over the waist-high ferns surrounding us. Talk about secluded and private. Ah, the joys of cycle touring ... and finding an impromptu camp spot.

We finally fried up the steak that had been bouncing in my pannier for the past couple of days. "If I don't get food poisoning," I said, carving off a tasty morsel, "this is perfect!"

"And we still have a 'World's Largest Cinnamon Bun' for dessert," Sharon reminded me, boiling a pot of tea.

Life doesn't get much better.

Rails to Trails

> **"The hardest thing to learn in life is which bridge to cross and which to burn."**
> ~ David Russell

I fell face-first into Sleepville at 8:30 PM, and didn't wake until a full 12 hours later. We required (and got) more sleep while cycle touring than when we had held down good paying jobs.

Our breakfast spot of choice was a rest area overlooking smooth as glass Lake Michigan with a lighthouse gracing a distant island. Just as we finished, a fellow approached. When he heard our day's destination he asked if we knew Saint Ignace's five mile-long Mackinac Bridge — the longest suspension bridge in the western hemisphere — didn't allow bicycles.

Nope, we didn't have a clue. Hmmm. What to do? All the way to the bridge, I worried, befuddled as to what would happen once we got to the dreaded no-cyclists-allowed bridge. Options spiraled through my head. Take our chances and ride across? Flag down a passing pickup? Catch a bus? How about a taxi? Maybe there was a pedestrian walkway? Could we push our bikes the entire five miles?

But, as usual, my worries were for naught. Upon our arrival, the Mackinac Bridge Authority dispatched a truck to pick us up. The friendly driver shuttled us across the Straits of Mackinac for the pauper sum of one dollar. "Mackinaw City is the Fudge capital of the USA," the shuttle driver told us. "They call the tourists 'Fudgies.'" He laughed boisterously. "The radio station we're listening to? Its call letters are 'FGE.'" He laughed uproariously again. It was good to see someone enjoyed their job!

Zipping along in the truck cab we glanced to our right and caught a splendid view of sparkling Lake Michigan; off to our left glittered sanguine Lake Huron. At mid-span our driver informed us we were 200 feet above the water surface. "In high winds," he added, "the centre portion of the bridge sways as much as 35 feet!"

We had begun our five mile long Mackinac Bridge shuttle ride in Michigan's Upper Peninsula. When the driver dropped us off on the other side, we had magically been transported to Michigan's Lower Peninsula. We kindly thanked our driver, and set off, bucking a hell-bent for leather, knock-down headwind. I glanced back at the bridge to see how much it was swaying.

Along Lake Huron's shore, we followed a route of flattened fauna: a nightmare of pancaked skunks, squished raccoons, and other non-identifiable remains smushed to smithereens.

"Gosh!" Sharon exclaimed, crinkling her nose. "This stuff falls into three categories. Gory: fresh — hot off the tread, tongue still sticking out. Fetid: days old stench — hold your nose or lose your lunch. And Offensive: weeks old, name-that-indistinguishable-patch-of-fur." The carnage stretched for miles. Considering how close cars cut past our churning legs, I wasn't all that surprised.

Near a mill, we spotted an abandoned railroad, and turned on to it, leaving the buzzing cars, relentless wind, and myriad squashed critters behind.

Cycling through whispering deciduous forest, leaves in the magical throes of autumnal change, was relaxing. However, we paid for the lack of traffic with slow travel. The track consisted of little more than loose gravel and sand. Our progress slowed even more when my rear tire suffered a flat. While I changed it, Sharon amused herself by digging around in the sand.

"Hey, look!" she announced, unearthing a rusty rail spike. "A memento for our first rails to trail ride in Michigan!" She handed me the iron object. I looked it over. She didn't really expect me to carry it as a souvenir, did she?

"Whew!" I breathed, hefting the spike. "I think it's made of leaverite ... as in 'Leave 'er right' there." I tossed it back onto the trail's side to await discovery by some other lucky passerby.

A porcupine waddled toward us. "Looks like a pincushion on legs," Sharon said. A marvellous defence shield made up for its poor eyesight. It padded closer, not worried about predators in the slightest.

"Do you think he's going to plod straight past us?" I chuckled when the walking pincushion was ten feet away and still doddering onward without a care in the world. Then, six feet from us, he stopped and raised a pointy snout in our direction and squinted, staring. As if figuring we were an animal larger than he wished to tangle with, the little porcupine wambled off the track and squatted in the weeds. Tucking himself into a ball, he waited for us to pass — his quilled backside presenting a prickly defence against a suddenly hostile world.

To Live and Die in Posun

> **"We make a living by what we get,
> we make a life by what we give."**
> ~ Winston Churchill

Gas stations became our one-stop shopping centre and home away from home. We washed ourselves and our clothes in an Onaway Shell station's washroom – leaving the sink cleaner than we found it. I shaved, filled our water bottles, bought groceries, and used the station's microwave to nuke the remaining half of our World's Largest Cinnamon Bun. Talk about home cooking!

After our snack, in an effort to slip the long-weekend traffic, we followed various backroads. "One more day until the holiday crowds return to work," Sharon sighed.

"Yep," I said. "You know, now that I'm on vacation full time, I hate long weekends! It's amazing how a person's perspective changes."

We fought a belligerent headwind through Hawk. Several trucks, filled with overflowing loads of potatoes, sped past.

In Posun, population 270, folks were preparing for their annual spud festival. A good time by one and all – a real outing for Mr and Mrs Potato Head.

I imagined the fun filled contests: potato sack races; potato baking; potato carving; potato mashing; potato peeling; potato digging; and, of course, potato hilling. Prizes for the best trained tater. Disqualification for those shouting "Pull my tuber! Pull my tuber!"

"Where are you from?" several Posun folks asked when they came over to inspect our loaded bicycles.

"Alberta."

"Where's that?" came the immediate response, followed closely by: "Never heard of it."

"Canada," we generalized. "Above Montana."

Still a blank stare, then the oft repeated phrase: "Never heard of it."

"Ah," Sharon murmured. "To live and die in Posun."

Déjà Vu

> **"How many roads must a man travel down before he admits he is lost?"**
> ~ Bumper Sticker

We pedalled toward Long Lake, and came across a road not on our map. The newly paved surface looked great. As we puzzled over our finding, a car stopped to see if we needed assistance. We asked the fellow if the road went to Long Lake. He assured us it did, and he threw in directions to a nearby county campground, as well. "They have *showers,*" he added with a knowing wink. He certainly knew how to entice cycle tourists after a hard day's cycling.

We headed off in the new direction and soon intersected a road with a name we thought we recalled our direction-giver saying. The road was gravel, but we pushed onto it anyway. The promise of showers holds a powerful allure.

A few kilometres farther, our fears were confirmed: we were definitely mislocated. A body of water appeared on our left when we expected it to be on our right. Even Sharon, able to navigate by sun or stars, had to admit she had no idea where we were.

She studied the map. After some time, she declared, "This thing is useless!" She scrunched up the paper and tossed it at me. The map's remnants bounced off my helmet. I stooped and retrieved it. Maybe I'd have to start a fire later.

A ways down the road, we spied a fellow working in his manicured yard; the lawn glowed an otherworldly green from abundant fertilizer and recent generous Michigan rains. A profusion of begonia-filled baskets hung from the soffits, throwing colour in every direction. Rose bushes, splendid in fragrant bloom, bedecked every corner of the property.

We stopped to ask directions. The fellow introduced himself as Martin. He was curious about our travels and asked questions. Whatever we answered, Martin seemed to find incredibly amazing.

"We cycled over 2,000 miles last month."

"Gee whiz! Can you believe that? Why, that's more than I drive!" Martin exclaimed. "Wait here," he instructed and disappeared inside.

"Maybe he has to confirm that what he's hearing is really what he's hearing," I said.

Sure enough. Martin reappeared with his wife, Ann. Shoving her to the forefront, Martin asked the exact questions he had moments before.

"Are you having an incredible sense of déjà vu?"

"Yeah," Sharon laughed. "Like all over again."

A rousing session of astound-the-homeowners concluded when Ann and Martin invited us to join them for supper. At the kitchen table, we plunked ourselves down to large helpings of chili and roast corn. Dessert was even better. We tucked into hot cherry pie topped with mountains of vanilla ice cream.

After dessert, Martin's 92-year-old Grandmother appeared from a back room. She spoke to us briefly, then shuffled away. Watching her go, Martin's eyes lit up. "She had me buy her a cane," he whispered. "She said, 'I'm getting old now; I should have a cane.' So I bought her one. One day, I was out working in a corner of the yard, hidden from view. I saw her come outside. Hobbling. With her cane. She looked all around. When she didn't see anyone, she propped her cane by the door and then went zipping around the yard, here and there, like *Flight of the Bumblebee,* checking all the flowers." Martin tilted his head back and roared. "Hell," he continued, his belly shaking with laughter, "I figure she goes jogging after we leave for work ... probably throws in a few push-ups and some cartwheels, too!"

It began to rain. Martin looked at the overcast sky and falling drops. Without hesitating, he invited us to stay. "We have an enclosed atrium that'll suit you perfectly," he said with a smile. "I'll show you the shower."

Sharon and I scrubbed ourselves pink as two crazy pigs in luscious scalding water, then floated off to slumberland, warm in the knowledge of being well-taken care of by our new friends.

We arose feeling more rested than we had in ages. Ann served up crispy bacon, over easy eggs, toast with strawberry preserves, and homemade applesauce "from transparent apples."

"Huh?" I said. "How come I can see the applesauce then?" Ann raised her eyebrows. I figured she'd either get used to my weird humour ... or she wouldn't.

Well fed, we said goodbye to Martin and Ann, and headed down the road in good spirits and with fresh directions.

Martin and Ann, on their way to work, soon overtook us in their vehicle — they honked up a storm and waved as if they hadn't seen us in years. We watched in silence as their tail lights disappeared around a bend. "I think we ought to get lost more often," I said, patting my stomach.

Grease Gremlin

> **"More than any other time in history, mankind faces a crossroads. One path leads to despair and utter hopelessness. The other, to total extinction. Let us pray we have the wisdom to choose correctly."**
> ~ Woody Allen

Seven-thirty AM and we were on the road. In a short distance, our wonderful wide shoulder disintegrated to a measly foot-and-a-half strip, littered with broken glass, potholes, and sharp rocks. Weaving a crooked path between the obstacles, Sharon's rear tire flatted ... twice ... air hissing from the puncture. But, each time, the self-healing tube spurted into action and cauterized the wound. She didn't even have to stop.

"I must be living right!" I boasted to Sharon about not having one flat on our entire tire-eating morning. In Au Gres, the tire gods got their revenge. My rear tire blew with such a vengeance the explosion could be heard a block away. A three-inch section ripped away from the tire's wire bead. My poor defenseless tube was shredded to bits. (Lesson: Don't be too flippant with the tire gods.)

"This one's going straight into the Dumpster," I announced, surveying the tube's mangled remains. *What caused the blowout?* I wondered. I checked the alignment of my brakes. I know you're not going to believe this, but they appeared perfectly fine, hitting the rim squarely. What was going on? In all our miles of touring, never before had I experienced such baffling tire troubles.

Tire beyond repair, I had the challenge — in a settlement of 800 — of finding a new one. I left Sharon lounging on a patch of grass beside our bikes and struck out on my quest (taking only an apple and a piece of cheese with me).

I entered a sporting goods store. No luck. Two variety stores produced the same lack of results. *Will I have to bribe someone in the trailer park for their ten-speed's old tire?* Dejected, but not totally without hope, I headed into a hardware store — and struck black gold! They had not one, but two tires in the size I was looking for. Attempting to appease the tire gods, I snapped up both, plus two new tubes, and a patch kit for good measure. Trifle not with tire-god karma.

Trotting back to where I had last seen my wife, I stopped short. Those were our bikes all right, but squatting on the grass beside them was a barely recognizable grease gremlin. Sharon, left alone to amuse herself, couldn't resist. She had cleaned my ultra-mucky chain and extra-gucky derailleur. In the process, she had transferred the sludge and grease onto every square inch of exposed flesh ... from her forehead on down. "Oh, baby," I winced. "*How* the heck did you get it in your knee pits?"

"Mosquitoes," she answered.

While Sharon cleaned up, I created what I thought would make the ultimate flat-proof tire. I cut the bead off my old tire, and inserted the beadless marvel — along with my Mr Tuffy tire liner — inside my new tire.

"Jeez," Sharon said, observing my handiwork. "I don't think that's a good idea." She wrinkled her nose. She figured there wouldn't be any room for air. "If you can get your tire onto your rim, that is."

Hmmm. She was right. I couldn't get the darn tire on the rim. "Maybe if I had a smaller tube and a larger tire?" I hypothesized.

Sharon shook her head. "Maybe a smaller head and a larger brain," she kidded.

I abandoned my grand experiment, and we headed off in search of lunch.

At Holland's IGA grocery store, along with peaches and bananas, we bought yogourt ice cream cones. "It's almost warm enough to enjoy them," Sharon said. Standing outside the exit, licking our treats, Mr Holland, the store's owner, strolled over. Soon, he was treating us to Slurpees and samples of a new Chiller drink they had just received that morning. We judged it two thumbs up. He liked us. Leading onward to the deli, he loaded us up with free pieces of spicy fried chicken. Au Gres was turning out to be not such a bad place after all.

Struck by the spontaneous generosity of some folks, we pedalled out of Holland's IGA parking lot. "You're not going to believe this!" Sharon yelled. "I've got a flat!"

I changed the tube for Sharon, and when I did so, I noticed something interesting. Sharon's tire was a size larger than mine. Sharon shook her head no. I nodded my head yes, and, grinning, stuffed my beadless wonder inside her tire. (It's similar to knowing the correct way to test a spark plug. The wrong way, of course, is to hang onto the plug while you crank the engine over. The right way: while you crank the engine a friend holds the plug.)

Mutant Ninja Turtles

> "There's no excuse for [rude]ness, except for maybe if you've been in a real bad train accident, and had to have a large part of your brain removed."
> ~ Lev L. Spiro

Ten kilometres out of Au Gres, we stopped again. It wasn't another flat, mind you. We were lost. Again. (Or were we just putting my new-found 'ask for directions and hope it'll lead to a supper invitation' theory into practice?)

Garry Charbonneau's careful directions enabled us to find our way to Bay City along a network of backroads. He did a marvellous job! For the entire distance, only a few cars passed us on the ultra-smooth roads.

At the entrance to Bay City State Park we stood around looking lost for too long. A woman, from a trailer next to the check-in office, wandered over and collected our fee. "I'll give it to the attendant in the morning," she said.

"That was lucky!" Sharon muttered as we pedalled off in search of a site.

After eating, showering, and doing laundry, it was near midnight. Sharon dragged me off "for company" while she phoned home. In the end, I was glad I had accompanied her. The call was eventful. And not just because I invented a new hop-from-one-foot-to-the-other-bug-swatting dance. Rather, we learned an offer was pending on our house. We skipped off to bed, footloose and fancy house-free visions hopscotching through our heads.

At 2 AM we were rudely awakened. A rowdy gang, astride raucous Harleys, thundered into the campground. Motors thudding, the dirty dozen roared around our little tent like Indians on the warpath circling a Conestoga. Whooping and clapperclawing, they rumbled a couple of tours around the suddenly wide-awake campground before mercifully exiting.

Moments after slipping back into unconsciousness, dazzling white car lights jarred me from my motorbikes-with-fluffy-pillows-for-mufflers dream. A late-arriver backed his vehicle into the site directly across from ours. Leaving his headlights to eloquently stream into our fabric abode, he casually set up his tent. "We *paid* for this?" I moaned for the second time in an hour. Our good neighbour spent long minutes unloading gear, vigorously slamming his car doors between each and every trip. "Just our luck," I groaned. "A 27-door model!"

I had previously fought a losing battle in my attempt to convince Sharon we should abandon commercial campgrounds. In the morning, her head aching and her body tired, Sharon had swung around to my viewpoint. "Official campgrounds are for the birds," she stated. "And noisy ones at that!"

From Bay City, we headed southeast on four-lane Highway 15, riding a foot inside our lane to avoid the potholes that lined the road's edge. All drivers passed us courteously. Especially truck drivers. Except one, of course.

A boll weevil truckie, dragging a two-trailer widow maker, burned up behind us. With a "might is right" creed, the dork blasted his air horn, poured on the coal, and — even though no traffic occupied the adjoining lane — scraped past our churning gams.

"Thanks!" Sharon screamed into the diesel fumes. "Now I won't have to shave my legs!"

Through the Saginaw Valley, traffic decreased as corn crops increased. We passed field after field of corn, corn, and more corn. After passing my millionth cob, I said (in a husky voice), "I'd make a joke here, but it'd be corny."

"I'm all ears," Sharon said.

"Hear about the divorced cob? He stalked his ex-wife."

"Yep, that is corny," Sharon agreed.

Munching buttery popcorn in Frankenmuth, self-proclaimed Bavarian capital of the US (minus the Alps), we ambled around town viewing the tourist trap. So authentic, tourists spoke German! It even had its own beer.

Outside an ice cream shoppe (when it's spelled like that, you just know it's going to be expensive), we joined a gaggle of white-socked retired folks licking pastel-coloured yogourt cones.

We followed them to the Cheese Haus where we sampled chocolate peanut butter cheese. A true gourmet adventure. "Only in the US!" one tourist commented. It smacked more of fudge than cheese. A woman beside us must have had the same taste sensation. "When I want to eat fudge, I'll eat fudge. And when I eat cheese, I want it to taste like cheese," she remarked sharply. Her cheesy comment didn't stop us from trying jalapeño cheese, watermelon-licorice cheese, and hot pepper jelly cheese. Great on crackers!

With strange-smelling breath, we excused ourselves from the Cheese Haus, and toodled down the street to a covered bridge dominating one end of town. A paddle-wheeler plied the Cass River, transporting bandy-legged tourists on a mini Danube cruise, oompah music blaring from tinny speakers.

Amused, but unimpressed, we abandoned Frankenmuth to the hordes of tourists and struck out for Vassar. Arriving at dusk, we found a secluded park. While I prepared supper, Sharon reconnoitred the nearby ravine for a tent site.

After eating, it was nearly dark. We pushed our bikes down a narrow trail and into concealing leafy growth. To our dismay, vehicle headlights on a side street shone directly down the trail.

Sharon groaned. "It would be like sleeping in a roving searchlight all night. I don't think I can handle another night of lousy sleep."

We scouted for an alternate site. One side of the narrow path abruptly dropped to a sluggish waterway. Shining our tiny flashlight in the opposite direction, I scanned the terrain for a possibility. Nothing but an inhospitable proliferation of thorns, rocks, and pointy sticks. "Even our Therm-A-Rests won't help with that," I said.

Abandoning our search, we pushed our bikes back to the park. Maybe we could set up in the cooking shelter? Falsetto voices brought us to a halt. Two teenage boys were in the picnic shelter, smoking. In their smoky haze and impetuous swearing they hadn't heard our approach. We eased our bikes onto the ground and laid on the grass; shadows enshrouded us in near-invisibility. The slimmest glimmer of moonlight penetrated the leafy canopy overhead.

"Oh, no," Sharon groaned. "I hope they leave soon." Instead, five more foul-mouthed cretins joined them. The pro-unofficial camping argument I had so successfully presented that morning evaporated like a puddle in the afternoon sun. "Oh, joy," Sharon sighed.

It soon became apparent that the delinquents aspired to be *Teenaged Mutant Ninja Turtles*. In an awful karate display, they kicked the garbage cans, denting the shiny new aluminum, and strewing plastic and paper innards over a wide area of freshly mown grass.

"Early Neanderthal," Sharon whispered.

After vanquishing Sir Garbagehead, the angry teens turned their wrath on their next defenceless victims: cement-anchored barbecues. After a succession of forceful kicks they succeeded in uprooting the metal posts. Amid high-fives and breathless cheers — convinced testosterone levels were at a high enough level — they departed.

"Home to catch Ninja reruns, no doubt."

"At least it'll get them off the streets," Sharon muttered.

Shaking our heads at the youths' idiotic behaviour, we erected our tent behind a nearby building, dreading another possible round of unwelcome visitors. Never being certain that an entire night would pass without interruption was definitely an uncomfortable part of unofficial camping. But, at least we hadn't paid for the privilege.

Sarnia Bob

"The smaller the mind the greater the conceit."
~ Aesop

The mortgage company approved the offer on our house. "I guess that makes it official," Sharon said. "No excuses now why we can't continue." We jettisoned any waffling concerns we had been harbouring and committed ourselves to our dream. After all, touring cyclists' have a rule: Never turn back.

Following backroads through miles of farmland provided us with enough corn crops to last a lifetime. "Build it and they will come," kept repeating in my head. Cornstalks towered over and around us. Wind rustled the papery dry leaves, sounding like whispering conspirators. Was it murmuring about our plans to ride around the world? It had big ears and probably knew all about our intentions. It must be impossible for farmers to keep secrets.

Before crossing back in to Canada at Sarnia, we stopped at a mall in Port Huron to mail postcards. My Avocet altimeter registered exactly zero feet climbed all morning. "That part of Michigan was flatter than the prairies!"

We entered the mall and discovered a food court. Eating there was an all-round bad experience. All those clean people! Spending their time (and money) buying useless stuff we no longer needed. We hadn't been on the road more than two months and already we felt removed from our previous lives.

Compared with nature's peaceful burbles, the mall's constant hubbub made us as jumpy as two cats on a hot tin roof. After the past weeks in mostly tiny villages, the crowd was a culture shock. And seated next to a blaring musical carousel ride — filled with screaming kids — did nothing to calm us. People gawked at us. What was it? What made them think we were different — something to be stared at? I knew I had changed on the inside, but had I changed on the outside, as well?

If being stared at wasn't bad enough, once outside the mall, we met Bob. He was from Sarnia, and had brought his wife to the States for a day's shopping expedition. He noticed our loaded bikes and hastened over with a few questions.

"How long are you out for?"

I took the plunge. After all, it looked as if we had sold our house. "Two year round the world trip." The words squeaked out, mewling like a newborn kitten, uncertain of coming into the light of day. Around the world? Unbelievable. I gulped as the words clawed their way out. Ringing in my ears, their harshness jolted me with reality. But I needn't have worried. Sarnia Bob paid no special mind to my reply. He may not have even heard.

"*I* bike 20 miles a couple of times a week," he bragged. "How many miles a day do you do?"

"As many as we can," I answered.

"No, really," he pressed. "How many?"

"Oh, eighty to a hundred or more," I answered. Unlike when we quoted those figures to curious Americans, Sarnia Bob didn't bat an eye (I could tell he was a Canadian from a mile off).

Not the slightest trace of attention in his voice, he asked, "Where are you off to next?"

"Toronto," Sharon answered.

"Via Point Pelee," I added.

Sarnia Bob finally blinked. He made an incongruent face and stuttered that those destinations lay in completely different directions. His mentality was of a racer, straight line, point A to point B, as fast as possible. No time to look up. No time to smell the roses. No time for detours. He didn't fathom the essence of bicycle touring. It's the journey, not the destination. Sharon pulled out a map with our highlighted route to Point Pelee.

"You don't want to go there," Sarnia Bob stated flatly, scrutinizing the proposed route: first south, then west, then back east along Lake Erie's shore, then north to Toronto. "That's a *long* way out of your way...," he mumbled. "I'd say you'd have at least a *hundred* extra miles!"

A hundred miles? This was the same fellow who hadn't batted an eye when I told him we were riding a hundred miles *a day?*

"*Who* wants to see Point Pelee, anyway?" he muttered. (Not only is it one of the country's most visited parks — well known for its remarkable birding and Monarch butterflies — it's also Canada's most southern point of mainland.)

When Sarnia Bob realized we weren't about to change our minds he revised his tact. "Well," he said haughtily, "if you're determined to go to Point Pelee, it'd be a shorter distance if you crossed back into Canada at Windsor."

Windsor!? Good one, Bub! Wouldn't that entail cycling through Detroit? *Detroit!* Now there's one of America's friendlier cities. Talk about adventures in cycling! Maybe it missed grabbing the American nation's "Murder City" title this year, but usually it's bobbing around in the top four. Detroit, population about 925,051, has in the neighbourhood — not a very good neighbourhood, apparently — between 395 and 615 murders per year. (Canada, with a population of over 30 million — and roughly 90% of that population living within 100 miles of the US border — usually registers around 550 murders per year.) I studied the map. Interstate 94 may have been shorter, and even if we had been allowed on it, we wouldn't have wanted to anyway. So, if we had been insane enough to cycle to Detroit, our route would have been south along the Saint Clair River, skirt Anchor Bay, then follow the shoreline of Lake Saint Clair. That route didn't appear shorter to me. And, we had no hankering to visit Detroit, nicknamed Motor City, historic heart of the American automotive industry, home of Ford, Chrysler, and General Motors, on bicycles. Sheesh.

When we politely declined Sarnia Bob's Detroit route suggestion, he felt compelled to supply us with directions to Toronto by way of Highway 7 (a good deal north of our intended Point Pelee route). After several minutes of explanation, he concluded his route spiel with: "I've never been on it personally, but it used to be four lanes. Now it's two, so it ought to have a wide shoulder." We thanked Sarnia Bob, eager to see him on his way. "I could give you directions past Toronto," he blathered on, oblivious to Sharon's growing restlessness (perhaps he wasn't the sharpest crayon in the box), "but I better stay in my own area." He paused. A sour look crossed his face — the exact one, I suspect, someone'd get if a wet mackerel slapped him upside the head. "Besides," he said, smacking his lips, "you've made it this far by yourselves."

Sharon swung a leg over her bike. We bid Sarnia Bob a final goodbye.

Out of Sarnia Bob's earshot, Sharon asked, "Have you ever noticed that a whole lot of people seem to have gotten shortchanged when it comes to having common sense?"

"I'm sure he was just trying to be helpful."

Sharon wasn't so sure. I think she had the distinct feeling that touring bikes were like squirrels: they attracted nuts. Or something like that.

We rode straight to the US-Canada Blue Water Bridge crossing before Sarnia Bob could hunt us down and assail us with more good advice. At the border, a chipper-looking guard made the mistake of asking a still-flustered Sharon, "Where have you been?"

She waved her hand vaguely toward the southwest. "Over there." One might say her answer took him slightly off-guard. His left eyebrow jutted skyward, but without another question, he waved us through.

"What a wonderful sense of geography you have," I kidded her as we pedalled away.

Sharon glared at me. "That Bob guy still had me rattled."

Geranium

> "The male is a domestic animal which, if treated with firmness, can be trained to do most things."
> ~ Jilly Cooper

We pedalled into Sarnia. Built along the banks of the turgid, turquoise and azure, Saint Clair River, it displayed gardens bursting with flowers. My favourites were dazzling red hot pokers. Heavy industry had spent a load of money disguising chemical plants and smokestacks. Everything looked clean ... as long as one only looked skin-deep. (Like my mother was fond of saying: "Beauty is only skin deep, but ugly goes all the way to the bone.")

Leaving Sarnia to the Bobs of the world, we arrived at a campground in Mooretown. In front of a travel trailer, two large women lay sprawled across lawn chairs. We wheeled over to them and discovered they wanted an exorbitant sum for a tiny plot of ground. *We only want to sleep here,* I thought, *not buy the place.* In hopes of wrangling a discount, I tried out my new spiel.

"How much is it for round-the-world cyclists?"

The two women shuffled in their chairs, eyes wide, mouths agape.

"That's more the response I have been looking for," I whispered to Sharon.

"In that case," the smaller of the two large women chirruped, "nothing!" She pointed to a piece of grass. "You can stay right here beside our trailer."

I nodded. Blankly. The woman's free offer hadn't registered in my teeny-tiny brain. Perhaps Sarnia Bob still had me rattled, too? Not one to quit when I'm ahead I added we were on our honeymoon. Which was true. Technically. But when they assumed we had *just* been married, I dumbly nodded again. (I like to think that what I lack in honesty I make up in charisma.)

"Newlyweds!" the woman exclaimed, her eyes twinkling. "And you're riding around the world on bikes? Honey," she said, giving Sharon a pensive look, "you must *really* love him." I was about to inform the woman that it had all been Sharon's idea, then, at the last moment, decided to keep quiet. From her ample bulk, I assumed she wouldn't understand how *anyone* on earth could *want* to do such a thing. Besides, I had already opened my big mouth wide enough. Was there room for another cycling shoe in there? *Sometimes,* I thought, *it's better to keep your mouth shut and let them think you're stupid, rather than open your mouth, and prove it.*

"Oh, yeah," Sharon drawled, giving me a sideways look, "he's good for a laugh now and then."

"Well, it sounds like you'll fit right in," the large woman replied with a shadowy smile. "My name's Pat," she said, thrusting a meaty paw toward us. Half-turning her torso, she jabbed a thick thumb toward a neat fellow two-thirds her size, standing in the travel trailer's doorway, tea-towel in hand. "That's my husband, Klaus," Pat said, a half-smile crinkling her lips. "He's part German and part Ukrainian ... I call him my little geranium."

I chuckled and waved. Already, I could tell we were in for an entertaining evening. "This is my sister, Judy," Pat said, introducing the even larger woman next to her. Pat gazed around, then pointed out a wee wisp of a feller running to another trailer over yonder. "That's Judy's husband," Pat said, giggling. "We call him 'Speedy.'"

The vast size difference between husband and wife struck me as comical. I smiled, pondering. *Do the biggest women always marry the smallest men? Was it one of life's little rules? Somewhat similar to those with the biggest butt, invariably always seem to sport the smallest fanny pack? Then again,* I thought, *perhaps it's all just an unfortunate optical illusion.*

"Are you hungry?" Pat asked, jolting me from my daydream.

"No, we're fine, thanks," Sharon answered. My stomach demurred with a reflexive growl.

"We've finished supper," Pat went on, "but it's no trouble for Klaus to fix you a burger."

I glanced toward Klaus. Still framing the trailer's doorway, he grinned, slapped the tea-towel over his shoulder, and about-faced into the trailer.

"Men never do anything unless people are visiting," Pat informed Sharon, beginning what would turn out to be a very long list of newlywed tips. "But if you have guests they will do everything — making it look like you do nothing. So," she said with a sly grin, "the secret is to always have lots of company!"

In short order, Klaus reappeared with two deluxe burgers and two cups of tea. Sharon and I sat at the picnic table. "Train your man early," Pat advised Sharon. "They take time, so don't waste a second!"

"Oh?" Sharon replied. "How long does it take?"

"Thirty-one years," Pat replied. I almost choked on a chunk of cheese. If Roseanne ever needed a stand-in, the woman could fill her shoes (and then some).

"I plan on writing a book on men and marriage," Pat stated.

"Good idea," I said. "What's the title?"

"I'm calling it *Pat's Pointers: A Guide for Today's Wild Wahini*. My motto: 'Make your man laugh at least once a day, and he'll never leave you.'"

Sounded good to me. Klaus delivered tea to Pat and Judy, then settled himself into a lawn chair. Talk turned to the usual questions of routes and how many kilometres a day we did. Then they shifted gears, asking what our parents thought about our trip.

"They're worried," we confided, "but they're supportive." Looking from a more senior perspective, they had said, "You only live once — so you may as well make the most of it." And, when they realized we were going away for a considerable length of time, they said, "You know, two, three, even four years are going to go by whether you do it or not." That was true. So, we thought, 'What would we rather be doing? Climbing the corporate ladder one shaky rung at a time (possibly sawed off midstep), or off exploring the big wide world?' Happily, travel won out. After all, who would voluntarily choose being cooped up inside all day breathing artificial air and seeing with artificial light when there are mountains to climb, roads to ride, rivers to swim, and new friends to meet?

Did I mention copious amounts of food to be eaten? Barely finished licking our fingers from our first helping, Klaus hustled over with another humongous burger.

"We decided we'd rather be doing this," Sharon said, "than stuck in some dead-end job."

"Just waiting to die," I added.

Pat lurched upright. "My dad's 80," she said. "And he's just waiting to die." She paused, her eyes moist. "I went to see him the other day," she said. "He greets me with 'Hi, Fat Pat.'" She frowned. Her head bowed. "I asked him, 'Dad, do you want to go to a birthday party next week?'

"'Probably be dead by then,' he says.

"Well, if you're not dead, do you want to go?

"'Okay, but I'll probably be dead. Don't make any plans around me.'

"Okay, Dad," Pat grimaced, enjoying her one-woman two-sided dialog. "He's so stooped over," she rebounded, giggling, "he reminds me of the letter 'n.' It looks like his suspenders are *way* too tight and they're pulling the poor old guy over. 'Hey, Dad! Your suspenders are too tight!'

"'Whaaaat?'

"Never mind." Pat paused. A crease furrowed her brow. "Yep. He's just waiting to die."

There was silence as we digested Pat's remarks. I decided then and there that I intended to wear out rather than rust out.

"So!" Pat burst out suddenly, breaking our ruminations. "Enough of my morbidity!" She looked directly at Sharon, ready to dispense more bang-up newlywed tips. "What do you guys do about sex?"

It was Sharon's turn to nearly choke.

"Well, I've got some advice for you," Pat said, "on how to avoid sex." *Oh, great.* "Can't use the old headache excuse anymore," she griped, pursing her lips into a beguiling pout. "Some dumb doctor loused that one up. 'Sex reduces stress and actually helps your headache go away.' Terrific! I've had to go and change my entire tactic since that sordid piece of research. Now I say to

Klaus, 'Rub my back.'" Her voice dropped to a whisper as she demonstrated. "The secret is to keep twitching your shoulder until he falls asleep."

I hoped Sharon wasn't paying too close attention.

"Men are quite ignorant about the female physiology," Pat continued. "Like, I'll wear pads for three weeks straight. 'Sorry, hon, not tonight.'" Her face twisted into a cherubic grin.

Hmmm. I'd watch for that one.

Pat was full of good ideas. "Another thing you can do is tell him to go to bed and you'll be right there. Keep checking every so often. 'Honey, don't fall asleep watching TV. Hon?' When he doesn't answer anymore, it's safe to go to bed." *Good thing we sold our TV!*

Klaus served mugs of hot chocolate.

"Speaking of 'safes,'" Pat went on, "the other day, our grandson asked Klaus, 'What's a condom, Grandpa?' Klaus tells him: 'An apartment building.' I felt it my duty to correct Klaus," Pat sniffed. "'It's a raincoat for a penis,' I told him. Don't want the kid gettin' no wrong ideas." I nearly spat out my hot chocolate.

After another round of 'helpful' newlywed advice, Sharon and I were ready to hit the showers. I rummaged through my panniers, searching for fresh clothes. "You can shower together if you like," Judy piped up. "The one on the end is for handicapped. It's nice and roomy!" I considered *that* the most helpful tip of the evening.

Sharon and I traipsed off happily to the showers.

"Hey!" Pat bellowed. "You're holding hands! *Newlyweds!"* she shouted. Then, in mock disgust, directed at Sharon I presumed, "You haven't learned *one* thing I've told you, have you?"

Fire House

> "Hope is the worst of evils, for it prolongs the torments of man."
> ~ Friedrich Nietzsche

In the morning, we phoned Sharon's mom and dad to find out if the sale of our house had been finalized.

"Still in process," they said. "Call back in a week, in case anything needs to be taken care of." It was an ominous sign.

We loped back to Pat's campsite. Pat and crew reclined in lawn chairs, lolling in the weak morning rays. Pat lounged in the same lawn chair (and the same position) as when Sharon and I shuffled off to bed the night before. She had moved though — at least she was sporting a different housecoat.

Pat wagged her head as we approached. She clucked her tongue, and chastised Sharon. "You haven't learned a thing!" she scolded anew. "I saw you over in the phone booth. Pair of fishing worms, that's what you two looked like."

Klaus scrambled up to make tea, toast and cereal.

"Your hair looks great," I complimented Pat, attempting to sidetrack her from her pet subject.

"Oh, yes," she burbled, coiffing the back of her head in an animated manner. "I was up every hour changing sides so it would be even."

"Yeah, you look like you were up half the night," Judy croaked in with her two cents, her inflection betraying that misty area somewhere between sisterly love and sibling rivalry.

"Could have been worse," I offered. "You could have been in a tent."

After another bowl of cereal, ready to hit the dusty trail, Sharon and Pat hugged like two bears. Then Pat surprised Sharon. She presented her with a tiny gold angel pin. Sharon accepted it with a smile, brushing away an unexpected tear.

We pedalled away, waving and waving. "Good thing we're not staying longer," Sharon said. "It's hard enough after one day." She was right. We had arrived complete strangers. A few hours later we were departing, feeling as if we were leaving family. It was truly amazing how folks 'adopted' us on such short notice and made us feel like long-lost kin. Even without Sharon's new angel pin, we felt truly blessed. All across Canada, generous folks opened their homes, and hearts, to us.

"How do you tell a happy cyclist?" Sharon asked, grinning. "Count the bugs in her teeth." With smiles plastered across our faces like wallpaper, we rode south through Mooretown and Wallaceburg — zigging and zagging — following mainly traffic-free country lanes.

At Mitchell's Bay, perusing our map over lunch, I sucked up several cups of tea (talk about being hydrated!). "Hey, check this out!" I said, pointing to the map. "There's a place near here named Lighthouse Cove!" (Being from landlocked Alberta, we loved lighthouses *and* coves.)

So, after lunch, we set off for Lighthouse Cove — just because we liked the name. "That's the beauty of unscheduled travel," I crowed. "We're free to choose anywhere we please."

And Lighthouse Cove didn't disappoint. In a powder blue sky, puffy milk-white clouds hovered on the horizon. At the water's edge, amidst neon green grass and waist-high shrubs, we found the lighthouse with its beaming white tower and faded red cap. A wrinkled reflection stared mutely back. Tranquility permeated the atmosphere. Sharon yawned. "This place could be named Sleepy Hollow," she decided.

Before I could agree, the sound of lapping waves shifted my tiny bladder into overdrive. "Jeez," I grimaced, "my back teeth are floating."

"Little wonder," Sharon frowned. "How many cups of tea did you drink at lunch? Five?"

"Six," I corrected, an indigent contortion straining my face. "Seemed like a good idea at the time," I said, sucking in my cheeks and hopping from foot to foot.

Instead of slipping discretely behind bushes, I did the civilized thing, and struggled to a nearby grocery store. I zipped in. The place was deserted except for one lone woman behind the counter, working on a crossword puzzle. She glanced at me in disdain. How dare I interrupt her concentration? In far too great an urgency to even pretend I was a customer, I hastily asked to use the washroom. The woman glared over the top of her horn-rimmed glasses and hooted, "Employees only!"

"I only have to pee," I beseeched, hoping to appeal to her maternal side. "I won't even use any toilet paper," I promised through clenched teeth, my feet tapping a little jitterbug dance.

She growled again, but pointed toward the store's rear. Perhaps she decided it was in her own best interest to grant me passage to the sacred room with its gleaming porcelain god? Or perhaps my impromptu jig was the most entertainment she had had since completing the *New York Times* crossword puzzle back in the summer of 79.

A few minutes later — bladder wrung out — I thanked the woman (she didn't even look up), and stepped back outside and into warm afternoon sunshine. I found Sharon dozing. "Talk about Sleepy Hollow," I said.

We pedalled away from the hamlet, the dark forest buzzing around us like a symphony of insect bebop. Mosquitoes hummed. Crickets chirped. Katydids chirruped. "More like Frog Hollow," Sharon grinned.

At Stoney Point, wild town kids greeted us. Complementing their barbaric behaviour, an assortment of weirdos plied the sidewalks. Both locals and weekenders seemed united in their unfriendliness. While Sharon foraged in a grocery store, I stayed outside and guarded our bikes.

One teenage hooligan roared up and down main street on a high-powered unlicensed dirt bike, ignoring yield signs, stop signs, personal and public safety. Within minutes he nearly caused four accidents. “His girlfriend just broke up with him,” a kid beside me said as I watched the motorcyclist’s bizarre antics. “So he’s trying to kill himself.”

“He’s going to succeed,” I replied. “The sad part is he’s going to take some innocent person with him.”

“All the world’s a stage,” the kid replied.

“Ain’t that the truth?” I responded, pushing out my lips. A throng of teenagers mobbed me.

“Where you guys from?” one asked acerbically.

“Edmonton,” I answered.

“I doubt it,” another gangly member spat.

Our exchange continued in that venomous vein. They would ask a question. I would answer. They would spit, and say “I doubt it.” I found it rather remarkable how much spit, and doubt, they possessed.

Sharon reappeared. They pounced, immediately asking where we were from. “Edmonton, Alberta,” Sharon replied. More spit. More doubt. They still weren’t convinced.

“Aw,” one drawled, “they probably rode here from Tilley.” (Tilbury was a small place a few kilometres away.)

With that proclamation, the gang drifted away. Sharon and I stuffed supplies into our panniers.

“Is it just me?” Sharon wondered aloud. “Or are the people here really unfriendly?”

“Gee, what do you mean?” I asked in feigned wonder.

“Well, the store owners went out of their way to inform me that no camping is allowed at their municipal park.”

The loser on the motorbike roared past at 80 kilometres an hour. “Not that we’d want to anyway,” I said. “No doubt the store owners’ warning was for our own safety.”

More than happy to be leaving Stoned Point, we headed out of town on double lucky Highway 77. Suddenly, the kamikaze motorbiker howled up behind us. He pounded past, hard, inches from our elbows. He downshifted, engine screaming, and turned at a right-angle into a plowed field to bounce over furrows like riding a bucking bronco. “Gawd,” Sharon shuddered, “I’m grateful that kid doesn’t have a car.”

We rolled into Comber with waning rays of light, and wheeled into a ball field. Four kids, aged five through eight, came running over, saucer-eyed, as fast as their little legs would propel them. “Do you want to camp here?” they asked. “Please!”

When we agreed, they accompanied us to the park caretaker’s house. A well-fed Dalmatian ran out and licked our hands. The caretaker turned out to be as congenial as his dog. "No problem," he smiled. (That's what I like to hear at the end of a long day! Maybe Ontarians weren't so bad, after all.)

We pushed our bikes to a picnic table. "Can we watch you set up your tent?" the kids asked. "Please!"

"Sure!" I replied. But even before I pulled the tent bag off my bike's rear carrier, the children's mother arrived. When they told her of the plan, she scolded the eldest, "You have papers to deliver first."

Sharon and I watched them go and decided to leave setting up the tent for later. By the time we had eaten and washed up, the eager kids were back, their haggard mother in tow. "This is big time entertainment!" she grinned.

We threaded the poles through their nylon sleeves, then, as we had a hundred times in the past, popped the tent up. From the kids' response, you would have thought our tent was a Big Top circus tent complete with three rings of non-stop action. The four children, oohing and aahing, took turns peering inside. "Perhaps they think we've hidden Dumbo the Flying Elephant in there somewhere?" Sharon kidded.

"This'll be Show and Tell on Monday for sure," the mom laughed, playing along, taking her turn to peer inside.

Jim, the kids' muscle-shirted father swaggered over and introduced himself as "a truck driver and Harley rider." I could tell right off we were going to be friends. After all, he rode a bike, too. Near the end of his summation of the area's history, Jim cautioned us, "Watch out for the wild cottage kids at Stoney Point if you go that way!"

"Too late!" I cried. Apparently we weren't the only ones who thought the Stoned Point rich kids a deplorable bunch.

The sun had long since turned itself in. The mother and father bid us good night, and rounded up their brood for home.

I headed to the porta-John. Upon exiting, I observed a glowing orange cloud hovering low in the otherwise clear sky. *Huh? Hasn't the sunset already finished?* I watched in wonder as a pair of lanky youngsters sprinted past the park's gate. *A break-in getaway?* Jim had mentioned there had been two break-ins the previous night.

Flashing red lights flickered in the darkness. A fire engine, its siren full blast, hotfooted it past. Fire engine! Orange glow! *Aha!* A fire! (It may take me a while, but I eventually get there.)

The blaze was one street off the main drag. Sharon and I — suddenly wide awake — hastened toward the glow. Orangish flames crackled and leaped, licking the black night sky like tongues of tiger ice cream. As we neared the hot zone, we recognized Jim leaning against the tailgate of a pickup — one of his young sons standing next to him. We stopped alongside them. "Someone's garage," Jim said. "It's filled with paint and other combustibles. Arson. Someone set it on fire."

A smoldering team of firefighters hosed down the structure with robust streams of water. Paint cans exploded like fireworks detonating on the fourth of July.

"I've lived through two house fires," Jim said, as a second fire engine rushed onto the scene. "The first time," he said, "my son was playing with a cigarette lighter in a closet — one of those gun-shaped lighters. He liked how it sparked when he pulled the trigger." More paint cans exploded. "Our entire house burnt down." Jim paused, then continued. "The second time," Jim related, "he was playing with matches under his bed."

The boy looked up at me, his blue eyes wide, his gentle features enlivened. "That stuff under the bed catches fire real easy," he whispered.

"Sounds like you've got a promising career as a Fire Chief," I wisecracked to the wee firebug.

An ancient fire truck barrelled up. A three-alarmer! "Must be having trouble with the paint cans," Jim remarked. "That old thing is usually reserved for parade duty only."

"It's a really big fire!" the little guy exclaimed.

A half-hour later — excitement burnt down — Sharon and I bid Jim and his fiery son good night and trudged back to our tent.

Surrounded by the ball field's high fence, we fell asleep peacefully. Some time later, a blinding flashlight beam lambasted me square in the eyeballs, jarring me from a wonderful deep sleep. "Get that light out of my face!" I commanded groggily, one hand groping upwards toward the offending beam like some cross-eyed monkey attempting to shove a cork back in a diarrhetic cow.

"This is the Fire Chief," a booming voice at the other end of the spotlight said. "We had an arson fire earlier this evening. I was checking around and saw your tent."

"I know," I mumbled incoherently. "We saw it."

"Where are you from?" he demanded. "What do you do? Why are you here?" A midnight session of *Twenty Questions* was shaping up rather well.

Oh, joy! I thought. *Now I'm an arson suspect. But, hey, no problem. I have an alibi. I was with that kid.* What kid? *You know — the one who started his house ... on fire ... twice. Terrific.*

Point Pelee

> **"Reptiles are a part of the old wilderness of earth, the environment in which man got the nerves and hormones that made him human. If we let the reptile go ... we shall no longer be exactly human."**
>
> ~ Archie Carr, *The Reptiles*

"Bring your water bottles in and I'll fill them with ice for you," a clerk in Leamington offered.

The ice turned out to be a good thing. It was September, but a summery blue sky with rows of cirrocumulus clouds helped pull us down the road to Point Pelee National Park. When we arrived, we received pleasant news. Bicycles were admitted free. "Now that's the kind of surprise I like," I said.

Point Pelee National Park may be one of Canada's smallest national parks, but it hosts a whopping half a million visitors each year. The park is well known as a bird watchers' mecca (it boasts 55 types of songbirds alone). Three-hundred-seventy species, from dainty black-and-white Avocets to knobby-kneed Yellowlegs, have been identified in the area. Some aficionados report they've spotted a hundred species in a single day!

Bird watchers are not the only ones to flock to the park to view its amazing variety of winged creatures. Butterfly admirers descend in droves, too. For a few days each autumn, thousands upon thousands of orange and black Monarch butterflies, travelling on their long migration to Mexico, stop and rest in a small grove of Point Pelee trees.

But, that's not all. As an added bonus, my favourite reptile, the non-venomous yellow-bodied Fox snake with its sleek black isosceles triangles, lives there, too (when threatened it secretes an odorous substance that smells like a red fox).

We pedalled off, keeping a watchful eye out for birds, butterflies, and slithering creatures. Tulip trees spread their flamboyant leafy branches overhead, offering a crosshatched canopy of shade as we cruised the deserted park path.

The road dead-ended. We abandoned our bikes and traipsed three kilometres along a boardwalk to the very tip of a 20-foot wide dagger-shaped spit of sand and gravel — Canada's most southerly point of mainland. (Canada's southernmost chunk of land, Middle Island in Lake Erie, still lay 14 kilometres away.)

Standing at 42 degrees latitude, I exulted "We made it!" I picked up a stone and chucked it as far as I could into the waves of Lake Erie. "I wonder what Sarnia Bob would say now?"

"This is truly amazing!" Sharon said. "Can you believe we're in Canada and we're standing at the same latitude as northern California? Why, we're farther south than Barcelona and Rome!"

"Unbelievable," I agreed, warily watching the Great Lake splashing on three sides of us. "Feels a little eerie to me."

Tomato Route

> **"Politics is the art of looking for trouble, finding it whether it exists or not, diagnosing it incorrectly, and applying the wrong remedy."**
> ~ Ernest Benn

"*What is this?*" Sharon asked as we pedalled along a tranquil country road. "The Tomato Route?" For the past few kilometres, hundreds of smushed tomatoes littered the gravel shoulder.

I laughed and stopped to pick up a couple of non-smooshed beauties the size of softballs. "Maybe this is a political parade route?" I bent again, and picked up another cherry-red beaut.

Sharon sniffed the air. "What's that smell?" she asked, her pert nose wrinkling.

"Wasn't me," I responded reflexively. Then I caught a whiff, too. "Hamburgers or something," I said absently, as another crimson beauty caught my eye.

"No," Sharon said. "It smells like ketchup." Huh? I scrinched my eyes and looked at her as if she was losing her French fries.

We hit the road, skirting slippery red spots. In a couple of kilometres, we came upon a giant multi-storey Heinz ketchup factory. *Who knew?*

"I guess it's true," I said. "Women have a better sense of smell than men." (Which explains a lot.)

I was still calculating how many litres of ketchup that factory held when we happened across a trail of carrots. "Let me guess," I joshed. "There's a V8 juice facility just down the road." I stopped and tossed a few of the orange vegetables into my pannier.

Sharon smiled. "If this keeps up," she said, "we'll soon have enough to make a salad!"

Androgynous

> **"There is a certain relief in change, even though it can be from bad to worse! As I have often found in travelling ... that it is often a comfort to shift one's position, and be bruised in a new place."**
> ~ W. Irving

Following unsigned country roads, we traversed to Wheatley, and headed north, away from Lake Erie's built-up shoreline. Hundreds of black birds lined telephone wires, three deep. As we rode past, a flurry of feathers would erupt as they zoomed skyward, performing displays of sweeping synchronized aerial acrobatics, only to alight farther down the line ... and do it all over again when we arrived moments later.

The birds led us to a camp spot amongst woods. We dozed off to unremitting insect droning. In the middle of the night I suddenly awoke. It was spookily quiet — not a peep to be heard. Complete and utter silence. During the day, crickets chirped loudly until we rode by, then they would quit — sometimes mid chirrup. Had something disturbed the insects to hush? *Or do they sleep too?* I wondered. I lay there a long time, straining my ears to the incredible lack of sound. I always thought the phrase 'deafening silence' was an oxymoron. But, lying there, marvelling how any place on earth could be so totally without sound, I could hear the roar of molecules bouncing off my eardrums. Or was it remnants of the Big Bang?

At 6:30 AM, the hum of motorized insects began — also known as the urbanite morning commute. We waited till 8 AM to get on the road, after most of the urban insects were off the highways and into their hive-like cubicles.

Skirting Lake Erie's shoreline, we followed Highway 3, the Talbot Road. Colonel Thomas Talbot was said to have been a stubborn Irishman. In the early 1800s, in hopes of attracting more settlers, he built a crude road along the lake from Fort Erie to Windsor.

Anna Jameson gives a wonderful account of her arduous 1837 Talbot Road horse and cart journey in *Winter Studies and Summer Rambles in Canada*. She describes the route as "scarcely passable ... dark pine forest and the rank swamp (my bones ache at the mere recollection!) and deep holes and pools of rotted vegetable matter, mixed with water, black, bottomless sloughs of despond! ... I set my teeth, screwed myself to the seat and commended myself to Heaven...."

A bicycle seat wasn't looking so bad, after all. And the road we cycled was heavenly smooth compared to the corrugated surface those first travellers endured.

Lake Erie sparkled, sunlight reflecting off small waves. I thought it odd that no cottages lined the waterfront as they had up till then. Searching for a spot to enjoy breakfast, we followed a path lined with old oak, weeping willow, and tulip trees to the edge of Lake Erie. Suddenly, with a start (and a sudden stop) we discovered why no vacation homes occupied the shoreline. There was a tremendous 75-foot drop, straight down to the water. *"Yikes!"* I gulped, looking over the cliff. "Makes it rather difficult to get to one's boat." But it made for one fine breakfast spot.

After our breakfast with a view, a sudden urge to make like a doggy in a flower bed struck me. All those fresh veggies we had found along the roadside? I needed a washroom. Pronto. Cycling gingerly, praying for something to turn up, I wasn't having much faith. In the middle of nowhere, I had about as much chance of finding a toilet as a one-legged dude did of winning an ass-kicking contest.

Then, ahead, I thought I saw something outhouse-shaped tucked amongst pine trees behind an old church. "That's my Man," I muttered, pulling into the church yard and leaning my bike against an ancient oak. I scurdled (that's scurrying and waddling combined) toward the outhouse.

I yanked the door open. Gauzy spider webs draped the interior — including the entire roll of toilet paper. But what shocked me more was the side-by-side two-holer greeting me — a tandem pooper! *What's this?* I wondered. *One for you and one for a very good friend?*

Nope. Closer inspection revealed it was a dual-purpose combination men and women's outhouse. I could tell right off that the hole on the left was for the men. It was nothing but a bare board. Apparently, real men were supposed to be like John Wayne — they liked it rough and tough.

In contrast, the hole opposite the men's displayed a padded cushy pink seat. "Talk about discrimination," I grumbled, dropping my drawers and setting myself delicately onto the rough-hewn plank. Watch for slivers. No sudden movements! Sitting on that butt-numbing board, I felt like Goldilocks. "This commode is too hard!" I glanced over at the soft and supple women's seat. Hmmm. *Hell,* I thought, *aren't I androgynous enough to use the comfy pink throne? After all, I always remember to put the seat down. And besides, who would ever know?*

Wiping cobwebs from the overstuffed seat, I lifted the lid and checked for spiders. I had no intention of letting a black widow bite unmentionables as they swung over the dark abyss. Plopping myself onto the pillowy-soft seat, I sat in momentary dignified repose. Apprehension cut my solitude short. Spiders, large and small, brown and black, bald and hirsute, scuttled forth from nooks and crannies. I watched with rapt attention as the biggest carpenter ant I'd ever laid eyes on crawled forth from a crevice. All two inches of the shiny minibeast shot straight for me. Shocked, I stood abruptly. Too abruptly. My shorts plummeted, blanketing the ant. I snatched them up and gave them a vigorous shake. But the corpulent six-legged brute had vanished. It was nowhere to be seen. Talk about having ants in one's pants! *Omigosh!* I thought. *I hope it's not looking for a new crack to call home!*

I quickly exited, wedging the door tightly closed behind me. Back outside in bright sunshine I composed myself, then sauntered around the corner to where Sharon waited.

"How is it?" she asked.

"Posh," I lied. "Five stars."

Sharon happily trundled off to use the facilities.

Paper-Thin Towns

> "**Live each season as it passes; breathe the air, drink the drink, taste the fruit ...**"
> ~ Henry David Thoreau

Towns we passed along Lake Erie's shoreline consisted of one long skinny street. Sharon called them "paper-thin towns."

Fresh produce had been an anomaly in the towns. When we saw a sign advertising a fruit stand we immediately stopped. A bin of cantaloupe caught my eye. I picked one up.

"Do you want to eat it right away?" the woman working at the stand asked.

"Oh, sometime today," I replied.

She took my chosen melon from me and replaced it in the crate. She chose another, held it up to her nose and sniffed its navel. She put it down, picked up a third melon, and repeated the sniffing process. After sampling several, she held one aloft. "This one's the ripest," she declared. It turned out to be succulent. (Once, after we returned from our travels, I tried the fruit woman's method at a local grocery store. I've got to warn you: other customers don't regard you fondly. "I'm checking for ripeness." "Sure, fun boy. Get a room." They thought I was out of my gourd.) Along with the ripe cantaloupe, we bought apples, plums, cucumbers, and tomatoes.

"How about some cheese?" I said, spying a large block.

"Sure," Sharon agreed. "It'll go good with our cucumber and tomato sandwiches."

She was so agreeable — I wondered if I might persuade her to lug another melon. "How about a watermelon?" I asked. "I'll pay for it, if you carry it," I offered.

"Naw," she declined. "It'll make me lopsided."

"I'll buy two."

Out For Blood

"You're alive. Do something."
~ Barbara Hall

Todd, a seasonal park ranger at Rondeau Provincial Park, told us he planned on heading west to look for work once the fall season was over. Government cutbacks had decreased his hours until he couldn't afford to live on what little he made. Our cycle trip impressed him. He asked us a ton of questions. After handing us a park map, he suggested several good picnicking spots. But, best of all, he said, "Feel free to help yourselves to showers." Words of welcome, indeed. The breeze that heralded my arrival wasn't exactly Oscar de la Renta. It wasn't even English Leather.

The showers were our first stop.

"Ah!" Sharon sighed, emerging squeaky clean. "Hot showers! Modern technology's finest achievement!"

Fresh as two daisies, we meandered down the smooth park road in search of a most excellent picnic site. There were few people, even though the park hosted an accumulation of quaint cottages. The place was deserted. We soon discovered why.

"Idyllic," I sighed, surveying a site alongside calm Lake Erie. We unloaded lunch supplies. Within seconds of sitting down, ferocious biting insects descended upon us in droves. And they were out for blood. Our lunch spot was about as far from idyllic as swamp land in Florida being Elysian Fields.

We swatted. We shooed. We hopped and we skipped. Even cursing didn't work.

Nothing deterred the ravenous hordes from their blood sport. The little beggars even bit right through our clothes! Unfortunately for Sharon, the gnats preferred succulent female flesh. By the time we concluded our abbreviated lunch, her ankles had swollen in size to rival our melon. *Why couldn't they have bitten her boobs?* I wondered.

"These are the worst of the trip!" Sharon screamed, flailing her arms, and heading back to our bikes to make a quick getaway.

"Much as I hate to agree, I have to agree," I said, following closely in her jet stream.

Todd drove up in a dark green Park's truck as we prepared to take flight and leave Rondeau Park to the flying pests and annoying midges. Todd rolled down a window. "I finally found you guys!" he shouted. "Everyone in the park is on alert, on the lookout for you two." Had I used too much water showering? Seeing my questioning expression, Todd said, "Oh, there's no problem. I just wanted to give you some park pins." He handed them over, then reached onto the seat. "And here's a patch for each of you, too. We're commemorating the park's 100th anniversary. Maybe you can sew it onto a pannier as a memento?"

We thanked Todd. "Oh, and one more thing," he said, smiling. "I asked my boss if you could stay in the campground for free and he said you guys can stay as long as you like."

"Great!" I chirped. "In that case, we'll stay a month." Sharon swatted another blood-sucking savage and looked at me as if I were more deranged than usual. Maybe I thought I could kill all the wee beasties in that time?

We chose a site close to the showers.

After setting up, Sharon and I struck out on Tulip Tree Trail. Big mistake! Hordes of biting insects chased us every inch of the way. A sign at the trailhead indicated the trail took 60 minutes. It took us less than 20. Running cuts down on the time.

"'Blood Transfusion Trail' would be more appropriate," Sharon said, huffing like an emphysematous Big Bad Wolf.

"Yeah, no kidding," I agreed. "Some of those little beggars were so fast I'm sure they had racing stripes."

Sharon soaked herself in citronella. But even that didn't help. She was still a major bug attraction. "This stuff works about as well as smearing honey on one's body to avoid a bear attack," she snorted.

"Yeah," I agreed, swatting at my own cloud of gnats. "Sort of like running in front of an auto to escape a falling grand piano."

Still, I thought her masochistic. Dusk descended. More mosquitoes (if that were possible) appeared — it was time for their bedtime snack. I sought refuge inside the tent. Behind screened protection, I heard the high-pitched whine of laughing mozzies.

Sharon, meanwhile, sat outside at the picnic table, cleaning her bike whilst hundreds of blood-suckers drilled holes in her. Covered in grease, she couldn't apply more bug dope or even swat the buggers. She made an easy target. It was like taking blood from a baby. They scored bite upon bite. By the time Sharon conceded defeat, the little rotters had driven her insane.

"Good thing we're not in malaria country," Sharon spat with uncharacteristic venom as she dove inside the tent. "I would have contracted it several times by now." She grabbed her journal. With obstinate determination she scribbled away. I glanced over. In capital letters, she had printed: MOSQUITO RATING SCALE.

1. Annoying: But can ignore them.
2. Irritating: Brush them away.
3. Curse and smack them.
4. Savagely swat: The stalk begins.
5. Swat and cheer: Beginning of unglued stage.
6. Erratic movement: Dance, swat, flail.
7. Fight, then flee. Swatting combined with swift movement away from invaders.
8. Irrational: Bugs begin to drive insane.
9. Resignation: Look like pin cushion; why bother?
10. Bugbarians declare victory! Call hospital. Need blood transfusion and padded cell.

Muggy

> **"Oh, what a bitter thing it is to look into happiness through another man's eyes."**
> ~ William Shakespeare

We awoke from a restless sleep feeling terrible. The humid night hadn't helped any and we were both so itchy. The combination made for an uneasy night filled with much scratching and moaning — not that kind of moaning, unfortunately.

Sharon woke to find her ankles swollen and rubbed raw. "I have a headache," she groaned, surveying her red and lumpy body. "I think there's too much mosquito toxin in my system."

"Let's get out of here!" I said, packing to a jitterbug dance.

Todd strolled over to say goodbye. "I told my mom about you guys and your trip," he said. He waved a cycle touring book in the air. "I want to buy a bike," he announced, "so I can come with you guys!" Meeting someone so enthusiastic about our trip was exciting. "Although," he continued, taking a hard look at our bikes, "I don't know if I could get mine to look like yours."

Sharon laughed. "You may not want to," she said. With new eyes I gazed at our bikes and had to smile. Laundry hung off various niches. Lashed on my rear rack, on top of sleeping bag, pad, and tent, was a half-eaten bag of whole wheat bread and a box of day-old doughnuts. We looked like 21st century vagabonds.

"It's a great way to see the world!" Todd enthused.

"It is," Sharon confirmed. "One of these days," she told him, "if that's your dream, you'll do it."

Todd nodded, and wiped his perspiring face. To say the conditions were muggy was like calling a hurricane a fresh breeze. It felt as though we were standing in a Turkish steam bath with the dial stuck on the kiln setting. A white haze hung in the distance, similar to when we'd cycled the Blue Ridge Parkway.

"Is there a forest fire?" I asked.

"Nope," Todd said. "It's Carolinian vegetation transpiration." Huh? We were a *long* way from Carolina. Todd chuckled. "Carolinian Canada is found only in southwestern Ontario," he explained, turning into Ranger Information Dude. "Carolinian flora may be situated amongst some of Canada's most populated and intensively farmed regions of tobacco and vegetable crops, but this entire area is unique in Canada with its profusion of species. Some of the vegetation established here isn't found anywhere else in the country, at least not natively, such as magnolias, prickly pear cacti, and sassafras for example."

Our botany lesson concluded. We thanked Todd again and pedalled away. Heading out the park gates, I turned for one last so-long wave. Todd was rooted in the middle of the road, looking wistful, like a lovelorn lad who had sent a dozen roses to an admired female, and had them returned.

Lightning Storm Alley

"The love we give away is the only love we keep."
~ Elbert Hubbard

If I thought it humid while standing in the shade talking to Todd, I soon discovered I had merely been taking up room in the sauna's doorway. The thermometer smacked up to a sweltering, treacle-sticky, 29 degrees Celsius. Pedalling felt like churning slow-motion through a bucket of Maple syrup.

We spent the day sweating past poor farm boys' huge manor brick estates with paved drives a half-kilometre long. Apparently tobacco was a far more lucrative crop than wheat.

In late afternoon, in the paper-thin town of Springfield, I slipped into a small grocery store just before closing to buy ham and cheese for our pasta. The tiny store had neither ham nor cheese. From the sparse items stocking the store's near-barren shelves, I tried to conjure another plan. But before I picked out supplies, a slim 30-something woman entered. She strode directly to me. (Sharon later told me that while sitting on the curb nibbling an apple, the woman had approached her. "Looks like you're travelling," the woman said. "Yep," Sharon replied — ever the great conversationalist — and resumed munching her McIntosh. And *that* was the extent of their "talk.")

The woman looked me over. "I've been talking to your partner outside a little." (At that point, I had no idea how little.) "And I've just invited you both for supper." Plan B was shaping up rather well. When I took too long to accept, she upped the ante. "I'll even throw in showers and an offer to camp overnight." That cinched it!

I emerged from the store sucking a horrid blue Freezie (I had been in there *so* long, I felt obligated that I buy *something).* Sharon agreed to Sherry's fine offer. No doubt visions of showers were skipping through her head.

We hopped on our bikes and followed the woman home like a pair of lost puppies.

Sherry introduced us to her three gorgeous teenaged daughters — Pam, Melanie, and Elana. In short order we sat down to roast beef dinner with all the trimmings. How did she know we were coming?

Only one person was missing: Sherry's husband, Bud. Still at work, he didn't usually arrive home until 8:30 PM. (How soon one forgets those time commitments!) As the substitute male, Sherry insisted I carve the meat. Tinges of pink leaked out as I sliced into it. "Perfect," I said.

"Just the way Bud likes it," Sherry observed ruefully.

After a bowl-licking dessert of raspberries and fresh whipped cream, Sharon excused herself to hit the shower. I was digging in for a second round of berries as Sharon slipped out the back door to fetch her toiletry paraphernalia. She bumped into Bud. In the dark, neither had seen the other.

"Whoa!" Bud gasped. "You scared me!" (Truth be known, they both looked pretty scary to me. Sharon, dishevelled and unshowered after a grueling day in the saddle, and Bud, a large, intimidating man with a bulldog jaw — the sort of fellow that looked as if nothing would scare him.)

I got up to meet him. Shaking his extra-large paw, I pitied the poor boys who called on his daughters.

At 9 PM, a half-dozen of Sherry's artistic friends arrived for the weekly, as Bud affectionately termed it, "stitch-n-bitch." Since Sharon and I were there as guests of honour, they, unfortunately, were on their best behaviour. Around midnight, after much laughter and rounds of story-telling, the crew bid us warm goodbyes and trundled off to their homes.

"Would you like to sleep on our couch downstairs?"

"Oh, no," I said, airily brushing aside Sherry's offer. "We're very comfortable in our little nylon home."

"Okay with me," she said, "but I wouldn't sleep out there." I thought she was referring to the bugs and the hard ground. She wasn't. "We live in what townsfolk call 'Lightning Storm Alley.'" There was a pregnant pause before she continued. "Lightning struck our dog's kennel last summer. She again paused dramatically. "When he was in it. Killed him deader than a doornail."

"Ouch," I winced. "That's dead."

But I still wasn't smart enough to retract my refusal. So, sometime after midnight, Sharon and I pussyfooted out to the backyard, way off our bedtime schedule.

It began to rain. I hoped there wouldn't be thunder — or lightning. Sherry's rattling information, coupled with large quantities of sugar and caffeine from two large Pepsi's, and a foolishly accepted late-night espresso, kept me wide awake — staring at the tent roof. Somewhat sombrely, I noticed Sharon had no such regrets — not a soda or coffee drinker, she was already well into sawing her second cord of wood.

The muggy night held no hint of a breeze. Raindrops dripped off the house's roof, plopping into an ill-placed aluminum pot. Plink. Plunk. Plonk. It sounded like a badly out-of-tune banjo player. Any effort to drown the beat was futile.

At 4 AM, a resounding thunder and light show did little for my beauty sleep. Jagged flashes of lightning raced across the sky. One harsh bolt — very close, *extremely* close — illuminated the tent in grim chalky light so bright I could have read a newspaper's obituary column. Talk about a large hit of visceral terror! Thunder pealed. My ears rang. Oppressive air sat as heavily on my chest as a sumo wrestler. I laid there — eyes wide shut — shivering, castigating myself for turning down Sherry's fine offer.

The storm wound down, booming off in the west like a retreating marching band. Maybe I could finally get some sleep? But no. Edison, Bud and Sherry's new pooch, had come outside for a pee break. He romped over to check us out. (His moniker was Edison because he was so danged smart. Sherry had told us that one afternoon, left to his own devices, Edison had completely – and cheerfully – ripped apart their old living room carpet. Insurance had doled out for a spanking new one. "That's raw intelligence," Sherry had said, patting Edison good-naturedly.) The dumbbell barked at our tent for a full half-hour.

Long after Edison lost interest in stalking the great grey elephant dozing in his backyard, I fell into fitful slumber. Minutes later, the girls left for school, screen door slapping six times with each departure.

"I think I'm done," I groaned as Sharon dressed. "Worst sleep so far," I muttered. "And that's saying something." Head throbbing, eyes bleary, I fitfully rose and staggered inside.

Bud had left for work an hour prior. I groaned again at the flood of work and commuting memories. Even though I was dead tired, I sure was glad that it wasn't me still slogging in the trenches. Sherry flitted around the kitchen, preparing toast with ham and tomato omelettes.

I thought it odd how we could barely have met someone, and less than 24 hours later, feel as if we'd known them all our lives. After a personal conversation-filled breakfast, Sharon and I thanked our gracious hostess and prepared to hit the road. Sherry wasn't about to let us go without a parting gift. She held forth two jars of her preserves: strawberry, and thimbleberry.

"I've never had thimbleberry jam before," I said, plucking the jars from her fingers.

"Thimbleberries taste a bit like raspberries," Sherry said. "But they're harder to pick ... the bushes have nastier thorns."

"We'll think of you when we eat it," Sharon said.

We pedalled off with wide smiles and full hearts. We had just had the good fortune of meeting more of those people who would never make the six o'clock news.

Big City Blues

"Nothing is so simple that it cannot be misunderstood."
~ Freeman Teague, Jr.

From Norwich to Mount Pleasant, we plied pleasurable back-roads. We were on our way to Etobicoke, where our friend, Michelle, lived. I had phoned her a couple of times and she was expecting us. But, for some reason, I had a bad feeling in my gut.

Around 3 PM, our quiet road turned into a vehicular homicide route. By 5 PM, 'rush hour' traffic was going full throttle, zooming hither and thither — no one getting anywhere fast. The road we were trying to cycle wasn't much wider than two cars. On more than one occasion we narrowly avoided becoming road pizza.

We arrived, in the dark, outside Michelle's high-rise tower. Past frazzled, past exhausted, we looked forward to a quiet retreat. A note protruded from a corner of the apartment's buzzer. It was for us. My lips pursed, like just before one recalls something bad. "Oh, oh," I said, gingerly removing the note from its envelope.

"Hi Guys!" it began, cheerily enough. "Gone to look at a new apartment. Maybe we can meet tomorrow? Love, Michelle."

Ooooo. Somehow, in my phone calls, I hadn't made it clear we wanted to stay overnight. "Reading between the lines," I grimaced, "it appears she doesn't expect us to be staying with her." I sighed and pinched my lip, puzzled how I had managed to screw up something so simple.

"Ironic," Sharon mumbled. "We've travelled 5,000 kilometres without much concern about where we'd be sleeping. Then, at a friend's, we're worried we don't have a place."

In the end, everything worked out all right. We just hung around until Michelle showed up and then asked her point-blank.

"Sure!" she exclaimed happily. "I just assumed you'd be staying at Glynn's (her brother's). I didn't think you'd want to stay with me, because I don't have an extra bed."

We assured her the floor would be perfectly fine.

And it was.

House Seller Blues

> **"The most valuable things in life are not measured in monetary terms. The really important things are not houses and lands, stocks and bonds, automobiles and real state, but friendships, trust, confidence, empathy, mercy, love and faith."**
> ~ Bertrand Russell V. Delong

First thing in the morning, we phoned Sharon's mom and dad to find out if any last minute hitches with the pending house sale had come up. Of course there had. Land Titles was throwing a hissy fit over our Power of Attorney handling the proceedings for us. They demanded a specific form be notarized by us before they would complete the transfer. If I'd only known him then, I would have gotten the Dean of Real Estate.

Stephen English, a friend and lawyer, faxed us the necessary paperwork. Steve and I used to play squash together a couple of times a week. A great guy; he'd usually let me win. He was successful in business, too — a shining example of how one could be a litigator and still not lose one's soul. "Integrity, balance, sanity," is what should have been inscribed on his business card.

With the forms in hand, we scanned Toronto's Yellow Pages and called notary publics for the remainder of the morning. What a hassle. Not a one would notarize the forms that day! I had forgotten life in the real world could be so complicated. (And I didn't miss it one bit!)

Frustrated, we took a time out, jumped on our bikes and escaped along peaceful Humber River. Geese paddled about calmly in a pool near a small splashing waterfall, cooling their heels, looking as if they didn't have a care in the world. "They know how to relax and enjoy life," Sharon observed.

In a green space, we dropped our bikes and laid on our backs, staring upwards, lost blissfully in the fine art of cloud gazing. "There's a notary with a pen stuck in his eye." After half an hour, my cloudy thoughts became more civilized. "There's one being chased by a bear."

We returned to the apartment and phoned Michelle at work. After explaining our predicament, she told us not to worry. When she arrived home, she drove us to a notary public who signed the papers for a king's ransom. But, at that point, beaten and whipped, we could barely muster more than a whimper and a scowl.

Papers signed, and notarized in triplicate, we faxed them back to Steve. *Good riddance forms and house!*

Pick-Your-Own

> **"If more of us valued food and cheer and song above hoarded gold, it would be a merrier world."**
> ~ J. R. R. Tolkien

On the road by 7 AM — bucking the stiffest headwind in a long while — my lead-possessed legs twirled in uncoordinated circles.

At one o'clock, after six hours on the road, we stopped for lunch — a paltry 20 kilometres from where we set off that morning! The headwind was pummeling us, giving us a tough reintroduction to hills after southern Ontario's flat farmland.

The only thing keeping me from heaving my bike into the nearest ditch was the fantastic display of autumn foliage — waves of amber and orange reflected in canal waters. On one low canal bridge, I lightened up a bit when I read what some wag had scrawled: DUCK. OR QUACK YOUR HEAD.

At a farmer's field, tired of pedalling face-first into a stiff headwind, we stopped and pulled out our map. Holding it down with both hands, I studied it for an alternate route. "Can't get much worse than this," I complained. A sudden whirlwind hurled a fistful of dust straight into my face. I coughed and waved my arms. "Just to prove me wrong," I spluttered.

But it wasn't over yet. An earsplitting explosion, not unlike a letter bomb detonating inside a Belfast postal centre, rocked the air. My front tire had exploded clear off the rim! The lifeless tube hung limply, shredded, spindled, and mutilated, appearing to have suffered a cruel fate at the hands of Jack the Ripper. My jaw dropped. "Very strange," I muttered.

"I think you're going to have to take a look at that," Sharon deadpanned.

What could be causing the problem? Nothing like this had occurred on our long-distance bike trip across the States. I removed the tire and checked the rim. Nothing. Rim tape? Nope, it appeared fine. How about under the rim tape? Any slivers of metal? Nope, again, I could find nothing awry. I hated to imagine a blowout like that while flying down a hill. In consternation I wondered, "What's causing these blowouts?"

"Hmmm," Sharon murmured. "I pumped your tires to 90 pounds this morning. I wonder if that caused it?"

"It shouldn't have," I answered. "They're rated at least that. But, come to think of it, since that time my rear tire exploded, I've been keeping them at 80."

I replaced the tube. Head tilted and one eye closed, I pumped the tire to a tentative 80 psi. Talk about gun shy. Replacing the valve top, I remembered something *was* different.

"You don't suppose my Mr Tuffy tire liners are the problem, do you?" We hadn't used them on long trips before. "That's the only thing I can think of that's different."

"Aren't they supposed to stop flats? Not cause them," Sharon smirked.

We mounted up and rode on without complications. I admit, though, I was a lot more cautious whilst zipping down hills. (And the next time I had a flat, I tossed the Mr Tuffy tire liner. Guess what? I'm not saying the Mr Tuffy tire liners were the cause, but the mysterious exploding tire syndrome went away.)

A pick-your-own vegetable farm came into view — a choice spot to acquire fresh veggies. Produce, from asparagus to zucchini, sprouted in every direction. (Okay, I'm not sure if they had asparagus, but there was corn, carrots, cucumbers....) One field, as far as my eye could see, held nothing but cabbage. "I can't imagine *all* the people in Canada eating that much cabbage!" I sputtered. "Maybe they export it to the Ukraine?"

"That's a whole lotta cabbage rolls," Sharon confirmed.

We leaned our bikes against a metal quonset hut, and entered the main building to obtain baskets. The heady smell of onion permeated the air, tickling our noses with its redolent scent. Baskets of already picked carrots sat on a shelf awaiting buyers.

"Can I buy half a basket of carrots?" Sharon asked the person in charge at the cash register.

"No," he replied, shaking his head. "We don't sell half-baskets of pre-picked. But you can pick half a basket for yourself in the field, though."

We took two baskets and plodded what seemed a mile into a long field and picked a few tomatoes. Sharon wanted corn too, but it was at the end of another field, about another mile away. I convinced her we didn't need corn.

Disillusioned by how far it was between vegetable patches, we even forgot carrots. We trudged back to the quonset hut with our red fruit.

"How much for these?" Sharon asked, plunking her basket onto the weigh scale.

"For you?" the owner answered. "Nothing."

"Nothing?" Sharon said, startled.

In our absence, the owner had been outside and discovered we were on bikes. "Anyone who can make it here under her own steam deserves something," he said kindly. Our mode of transport had once again opened people's hearts.

"These are for you, too," he said, motioning to a couple of plump paper sacks sitting on the counter beside him. The bags bulged with new baby potatoes, cucumbers, celery, onions, and, oh yes, a few carrots, too. A woman approached and handed us souvenir pens. "To remember us by," she said warmly. "You'll think of us whenever you write a postcard."

We wholeheartedly thanked the owners for their generosity. They responded by throwing in cobs of corn. How much room did they think we had in those bike panniers?

Grinning ear to ear, we swayed down the earthen farm road and back on to the main route. With heavy bags (but light hearts), we skipped our way to Keswick. The park at Cook's Bay suited us for the night (though I had to wonder about a sign in the parking area: NO UNDRESSING IN CARS).

Surly Trucker

"When I am dead, my dearest,
Sing no sad songs for me."
~ Christina Rossetti

Rambling along Beach Road, on the shore of Lake Simcoe, we marvelled at waterfront 'cottages' the size of mansions. Our halcyon ride ended at an intersection to a feeder route for the infamous bicycle-eating Trans Canada Highway.

Heavy long-haul truck traffic plied Highway 48. We had been doing well until we met three oncoming flatbeds — each carrying a house. Complete with verandas (I'm not making this up). I didn't hear celestial music, but I did experience another near-death episode. The wide loads hung halfway into our lane. Suddenly a car sped past us, hurtling head-on toward the wide loads. At the last possible moment the car driver swerved back into his lane, scarcely missing getting wiped out by the lead house.

"Try to explain *that* to your insurance agent," I chortled. The titter died in my windpipe. From a thousand paces behind, a teamster airhead laid loud and long on his horn — not slowing one scintilla. Another piranha from the carnivorous might-is-right fish school of hard knocks.

Two oncoming houses slipped past us. Sharon, behind me, waggled in her lane, attempting to slow the rearward trucker till the last oncoming house was safely past (we had learned that if we appeared a wee bit unsteady, car drivers gave us extra room). No way, José. Not this beef jerky.

His 130 decibel Grovea air horn strafed us again. The hell-bent for leather poo-brain steamrollered closer. One hand flashing his lights. The other yanking his horn chain. Both feet tromped on the accelerator.

The third and final oncoming house driver maneuvered his new address as far to the right as possible — the big rig's tires chewing embankment gravel — bungalow dangling precariously over the ditch like some clownish off-balance high wire act.

Sharon, cat-like, saving one of her nine lives for later, ditched her bike onto the loose gravel. Foolishly, I stayed my course, anchored to a skinny ribbon of asphalt (barrelling a fully loaded bike onto gravel is a mite trickier than it may first appear).

The freighter roared within ramming distance. Nearly on top of me. Six-hundred rampaging horsepower. Raging like an iron Minotaur. Seventy tons of death. I held my breath. *Think thin! Think thin!* I repeated to myself, tucking my elbows in while adhering to my skinny strip of fogline paint like Lycra on Pamela Sue Anderson.

A thundering *whoosh* as Fat Daddy's tractor and twin trailer units scorched past my quivering thighs. A blur of steel and grey. A hairbreadth away. Hot fumes from the engine bounced off my nostrils. My heart thudding, I could have reached out and filed my fingernails on the trailers' box. I felt gadfly small (with brain to match). Eighteen torrid tires smoked past, hammering sickeningly at head height like a dozen and a half hard rubber mallets.

Whew! In my peripheral vision, I noted my left arm was still attached. I gave thanks. But the fun wasn't over yet.

Past me by mere inches, the crank hack swerved his bucket of bolts onto the gravel shoulder directly in front of me. Grit, dust, sand and rock fragments spat in all directions. Like legions of angry hornets, they stung my bare arms, legs, and face. Belches of black sooty diesel exhaust farted up the oil burner's dual chromed smokestacks. The surly trucker kept his rig of death on the gravel shoulder for the next kilometre. A plume of wavery dust hung in the air, like an achromatic spectre of the Grim Reaper.

I almost laughed in relief. Guess he taught me! As my brother, Rob, used to say in his long haul trucking days, "If you can't run with the big dogs, stay on the porch."

"My God!" a disembodied voice behind me shrieked. "What the *hell* are you doing?" Sharon screamed. "Just because you're allowed on the freaking road, doesn't mean you have to prove it! There's no glory in being *dead,* ya know! Dead right or dead wrong, it doesn't matter. Either way, you're still dead!"

Severely lashed, I would forevermore walk with a limp, seeing how Sharon chewed my ass off. A few kilometres farther, we exited onto a side road and made it through Pefferlaw, experiencing no more Big Mack attacks.

My heart rate had just about returned to normal when I had yet another close encounter of the near-death kind. A van, pulling a utility trailer, almost clipped us. But unlike the trucker, he gave no warning whatsoever. No traffic was oncoming and, with the wind in our ears, we hadn't heard his approach. He didn't move over one bit. The utility trailer, wider than his van, virtually skinned our legs. When the truck driver had missed me by one inch, I was quite certain he had meant to miss me by one inch. When the van missed us by a hair, he was just plain lucky.

"My God!" Sharon gasped, for the second time in as many hours. "Didn't he see us? For crying out loud ... one little wobble and it all would've been over."

Ontario was home to the worst collection of road hogs we'd ever had the misfortune to meet. I wondered how many were slaughtered daily?

The Long Way

> **"Even if you are on the right track, you'll get run over if you just sit there."**
> ~ Will Rogers

Mid-September. A sharpness was in the air. A fellow in Cannington greeted us with, "You two are out *very* late in the season."

"We've cycled in weather colder than this," we assured him. (A foot of snow at Oregon's Crater Lake one June leapt to mind.)

"Where are you going?" he asked. "Eventually, I mean."

"Vancouver," I replied. "The long way."

"It'll be snow before you get there," he warned, bushy eyebrows jutting skyward in haughty concern. A simper — like some folks get when secretly getting pleasure from delivering bad news — creased his thin lips. "Thunder Bay had frost in August."

"Cool," I said.

"No cool about it," he snorted, miffed at my lack of reaction to his frosty news. "That's damn cold. Where are you from, anyway?"

"Edmonton."

"Oh," he said. "So you know about cold then."

I nodded.

"Where are you headed now?"

"Gaspé," I replied. My response shook him. Gaspé, after all, is in the exact opposite direction from Vancouver. I could see the lights were flashing, but no train was coming.

"Then what are you going to do?" he stammered, trying to regain his equilibrium.

"Fly," Sharon interjected.

"Ah," he brightened. "To Vancouver."

"No," I responded. "Spain." That information perplexed the poor fellow even more.

"Well," he said, suddenly grabbing my hand and pumping it. "Good luck."

As his figure receded down the sidewalk, Sharon turned to me. "Don't you think it'd just be a whole lot easier if you simply told people that we're cycling around the world? Instead of 'Vancouver ... the long way'?"

I shrugged. "I like derailments."

Golden Moments

> **"Cherish all your happy moments: they make a fine cushion for old age."**
> ~ Christopher Morley

The sun rose a glowing ball of red. The intense natural beauty caused me to forget the previous day's clueless metal-caged road barbarians. All seemed right with the world.

Two school kids on BMX bikes raced past, then made a hard left a couple of hundred metres farther along. Following them, we discovered a Rails to Trails path. Soon, we were wending our way past old wooden fences, beneath a canopy of maple and oak. Vibrant red and gold leaves surrounded us, the trees in throes of a breathtaking autumnal clothing change.

"The locals know where the good trails are," Sharon said. "This is our most scenic route in days."

"And we don't have to worry about being sideswiped by motorhomes, trucks, buses, vans, cars, or houses," I reminded her. (Guess I hadn't forgotten the clueless hog's heads after all.)

Near Warsaw, we stopped and asked a fellow in his yard for directions to a nearby county road.

After furnishing the directions, he cautioned, "You folks know how dangerous camping 'freebies' are, don't you?" We nodded. "One time," he continued, "I stayed in a free camping spot alongside the road, and a child was abducted during the night. I've never used a freebie site since." We thanked him for his advice and prepared to push on. "If you want," he offered, "you can camp in my backyard down by the stream." Sharon and I smiled. His message seemed to be: 'Don't take freebies from strangers ... unless I'm the stranger.'

Sharon and I usually tried to hide a bit when we chose a free camp spot. And, of course, not having a vehicle sticking out like a sore thumb on the roadside, once we're off the highway a ways, we become nearly invisible. Sometimes, embarrassingly so. One night, in Nanaimo BC, we had set up under the stars in the midst of shrubbery. Around 2 AM an amorous couple roused us, making whoopee a mere five feet from us. My only complaint: I wasn't wearing my glasses.

As we grew wiser, we abandoned camping in towns altogether. Quick learners that we are (it only took us a few years), we finally figured out we had a better chance of uninterrupted sleep if we hit a town late in the day, bought food supplies, then headed out into the countryside, on the lookout for a concealing grove of trees.

We turned down the man's gracious invitation — not because we didn't trust him. Rather, it was because Sharon had phoned Claren and Kevin, friends formerly from Edmonton, who had moved to Ottawa, then Kingston. They were expecting us the following day at their new home in Kingston. To have any hope of showing up as planned, we had to put on some miles. Oh, to be tied to a schedule!

Partway to Norwood, Sharon realized she had asked for directions to the wrong town. "There's too many places named Something-wood," she griped. Maybe we should have accepted that camping invitation after all?

Back on track, we stopped for supper beside Rice Lake Waterway. A 73-year-old woman toddled over to talk with us. "We've come to Hastings to look at a yacht that's for sale," she informed us, beaming. She and her husband were from Phoenix. "We intend to buy it," she said in a bubbly tone. "Then we're going to spend three years exploring some US waterways." Her grey eyes fairly danced with excitement as she shared their dream. "And after that," she said, "we're going to sail up the coast of North America to Alaska."

We smiled. What an adventure! It was moving to see a long-married couple still so very much in love with each other and still eager to experience new adventures together. Sharon and I hoped that we, like them, would share many golden memories together.

Riding Under A Nuclear Sky

> **"Too much of a good thing is wonderful."**
> ~ Mae West

Autumnal equinox arrived without fanfare. I found it intriguing: Twice a year, on the vernal and autumnal equinox, everywhere on earth receives an equal 12 hours of dark and 12 hours of light. Compared to the long hours of light we had enjoyed in July, the third week of September had drastically less daylight. No longer could we dawdle as we had in the past and still rack up a good number of kilometres before darkness enveloped us. After all, we wanted to make it out of Canada before winter snowed us in.

And if we wanted to be in Kingston before nightfall we had to get a move on — we still had quite a few kilometres to go. At 6:30 AM, morning light had just begun to paint a faint rosy blush on the distant eastern horizon.

We pushed our bikes out of a secluded spot from behind a stand of evergreens in closed-for-the-season Ferris Provincial Park. In the early dawn, we were the only ones up for miles around, and were enjoying the all encompassing silence. A hearty "Hello!" startled me.

"Good morning!" I replied reflexively. "Beautiful day for a walk," I stuttered. As soon as the words left my lips, I noticed the walker's mittens. Maybe it was still a bit cool. Her breath puffed out in smoky wisps as she laughed in agreement.

We rode some of the morning wearing our fleece pullovers. By the time we cruised through Stirling at the day's 30 kilometre mark, we were perspiring like overweight recruits on a cross-country run. Pedalling hard, we were racking up the kilometres, our goal being to reach Claren and Kevin's before nightfall.

Our first stop of the day came at lunchtime in Belleville. The morning's workout had piqued our appetites. We bought a grilled chicken, and, overlooking Bay of Quinte, devoured the bird in short order to little more than a heap of steaming bones. After our chicken-feast decimation, we crossed onto Picton Island with its delightful collection of country cottages. Drinking in a view of tranquil Muscote Bay, we wound our way along Prince Edward County's sporadically trafficked roads.

At 4 PM, we arrived in Picton, lightheaded, still several kilometres from our destination. Our legs shaky, delirium was just a short step around the corner. We needed food. Sharon's ashen face broadcast fatigue and hunger. I wasn't feeling so hot myself — lack of glucose is nasty business. Not only was I out of energy, but it felt as though rats were gnawing my stomach lining. "How about if we eat at Lake on the Mountain Park?" Surely, I thought, we could make it ten more kilometres to the park.

But when we reached Glenora Ferry, Lake on the Mountain Park was still two kilometres away — and all of it uphill (I guess that's where the 'mountain' part of the name came in). "Forget that!" Sharon announced, and clomped onto the waiting ferry like a weary Clydesdale.

During the short crossing we tore into granola bars and fruit leather. I had visions of fastening my handlebar bag around my ears like an old mare's feed bag.

We gulped down every food item in our bags. By the time the ferry reached the other side, our hunger had vanished. We hopped on our bikes and sprinted along Highway 33, making good time — considering our quasi-twilight state of existence. Five kilometres farther, two touring cyclists headed toward us. Often, touring cyclists will stop and jaw with each other — exchanging war stories, routes, and good bakeries. But we were on a tear, and didn't plan on stopping. I had decided we would pass them with a cheery wave. However, they had other ideas. Both cyclists darted across the road and swerved to a dead halt in front of us. Sharon and I jumped on our brakes and barely stopped before knocking them down.

Unfazed, the front runner thrust out a gloved hand. "Hi!" he chirped. "We're from England!"

"Nice running into you," I drawled.

The jawing began. On the road since May — almost five months — they had begun their trip in Vancouver, ridden to Québec, and were on their way back to Toronto to catch a flight home. "I can't believe it!" the rearward bloke deplored. "In two weeks we're flying back to England! It all seemed so far away when we started.... It's hard to believe how fast the time has flown." His voice trailed off. I wondered, after living free for five months, how they were going to manage the adjustment back into the 'real' world. Wearing cycling gloves at the office water cooler? Roasting wieners over a garbage can? (Really though, my concern should have been how *we,* after our much longer sojourn, would pull off re-entry. But, at the time, I had not the slightest inkling that we would never be normal again.)

The front fellow nodded. "We've been watching the BEST-BEFORE dates on milk," he said with a chuckle. "For a long time we had far more days than the date. Now," he said, and he practically whimpered when he said this, "the expiry date is after when we'll be leaving." (Still in a delirious state, I wondered if milk dates were perhaps a metaphor for life — we all had a 'best-before' date. Perhaps that's why some folks have such a sour outlook on life? They're past their 'best-before' date.) The English bloke composed himself. Stiff upper lip and all that. "All very depressing," he muttered.

"Quite," the second chap concurred. "Quite."

At 5:30 PM, still shaking their heads, they shoved off. Sharon and I, our bellies again well past empty, had 50 kilometres to go.

Not long after, in a hunger-induced state of violent mental agitation, we goose-stepped through Adolphustown, conned our way through Conway, blasted through Sandhurst, washed through Bath ("cleanest folks around!" Sharon declared), and guardedly sprinted past Millhaven Penitentiary.

After pedalling kilometres in a trance-like state, we became woozy. I spotted a roadside corner store and pulled off the road. Sharon, collapsed over her handlebars, white as a ghost in a freshly laundered sheet. Near collapse myself, I managed to get off my bike and tromp inside. Suddenly possessed of five thumbs, my uncoordinated fingers fumbled for change to buy a half-dozen chocolate bars.

"Do you want a bag for those?" the clerk asked, watching me with concern.

"Naw," I slurred. "I'm gonna eat 'em here."

Back outside, Sharon wolfed down her allotted three candy bars. And off we dashed. Daylight was rapidly abandoning us. Fuelled by hits of chocolate, we rocketed along at 30 kilometres an hour. Then, a crosswind blowing off Lake Ontario blindsided us, hampering our best efforts. We churned away, sweat streaming down our temples. The only thing that kept us cranking? The vision of showers at our good hosts' home.

At Collins Bay, on the outskirts of Kingston, daylight failed us completely. We stopped and basked in a nuclear explosion sunset (sunscreen SPF 1 million). Deep pinks, husky reds, lurid purples, all radiated in a polychromatic burst.

Evaluating our predicament we stopped at the first pay phone we found and called our friends. Alas, there was no answer. Claren, a Chartered Accountant, and Kevin, an officer in the Canadian military (yes, Virginia, we have an army — we just don't let them have any weapons), hadn't arrived home from work yet.

We rode on doggedly, our VistaLites flashing red, while keeping as far right as practicable. When we arrived in Kingston it was in pitch blackness. We stopped outside a Mac's convenience store, and I phoned our friends again.

Kevin answered. "Man, it's dark out there!" he chuckled. "I have a bike rack," he said. "I'll come and pick you up. Where are you?"

"We're beside the Mac's at —," I said. "Hang on. I'll run to the corner and check the street names."

"I know where it is," Kevin said. "I'm on my way." The receiver clicked in my ear.

"He's on his way," I told a relieved Sharon.

It took longer than expected for Kevin to show up at our location. And when he did, it was our turn to chuckle. When I had told him we were outside "Mac's," Kevin had misinterpreted it as "Max" as in Kingston Maximum Security Penitentiary. He had spent the past several minutes driving past the penitentiary on the lookout for us.

"After my third pass, I figured it out," he said, laughing.

"Only an armed force's officer would make that mistake," I kidded him. "You must have forgotten you were dealing with civilians. Did you realize that on your second pass you were a 'repeat offender'?"

We loaded our machines onto the small bike rack and Kevin whisked us home within minutes. Amazing how fast cars go. Headlights are pretty nice, too.

The Canadian Armed Forces had recently transferred Kevin from Ottawa to Kingston. Claren was still holding her government job in Ottawa and only came home on weekends. The price of success? She had arrived home only seconds before us.

They gave us a tour of their new residence. It featured gleaming hardwood floors, antique French doors, and plenty of large windows. "Officers are treated pretty good in Kingston," Kevin understated.

They set about pampering us. While we hit the showers, they ordered in massive boxes of cheese-laden ultra-gooey super-deluxe pizza. Sharon and I ate. And ate. And ate some more. Our friends' eyes expressed admiration for the amount we could pack away — or was it a look of shock at our gluttony?

After 'stuffer' (when one eats *that* much, it can't reasonably be called 'supper' – at least not with a straight face), filled to the brim, not even room for one little wafer, we bid our wide-eyed hosts good night, and retired to a comfortable bed complete with matching feather pillows.

"Hmmm," Sharon murmured dreamily, as she slipped under the warm covers. "I could get used to this."

Hold the Anchovies

> **"Ice cream is exquisite — what a pity it isn't illegal."**
> ~ Voltaire

Claren took us shopping – for bike gear, of course. When Dave, at the Frontenac cycle shop, learned we were bound for overseas destinations he handed us reflective Canada flag stickers. "They work great on helmets," he said. "Folks are very friendly to Canadians overseas," he added.

"What's the difference between Canadians and Americans travelling in Europe?" he asked. I shrugged. "Canadians have a small Canadian flag on their backpack." I nodded. "Americans," he continued, "have a large Canadian flag on their backpack."

Heartened by the good news, I bought a Specialized Tri-Cross knobby tire for my bike's front end. If uncaring or inattentive drivers were going to run me off the road, I intended to hit those gravel shoulders with aplomb. It was true that knobbies required additional energy to overcome their greater rolling resistance, but the control, and confidence, I gained when off-tarmac more than made up for any extra friction – besides, on a fully loaded touring bike, I wasn't going all that fast to begin with. And there was a bonus too: after installing the heavier-duty knobby tire, I suffered fewer flats. So, when I factored in the amount of time usually spent patching tubes and changing tires, I may have even come out slightly ahead.

Returning from our successful shopping foray, Kevin (bless his little military heart), encouraged us to pack away the calories. "Yes, sir!" I said. (I always obey orders from an officer.)

Kevin ordered more stacks of calorie-rich pizza; he barbecued enormous slabs of beef; Claren stuffed us with baked apple pies; they drowned us in buckets of ice cream. What amazing hosts!

Claren had received a letter from Sue, one of our longtime cycling buddies, and ex-workmate of Claren and Sharon. We had made prior arrangements to meet Sue and Vicky (the same Vicky who had led us out of Edmonton so many days before) for three weeks of cycle touring in Portugal and Spain.

Above: When cycle touring we like to load up just a few of the barest essentials. Oh sure, this custom-made BOB is a bit sluggish on the uphills, but that couch sure is sweet after all day on a bike seat.
Previous: Enjoying one of Canada's best-kept free camping secrets.
Below: Fields of tangy scented, lemon-yellow canola chased us along our prairie route. The homestead: "One more payment and it's ours."

Above: I asked a fellow how this dusty Alberta prairie town got its name. "From that rock over there," a youngster answered. Sure enough, engraved into a granite boulder yonder was the village name: "Scandia."
Previous: Weather-ravaged split rail fences still get the job done.
Below: In Ottawa, Ontario, the nation's capital, Sharon rides along the Rideau canal—in the winter, it becomes the world's longest skating rink.

Above: Splendid New England fall foliage reflections.
Previous: A secluded rail-trail off the beaten path.
Below: Sharon enjoys tranquil cycling with little traffic.
Over: The most pleasant road we have ever been lost on.
Over 2: Scenic British Columbia is a favourite haunt of touring cyclists

Sue's letter said that she and Vicky were meeting Sharon and me November 20 in Lisbon, then flying back from Malaga. All as planned. *That fateful idea of mine is coming together rather nicely,* I thought smugly.

"See?" I said to Sharon. "And you were all worried it wasn't going to work out."

But then Claren read the bombshell: "For two weeks." Huh? Hadn't we planned three weeks? Reading further, we discovered Sue hadn't been able to get an *entire* three whole weeks off work. Ah, life in the corporate world. I scoffed. "Why doesn't she just quit?" Seriously though, I wondered if two weeks would give us enough time to ride from Lisbon, Portugal to Malaga, Spain? Sharon's rigid jaw betrayed apprehension. Schedules and deadlines reared their ugly heads.

Early Monday morning, the weekend over, we said goodbye to our hosts. Were we already leaving our comfy surrounds? Hell, no! But the two of them had to go to work. Someone had to pay for all that pizza and ice cream we were packing away.

"See you in Ottawa!" Claren said before jumping in her car and speeding away to her job in the nation's capital, a *mere* 180 kilometres away; Kevin studiously packed his rucksack, getting ready to depart on a week-long outdoor training mission. (I try — with varying degrees of success — to keep items in my panniers in some semblance of order, but compared to the army I'm in complete disarray. I had no idea the military was so regimented. Kevin showed us a list that instructed him where to pack every single item — right down to the little pocket where all soldiers keep their extra set of underwear! Important to know, I suppose, when someone is shooting at you. I know I'd certainly need clean undies after that.)

With our hosts out earning a living, Sharon and I had the run of the house, complete with large screen TV and matching La-Z-Boys (with built-in chip and beverage holders). With such outstanding hospitality, how would we ever pry ourselves away? "Ya know," I drawled to Sharon while dipping a nacho into creamy bell pepper dip, "I'm beginning to like this biking stuff."

For two whole days, rain deluged the area (oh, darn). "I'll bet Kevin is having a *terrific* time on his training mission," I mused, gazing out from our snug and dry confines and imagined the poor guy crawling around in the muck and oozy mud. Ironically, massive electrical storms knocked out the power several times.

By the third day, we determined the rain was unstoppable and it was never going to clear (ever). We pulled on our rain gear, double-bagged our cycling shoes, and departed for Ottawa to meet Claren. "At least the wind is at our back," Sharon said, attempting to console me.

"Ah, yes," I answered. "I was getting tired of the pampered life anyway." Sure I was.

Bicycles For Sale

"[R]ecognize that a person can be whole and well in the best sense of these terms even if disabled — say, without a leg or an arm, blind or deaf, or suffering from paraplegia or mental retardation. Such a person can be inwardly sound as a bell, with a warm and joyful heart that doesn't constantly grumble and rail against life."
~ Markus Baum

Our ride to Gananoque was uneventful other than the rain and one van cowboy who passed a line of traffic on a double-solid blind corner. Sharon and I, in the oncoming lane, had to swerve off the road to avoid becoming pothole filler. My brand new knobby front tire was already proving its worth.

"When people buy vans," Sharon asked, "do they have some kind of operation that sucks out half their brains?"

"Naw," I answered. "I think it's more likely the detrimental effects from a lifetime of substance abuse."

A bike path connecting Gananoque to Brockville ran 50 glorious van-free kilometres. Not having to worry about fluffy-headed van drivers was liberating.

I stared at the thousand little green islands dotting the Saint Lawrence River. "How'd you like to live on one of those islands?" I asked. "Really get away from it all."

"No man is an island," Sharon responded.

"True," I agreed. "But some are peninsulas."

Rideau River Provincial Park campground was our intended destination. But, in Merrickville, somewhat short of our goal, we admitted defeat. Nonstop rain had thwarted our progress and brief daylight hours had foiled our best efforts.

By the time we stopped, my 'storm shelter' gloves were two waterlogged sponges. My frozen fingers felt about as ungainly as the clumsy feet inside my soaked shoes. I tripped into a nursing home, planning to ask permission to set our little tent on the large expanse of lawn out back. A *goosh-goosh* emanated with each step of my saturated cycling shoes. With each footfall, tiny air holes in the shoe's toes fabricated a miniature watery fountain display.

No one manned the nurse's station. I waited patiently. In a few moments an aged patron rolled up in a wheelchair and stopped directly in front of me. "Can I help you?" she asked, gazing up, a wooden-toothed smile dimpling her sallow cheeks.

A drop of cold water dangled from the tip of my endlessly dripping nose — not unlike a faucet in need of a washer. "Do you work here?" I asked. I had expected someone younger.

"The girls are in the dining room," she answered sweetly. "Do you have a message I can relay?"

I explained to our good Samaritan that Sharon and I were bicycling across the country.

"You have bicycles to sell?" she interrupted.

"Huh?" The woman was as deaf as a post. My simple question wasn't going to be as quick or as easy as I had first imagined. I tilted my head upwards, thinking. An icy rivulet streamed down between my shoulder blades. At that moment, I admit, the old lady's idea of selling our bikes didn't sound half bad. But, being slow, instead of shouting "Sold!" I carefully re-explained my quest — pausing at appropriate intervals; enunciating syllables like a sopping Mr Rogers — hoping the information was sinking in and being interpreted correctly. I finished what had quickly deteriorated into an ordeal. It would have been quicker if I had written it down. But she was probably blind too.

"You want a safe place to store your bicycles?"

"Huh?" I said again. *Working here would be fun!*

She had caught that we were from Alberta (why had I mentioned that in the first place?). "Do you know where Wainwright is?" she asked, looking up at me with those sweet eyes. Without waiting for my response, she carried on. "I have a friend there. She has a 4,000 acre pig farm."

Sharon's going to make pork chops out of me, is what I thought. Ah, yes, Sharon. She was still standing outside with our bikes ... in the dark ... in the pouring rain. That was, if she hadn't already sold them.

Fortunately a nurse appeared and rescued me before I had to admit myself. "No, you aren't allowed to camp on the lawn," she said, but she gave me directions to a "town park alongside the canal, where you will be more than welcome to spend the night."

I exited to the awaiting Sharon. "Along the canal?" she said before I had a chance to even open my mouth.

"How? How did you know that?" I stammered.

Apparently, a more astute patron, having overheard my lengthy but-going-nowhere hallway conversation with deaf Granny, had come out and supplied Sharon with the information.

"About ten minutes ago," Sharon laughed.

Modern Art

> **"Skill without imagination is craftsmanship and gives us many useful objects such as wickerwork picnic baskets. Imagination without skill gives us modern art."**
> ~ Tom Stoppard, *Artist Descending a Staircase*

A serene backroad slipped us into Ottawa, the nation's capital. Many non-Canadians are under the impression that Toronto is our country's capital. But they're incorrect. Toronto is the centre of the universe. (In Spain, I got into a lengthy argument with an older fellow who absolutely insisted Toronto was Canada's capital. Each time I shook my head and said "Ottawa," he would even more emphatically shake his head and come back with "Toronto." Finally, a better educated Spaniard came to my rescue. Yelling "Ottawa" at the top of his lungs, he lashed the elder into submission. Or so we thought. The older fellow hopped in his car and drove off with one last shout of "Toronto!")

A bike path, lined with autumn leaves and well-tended flowers, paralleled the canal. It whisked us merrily downtown and deposited us outside the Ottawa Art Gallery.

We locked our bikes to a railing and went to go inside. But before we even entered, someone's perverted idea of art assaulted our senses. In an attempt, perhaps, to put patrons in the correct frame of mind to view modern art, some sicko had staged his interpretation of Monty Pythonesque art. Laying on the sidewalk was an exploded pigeon: grey head; clawed feet; clump of feathers. Dumped alongside the poor bird's remains was a smart heap of corn and a wriggling ball of fishing worms. "Just one little wafer...."

Hours later we exited. Thankfully, the art authorities had confiscated the revolting exploded bird display. Even better, we found our bicycles and panniers and all their contents exactly where we had left them several hours prior.

"Our bikes have been here so long," Sharon joked, "people probably were beginning to think they were part of some special modern art exhibition."

"Yeah," I agreed, nodding my head. "But wouldn't our tires be exploded?"

Priorities Straight

> **"I've caught this magical landscape and it's the enchantment of it that I'm so keen to render. Of course lots of people will protest that it's quite unreal, but that's just too bad."**
> ~ Claude Monet

Claren, after her workday ended, escorted us to supper at a fancy Chinese restaurant. She invited us to stay with Val and CJ, her cousins. We happily accepted and trundled off to meet them. Val and CJ were a cheerful couple, but their long day at work had exhausted them. Sharon and I were tired too (all that brain power trying to figure out modern art). No one complained too bitterly when we called it an early night.

In the morning, proving all bike paths lead to Canadian's favourite outdoor store, we followed a looping path past the under-construction rear of the parliament buildings, and stopped in front of the local Mountain Equipment Co-op. Alas, we were too early. The store didn't open till 10 AM.

"Maybe the staff are out doing morning training runs?"

"Speaking of training runs," Sharon said, "my rear tire feels weird. It has more play than it used to." After riding so many days and kilometres, Sharon had developed a keen awareness to her bike's handling. Unlike me, she seemed to have developed an almost intuitive sense when something wasn't exactly right. "It's been getting worse lately," she added. We rode to a bike shop to get it checked out. Alas, the bike shop had a notice that they didn't open until noon.

"We must be in a government town," I sighed.

So, while waiting for our stores to open, we hit a food store (time flies when we're eating). Sure enough, by the time we finished our bagels and juice, Mountain Equipment Co-op had opened.

Sharon, not usually one who enjoys shopping, eagerly bounded forth and picked out a new Gore-Tex jacket. "This will be perfect for our overseas travel," she said. "My old one is more like a J-cloth than Saran Wrap."

"Wow!" I exclaimed. "The designers of this jacket must actually cycle themselves." The new jacket's features seemed constructed with cyclists in mind: multiple lines of reflective strips; zippers under the arms and another across the back for venting while riding uphill in the rain; and, best of all, it possessed a long tail that covered one's backside even when bent over the handlebars to keep the mud-skunk stripe off one's butt. It was so well thought out I almost bought one for myself. Almost. It doesn't rain in Europe does it? Instead, I turned my attention to a fleece hat embroidered with a row of colourful Aztec symbols. Mornings had grown decidedly chilly! (Guess I figured I might as well look natty when I'm soaked.)

"Whoa!" Sharon said, after we had paid for our items and were back outside. "Great hat!" She snatched my purchase off my head and fastened it around her own. I sighed. I hoped that meant she was going to return my old toque she had so forcefully appropriated earlier in the trip. It somewhat reminded me of when waiters ask if we'd like to order dessert. I always get something. Sharon always does not. When *my* dessert arrives, Sharon asks for "just a bite" and proceeds to eat half. Being as clever as I am you'd think I'd learn to order two. That way, when she only eats half I could offer (magnanimously, of course) to finish her leftovers. But I had to admit: she looked darn cute in my new hat.

At noon, we trekked back to the bike shop.

The store was open. But the mechanic hadn't come in yet. "He went mountain biking in Gatineau Park," the owner explained. "He'll show up eventually. Ah, probably he will, anyway."

"It's good to see that someone has his priorities straight," Sharon laughed.

Shortly after 1 PM the mountain bike riding mechanic cruised up — plastered in mud from his helmeted head to his toeclipped shoes. But a white-toothed smile extended from ear to ear.

Whistling a cheery tune, he set to work, tightening the axle cones on Sharon's 15-year-old rims. "That should fix the problem for another 15 years," he proclaimed, holding aloft his two chromed cone wrenches. "No charge," he grinned. "Take it for a spin and come back if you want it adjusted more."

I'm not sure what the mechanic had in mind for a test ride, but we toured almost an hour, past the Prime Minister's residence on Sussex Drive (couldn't see a thing except fence), then up and along Rockcliffe Drive where we discovered a huge park and picnic area. I hustled over to use the washroom. A sign inside read: NO WASHING FEET IN SINKS. *Huh?* I wondered. *Do they get a lot of touring cyclists?*

Lolling in the weak sunshine, we ate until our appetites were sated (but feet unwashed). Leaving the park to the dog walkers, we followed another bike path along the famous Rideau canal. (In the winter — which with the biting wind, didn't feel that far off — the canal freezes over and becomes the world's longest skating rink.)

Windblown leaves littered the paths in a kaleidoscope of autumn colour. But it was another sign that caught my attention. In a local 'Stoop and Scoop' bylaw, it depicted a rather beady-eyed mongrel, squatting, and staring back at a whopping pile of steaming poo. Under the picture, a caption read: THINK ABOUT IT. I did. Only in Ottawa, I decided.

The afternoon turned windier; a decided nip hung in the fall air. Cruising along smooth bike paths, surrounded by green space, Ottawa struck us as being like one big university campus.

We met Claren after she finished work. When she suggested a drive in the Gatineau Hills to view the vibrant expanses of autumn leaves, we quickly accepted.

Inside her car — the heater flipped on high — we crossed the Chaudières Bridge and entered Hull, Québec. The Gatineau Hills, just a 15 minute car drive from downtown Ottawa, rose out of surrounding farmland looking like a delicious bumble berry pie. Sugar maple, birch and beech, and sumac bushes populated the gentle slopes, leaves blazing tasty wild raspberry reds, honeysuckle oranges, and gooseberry yellows.

We stopped at an overlook and viewed the tapestry. "Looks like Monet's been here," Claren beamed.

We continued on a gravel road all the way to Meech Lake — site of the Prime Minister's summer cottage and infamous Meech Lake Accord. (The Meech Lake Accord 1982: the federal parliament and nine out of ten provincial legislatures agreed on the Constitution Act (Québec wouldn't sign), which brought the constitution from Britain home to Canada on April 17, 1982. The Meech Lake Accord 1987: Québec signed after it was agreed that they would be recognized as a "distinct society.")

A short distance before the cottage, we approached a locked gate. Security guards manned the entrance 24 hours a day.

"Now there's an ultra low stress job," I grinned, watching the guard sitting on a chair and thumbing through a newspaper. "Sitting in the forest, listening to cheery birdsong while watching the leaves change colour. Some people have all the luck. How do you get a job like that?"

"The Prime Minister's brother-in-law?" Sharon said with a chuckle.

As we bumped to a stop on the rocky road, Claren said, "I can tell the Prime Minister helicopters in."

No such luck for us. Claren maneuvered the vehicle in a three-point 180 degree change of direction on the narrow, crushed rock road, and we jolted our way back to Ottawa.

Free Camping

"When we are capable of living in the moment free from the tyranny of 'shoulds,' free from the nagging sensation that this moment isn't right, we will have peaceful hearts."
~ Joan Borysenko, *A Woman's Book of Life*

After a second night at Claren's cousins, Val and CJ's, we said goodbye and slipped out the back door. We cruised a smooth bike path, surrounded by an enormity of green space, to the Parliament buildings. I had an idea: I wanted to set up our tent on the Parliament's lawn and have Sharon immortalize the occasion on film (I'd always wanted to camp on Parliament Hill).

"I don't like this," Sharon hissed when I told her my grand plan. I think it's safe to assume she wasn't exactly a willing participant in my grand scheme.

"You don't even have to help set up the tent," I said, attempting to persuade her. "You only have to take the picture."

It was 10 AM. Nine tour buses already lined the curb. A huge prayer rally, via satellite, was assembling. Hundreds of folding chairs filled the expansive lawn. Dozens of RCMP officers strolled about, making sure everyone behaved themselves. Security guards paraded around too, keeping an attentive eye on the milling crowd. Who knew how many plainclothes officers were lurking about?

"You're going to get arrested," Sharon stated flatly.

"Fine," I said, sizing up the situation with the determination of a SWAT commando. The best location? *As far away from the crowd as possible,* I thought. My plan was to pop up the tent, dive in, smile, and have Sharon snap a quick shot. I estimated (from all our previous practice) I could assemble and dismantle the tent within two minutes. Police officers, guards, and the others shuffling about, would never know. Or so that was the plan.

"How about if you set up in the back?" Sharon suggested.

"No way!" I exploded. "There's construction back there."

"Let's get out of here," Sharon insisted. "You can't leave the country with a criminal record, you know."

That was true. But I had made up my mind. Not that I'm stubborn or anything. "See the flowers over there," I whispered, nodding in the direction of a colourful display. "We'll lean our bikes against that lamppost. I'll pop up the tent in front of the flowers. Clock tower in the background. It'll be classic."

"I'm *not* helping you," Sharon reiterated. "And I'm not visiting you in prison, either." Her eyes narrowed to slits, she shook her head and flashed me one of her "you-and-your-crazy-ideas" looks. I'm sure she figured I was a couple of potatoes short of a full sack.

We pushed our bikes over to the flowers as unobtrusively as fully loaded touring bikes sporting bright pink and fluorescent yellow pannier covers with Canada flags flapping atop neon orange safety poles could be.

Leaning my bike against the lamppost, I suddenly realized: I was nervous! *Suppose I did get arrested?* Committed to the reality that I was going to do it, I yanked the tent bag from beneath its straining bungees. *Gosh. It looks remarkably like a gun bag.*

I dropped the bundle onto the grass, untied it, drew forth three lengths of shock-corded aluminum poles, and quickly snapped them together. Believing I would look less suspicious, I didn't glance around. With a single, spreading-a-bed-cover flapping motion, the tent unfurled. Eyes low, I threaded the poles through their fabric sleeves, popped the tent up, hopped in, and flashed Sharon a winning smile.

Hmmm. Sharon seemed to be taking her sweet time in the shutter release department. Good help is so hard to find. Pay back for dragging her through the whole charade? She *finally* clicked the shutter. I jumped out and flattened the tent. With one pole removed, I peeked up. A woman had walked over and was talking to Sharon. We had been spotted.

What? The woman, a tourist from France, was requesting I reassemble the "little house" so she could take a picture.

"I don't think so," I mumbled.

"For France!" she insisted, waving her instamatic.

Huh? That was supposed to convince me? Not knowing why, I complied (that docile Canadian upbringing?). I popped the tent up again and plopped myself down in front of it.

She was mercifully quick. But then she demanded that Sharon join me, and she'd take a picture for us. Sharon handed her our camera, and with a radiant smile skipped over and sat down beside me. I couldn't believe it!

The woman pushed the camera's button. But before we had a chance to get up, another tourist trotted over. She took a snapshot of us, too. Then, beginning to border on the theatre of the absurd, an entire busload of forty or so bandy-legged oldsters, like a gaggle of squawking geese, tottered toward us, cameras winking. Bus drivers eyeballed our predicament with wide grins.

The tourists encircled us, shutters snapping like alligators on two monkeys. Sheesh. If I had known we were going to be a major tourist attraction, I would have charged. "Five bucks to take a photo of the crazy Canucks about to be arrested."

A trio of police officers loped down the sidewalk toward us. Sharon and I wisely jumped up and collapsed the tent in a takedown so precise even General Patton would have been proud.

We swung our legs over our bikes and beat a hasty retreat — the assembled crowd parting to let us through like a suspender and garter-belted Red Sea. The throng cheered and waved. Cries of "Bon voyage!" rang in our ears.

"Now this is more like the world tour departure I had envisioned!" Sharon said, beaming and waving like royalty.

Transi de Froid

> **"Everybody talks about the weather, but nobody does anything about it."**
> ~ Mark Twain

Uncle Dennis and Aunt Rolande, who lived in nearby Orleans, invited us for supper (a cyclist's favourite meal ... followed closely by breakfast or lunch).

Sharon and I cycled a meandering path along the Ottawa River. People were out bike riding, fishing, or roaming hand in hand, viewing fall colours, and enjoying the uncommon warm day. A few were even taking advantage of the late summer-like temperatures, lazing on the riverbank in sunshine as sweet as golden honey.

We arrived at Dennis and Rolande's too early for supper (but hungry, of course). When my stomach roared like a distempered lion, Rolande flew into action, throwing together garden tomato and crisp lettuce sandwiches to tide us over.

After catching up on family news, Dennis, revealing his and Rolande's love of travel, said, "If we didn't have other commitments, we'd join you in a moment."

"It probably won't be long before we load up our VW van and hit the road again," Rolande concurred.

Using a recipe acquired from their five-month Mexico trip, Dennis began supper. He constructed massive tacos — our favourite kind!

The following morning, Sharon and I waved goodbye to our relatives. We cruised a quiet byway as it flowed along the curving Ottawa River. Although we were still in Ontario, the towns we came upon struck us as being more French than English.

The prevalence of the French language surprised us. Even business signs were in French. And everyone we overheard was speaking French. Anyone who spoke to us used French first. (When we responded, they quickly switched to English.) We weren't even out of Ontario, but already it felt as if we were in a foreign country.

A *very* French man, animated in both gestures and language, supplied us with route directions (though not before telling us we were "crazy" and that we were going to "freeze to death"). A north wind funnelled Arctic air into the area. His advice? "Get a motel room." That wasn't his only advice for us. "Don't ride on the sidewalk. The police will fine you." Then — rather darkly I thought — he cautioned: "There's a lot of crazy drivers around here. Make sure you wear your reflective vests."

"Yeah," I responded. "That way if they hit us I'll know they were aiming."

Down the road in L'Original we arrived at a gas station — cold, but unscathed. The attendant filled our water bottles while confirming the earlier weather report. "You'll be risking pneumonia by camping in this weather," he said. "The forecast is for one degree." He shivered. "That's too cold to sleep outside!"

We found an abandoned ball field and, fingers and toes like ice cubes, set our tent in a dugout. "That forecast temperature may have been a tad on the optimistic side," I shivered.

"The good news," Sharon said, "no mosquitoes."

"You always look for the silver lining," I said, my teeth chattering in an attempt to smile.

Sharon wore her newly acquired fleece hat to bed. And still she was unhappy that it was taking "forever" before she was sufficiently warm enough to fall asleep. (Swathed in a near-identical conglomeration of nighttime wear: double layers of socks, shirts, pants, jackets, mittens, and hats — neither of us were too warm.) Perhaps that fellow had been right: it was too *transi de froid* to sleep outside; I was crazy; and we *were* going to freeze to death.

Québec Welcome

> **"CAUTION — I Brake For Stop Signs!"**
> ~ Bumper Sticker

At Hawkesbury we crossed the Ottawa River, and entered the *belle* province of Québec. *Bonjour!* My plan was to cycle around the Gaspé Peninsula while checking out the fall colours, then head back to Toronto and catch a cheap flight to Spain. But, with the weather being so cold, Sharon wasn't keen on my plans. She argued we should head for Montréal and catch a flight to warmer climes immediately.

I persuaded her. "How about we try it for a ways, and if it's too miserable we'll turn around." (Unfortunately, going around the Gaspé Peninsula is similar to a swimmer making it halfway across a lake. Then, deciding they can't make it all the way, turn around and swim back.)

Sharon, still not entirely convinced, followed me along the river, heading for Lachute. Immediately we noticed that Québec's motorized wheelmen were far friendlier than their neighbouring clumsy oafs in Ontario. (Of all the places we've cycled in North America: Québec drivers are second only to Washington State for the most courtesy extended to cyclists.)

"Is it because of the French love for cycling and the Tour de France?" Sharon wondered aloud, impressed with the considerate attitude of motorists.

With better drivers, rather than concentrating solely on not being untimely dispatched by vehicles, we were able to look around and enjoy our surroundings. A church's brilliant white steeple glared in the sunshine, poking forth from an ocean of multi-coloured leaves like a submarine's periscope. "Looks like a great place for the night," I said, surveying the church's ample lawn. A vicar was outside, checking his remaining hardy blooms.

I wheeled over to the holy man. "Je'm'apelle Neil Anderson," I began.

"Say," the monsieur said, interrupting his gardening and suppressing a snicker, "you're not from around here, are you?"

Sharon affirmed his sleuth work and asked if we could camp outside his church. "Pick any spot you like," he said. Then, he hastily added: "Mind the flowers!"

The next morning, sidestepping the church's immaculate flower beds, we followed peaceful Route 344 — *Chemin de la Grande Côte* (Way of the Large Coast) — past Montréal's teeming millions. All along the *Riviére des Mille-Îles* (River of the Thousand Islands), there wasn't one spot without a building. That wasn't causing us concern, however. Rather, it was the vast number of stop signs we had to contend with.

On the main route, four-way stops at each street forced us to a halt. "Does Québec have a fetish for stop signs, or what?" I asked, after having stopped a dozen times in a kilometre.

"No kidding," Sharon complained. "All this stopping and starting is killing my knees."

"Mine, too," I agreed. "Not only is it taking us forever to get anywhere, but I'm not sure the over-abundance of stop signs is making travel any safer. Maybe even less safe," I grimaced, watching a motorist whiz through a four-way stop, barely letting up on the accelerator, let alone coming to a stop. With so many stop signs, motorists tended to ignore them. Sharon and I, meanwhile, stopped at each and every one, scanned both directions twice, making darn sure the coast was clear before scuttling across!

We also found it frightening that a two-way bike lane we happened to be following was abutted to the very edge of the main highway. The bike lane markings indicated we were to ride in the lane closest to *oncoming* traffic! Our only saviour: separating us from an onslaught of vehicles was a thin white line! A freightliner pounded toward us.

"Aren't engineers brilliant?" Sharon shuddered.

Feeling like two toads about to meet a steamroller, we hopped as far over to the left as the path allowed. The truck rumbled past, not more than two feet away. When the whirlwind and truck's thudding (or was that my heart?) receded enough to make myself heard, I answered Sharon's brilliant engineer question. "Yeah," I said, "but it's too bad more of them aren't cyclists."

Disturbance At Duck Pond

> **"Youth cannot know how age thinks and feels. But old men are guilty if they forget what it was to be young."**
> ~ J. K. Rowling, *Harry Potter and the Order of the Phoenix*

In Rosemère, alongside a tranquil duck pond, we sat at a bench, eating lunch. Feathered friends paddled about. A few dozed in the long grass. All was peaceful. At least until a troop of middle-school aged boys appeared with their bag lunches.

The seven youngsters didn't eat much. They began their lunch hour by chasing the resting ducks and swans into the pond. Satisfied at having ruffled a few feathers, they tore their bologna sandwiches into hunks and hurled the chunks into the water. They bit into apples and chucked pieces at the duck house. For dessert, they tossed chocolate-covered cookies into the drink. *Dejeuner* completed, they stooped at the pond's edge, filling plastic sandwich bags with water. Flinging the water-filled missiles high into the air, with seemingly laser-guided accuracy, the bags exploded in sloshy plops on the duck house roof.

"Hmmm," I said, watching their antics. "Today's youngsters may not be as environmentally sensitive as I had presumed."

"And a lot of parents are wasting time and energy sending lunches to school," Sharon observed.

"Well," I said, "at least the ducks get to enjoy an extra feeding on weekdays. If they don't get beaned by an apple, that is."

The group of seven, punching and play wrestling one another, headed off on other conquests. Four 12-year-olds approached from the opposite direction.

"Ohhh," I groaned. "I feel sorry for those poor ducks. I wonder how many times a day they have to suffer unthoughtful kids' abuse?"

But these boys were different. Whereas the first group had completely ignored us, not even saying hi, these boys came straight over. And they began speaking to us in English right off the bat. Cued from the Canada flag on our flagpoles?

The contrast between the two sets of youngsters was nothing short of astounding. The second crew was as refined as the first had been uncouth. One child in the second group was deaf. While two boys took turns asking Sharon and me questions about our trip, a third boy signed the replies to their deaf friend.

"Are you doing a Tour du World?" one lad asked. When I nodded, he continued, "As soon as I saw those panniers, I knew you weren't out for a ride around the park. I've always wanted to ride across Canada." The boys spoke with us for close to half an hour before excusing themselves and heading back to classes.

"Maybe," I decided, "youth aren't a total write off after all."

We departed our lunch spot and searched for a tourist information facility to obtain a Québec road map. I received my first taste of what we might face cycling in a foreign country.

A sign (in a promising manner) read: INFORMATION. I popped the door open and stepped inside. Surprise! A room full of computer teachers stared back at me. Taken completely off guard, I laughed out loud. I gave a little half-wave to the stunned onlookers, and about-faced out the door. The next place I tried turned out to be a restaurant. "Sheesh," I whispered, throwing my hands up in despair, "who needs a map anyway?"

"Yeah," Sharon agreed. "It'll probably be in French anyway and we won't be able to read it."

We abandoned our map quest, but found our language problems still persisted. In late afternoon, on the bank of the Saint Lawrence River, we approached a unique café made from an old double-decker bus. The café was closed. But picnic tables alongside the bus begged to be used.

We sat down and fired up our trusty stove. After eating too much for dinner, as usual, we didn't feel like riding any farther. "Maybe we can set up behind the bus," I suggested. An old maid, in her front yard across the road, squirted a few bedraggled zinnias that hadn't yet succumbed to frost. I hustled over and asked her if she thought it would be all right if we camped by the bus.

Unfortunately, the old woman knew approximately the same amount of English as I knew French. Next to none. Somehow, we managed to hold a lengthy conversation. Eventually we got around to the topic of camping beside the bus. "I don't own it," I presumed she said with an offhand wave, "but go ahead anyway." Sometimes it was handy being one's own interpreter.

I shuffled back across the nearly traffic-free road and regaled Sharon with the good news. We happily set up our tent behind the café bus. Shipping vessels swept past noiselessly in the dark, plying the mighty river. Huge wakes, panting like dogs after chasing rabbits on a summer's day, lapped against the bank, lulling us toward sleep.

Moneybags

> **"To dare is to lose one's footing momentarily.
> To not dare is to lose oneself."**
> ~ Soren Kierkegaard

Overcast and moody, the wind picked up a notch. "Will I ever be warm again?" Sharon wondered aloud. The temperature had approached frigid. Wearing all our clothes, and hats, and gloves, we sat at a picnic table and shivered while trying to coax our reluctant little stove to life. Even when the sun occasionally peeked through cloud cover, it didn't warm us sufficiently.

"There's only one thing to do," Sharon said, slapping her mittened hands together and packing up the uncooperative stove. "Let's ride!"

We hopped on our bikes and pedalled off into pinching air. As long as we were pedalling, we weren't cold, other than the distressing tidbits of ice that had replaced our fingers and toes.

A ferry transported us across the Saint Lawrence River to the town of Sorel. Perhaps it'd be warmer on the *south* side? We followed a small route to Pierreville. As soon as we stopped pedalling, our skin chilled and turned to goosebumps. Crouching on the bank of Riviére Saint Francois, we shivered through lunch.

We had stayed in Canada so late in order to view the magnificent fall colours. But we forgot to take into account that those who had recommended an autumn leaf tour stayed in B&B's and drove cars. They certainly didn't camp at this time of year.

"Maybe we should head for Europe *tout de suite,*" Sharon said, her teeth chattering. Cold days (and even colder nights) already, she worried that our route around the Gaspé Peninsula — farther north — would put us into seriously severe weather.

"The leaves look awesome," I shivered. "But maybe viewing autumn spectacles is best done from behind a car windshield."

"Yeah," Sharon agreed. "With the heater turned on high."

Thinking warm thoughts (like we should be cycling Hawaii), we headed back out onto the road. I attempted to distract Sharon from her freezing hands and feet by immersing her in commentary about the stunning scenery. For a couple of kilometres, maybe she almost forgot her numb toes?

We passed narrow strips of farmland. "Did you notice how land was divided in the old days?" I asked. Many holdings were about a hundred feet wide, and ran down to the very edge of the river. The strips were a good visual depiction of how important it was in forefathers' days to have access to the river highway.

We eventually made it to Deschaillons. Cold and tired, we were not in good moods. "I don't know how long I can stand cycling in conditions like this," Sharon said, through clenched teeth. But, once again, the universe was friendly. The moment we stopped in a Metro grocery store parking lot, a fellow with a shock of white hair peppered with flecks of black like burnt wood sprinkled on snow, approached — just like he was waiting for us.

"Where are you staying tonight?" he enquired.

"We don't know yet," Sharon answered.

"Well," he said, "I've got a place for you." He extracted a card from his wallet and wrote his name and address on the back of it. Thrusting it into Sharon's claw-like hand, he then instructed us on how to best find his home.

While Sharon watched the bikes, I foxtrotted into the grocery store, ecstatic that we were soon going to be out of the elements and into a warm haven for the night. Life was good.

"Une poulet barbecue," I said to a fella manning the butcher department, and pointed to a rotisserie chicken.

"Touriste?" he asked.

"Si!" I answered lustily.

With chicken in hand, we left the hen house, and cycled off to locate our night's accommodation.

What a place it turned out to be! When we looked over the bank from Maurice's main cottage, we couldn't see anything for 500 feet below except bush and the mighty Saint Lawrence River surging past in silent brown fury. The grade down the bank was an astonishing (and scary) 50 percent! Against Maurice's protestations, I rode my bike down, braking and skidding my rear tire the entire way. At the bottom, the road made an abrupt 90-degree turn. I narrowly averted plunging over the brink.

We arrived at our private cottage. After eating the spicy chicken, we indulged in bubbling hot showers, then trekked back up the hill — bent nearly double on the steep slope — to visit our new friends, Maurice, and his good wife, Jacqueline.

They had mugs of hot chocolate waiting for us. We learned that the cottage at the bottom of the hill had been in their family for 30 years. The cabin they were living in, at the top of the bank, was over 150 years-old — ancient by Canadian standards. Maurice had remodelled the place with old weathered barn wood, giving it a warm and cozy atmosphere.

Maurice, 65, told us he had retired at age 54 from the suitcase selling business.

"You must have made a suitcase full of money to retire that early," Sharon said with a grin.

"When do you find time to use two cottages?" I questioned.

"Actually," Maurice answered, "we own another cottage in Gaspé. And a fourth in Florida."

"You really did make a suitcase full of money!" Sharon exclaimed.

"With the brisk weather, Florida is sounding mighty good," I said, cradling my mug of hot chocolate tighter.

Maurice smiled. "We had a motorhome before we owned the cottages. We travelled all over the States for five years.

"One night, in a Florida campground, we woke to find a robber in our motorhome. Can you believe this guy had broken in while we were *sleeping* inside?" Maurice shook his head at the absurdity, not to mention the audacity, of the crook's actions. "Before going to bed," Maurice recalled, "we had set the table for breakfast. Without waking either of us, the guy had broken in and stolen the money from Jacqueline's purse. He had removed the entire set of dishes from the table — including the cutlery! — and had them in a sack. All without waking us! Then, when he couldn't find my wallet, he tiptoed over to our bed and gently shook my shoulder." Maurice chuckled at the memory. "I guess he didn't want to disturb Jacqueline's beauty sleep!

"When I opened my eyes and saw this guy standing over me I screamed so loud I'm sure I woke the entire campground! So much for Jacqueline's beauty sleep. The guy turned and bolted for the door. A high chain-link fence surrounded the campground. He vaulted over it, making a clean getaway — taking our dishes with him!"

I frowned. "See?" I said to Sharon. "Maurice's story confirms my belief that camping in the bush is safer than staying at official sites. In campgrounds, the crooks know where to find you!"

Sharon rolled her eyes.

After more stories (Maurice's mom had 20 kids! He was number 15 ... I'll bet he never had to worry about eating leftovers!) and more hot chocolate, Sharon and I slipped out the door and into the dark. Hanging on to one another for support, we rappelled down the steep bank. Safely back at our cabin, we savoured another hot shower before hitting the hay. We slept in absolute comfort and warmth for the first night in weeks.

After a leisurely breakfast (we were in no hurry to leave our comfortable hideaway), I hopped on my bike, ready to tackle the monster slope.

"You can't be serious," Sharon said, shaking her head and pushing her bike toward the steep incline.

But I wasn't as smart. In dour jut-jawed determination, I took a flying start down the short straightaway, legs churning like a crazed hamster on an exercise wheel. I flew around the 90-degree corner, and smacked into the incline. Pedalling with all my might, grunting like some bull who had polished off a sackful of beans, I made it all of 30 feet before coming to a complete standstill. I wobbled, stuck in my toeclips. Just before toppling onto the tarmac, I managed to free my foot. That would have been embarrassing!

Stubbornly (or stupidly), I turned around and got an even faster start, charging the steep grade like a determined bantam rooster. I succeeded in clawing my way a record-breaking five feet farther. Sharon, half-dragging, half-pulling her bike, passed me, shaking her head at my wackiness. "Poultry in motion," she clucked.

My third attempt ended poorly — the shortest of all.

"You'll be worn out before we even start," Sharon called to me from the top of the bank.

Muttering to myself, my legs quivering from all-out exertion, I wearily admitted defeat, and tugged my bike up the cliff.

Maurice and Jacqueline were waiting with their camera. "We sure admire what you two are doing," they said, clicking off several frames. They had no idea how much they boosted our spirits!

With renewed enthusiasm, we continued toward Québec City, the wind pushing us, the sun warming our smiling faces. We passed farmers out in orange-dotted fields, gathering pumpkins for market and Halloween festivities. Sailing past, we waved to them spiritedly, feeling a bit festive ourselves.

Big Dipper

> **"Reach high, for stars lie hidden in your soul.**
> **Dream deep, for every dream precedes the goal."**
> ~ Pamela Vaull Starr

North America's only walled city awaited. Québec City, built on the north shore of the Saint Lawrence where the great river narrows to a mere kilometre ('Québec' comes from an Algonquian word meaning 'narrowing of the river'). Maurice assured us we would love the old city's history, architecture, and its culture. We could scarcely wait to visit.

Ten kilometres from the old city we came across an official campground. Our plan was to pedal around Québec City unencumbered by heavy panniers. So, even though the camp fee was outrageous — and Maurice's motorhome break-in story did little to placate my fears of campgrounds being crime-free havens — we anted up and left our belongings while we explored.

At the Plains of Abraham, under a cloudless blue sky, we sat in profound tranquility: the exact opposite I'd bet of that fateful day back in September 1759, when British Major-General Wolfe took on the troops of French Lieutenant-General Montcalm. It was a fierce battle that mortally wounded both men. As I drank a bottle of Clamato juice I tried not to think of the sea of blood that must have flowed on the field that terrible day. (In 1760, the French attempted — and failed — to retake the city. Later that year, British forces captured Montréal and New France fell. Back in Europe, France reportedly took the defeat rather lightly. One government official was said to have casually dismissed Canada as nothing more "than several acres of snow." And, at times, I find it difficult to disagree with his candid assessment.)

We rode around the edge of the Citadel — a massive military fortification built between 1820 and 1831 — atop the Cap Diamant escarpment. The lofty location gave defenders of the city a commanding view of anyone approaching by way of the Saint Lawrence River or the Plains of Abraham. Across the river at Pointe-Lévis the British military, fearing attack during the American Civil War, had constructed three forts. None ever suffered assault (other than from tourists, that is).

We rode through the historic Saint Louis gates and into Québec City's quaint old quarter. Historic buildings, cheek to jowl, lined the hilly streets. "This is like living Canadian history!" Sharon said as we wheeled about town, observing places we had previously only read about. Our favourite was romantic Chateau Frontenac with its impressive view of the Saint Lawrence River.

"Too bad we can't afford to stay even one night," Sharon lamented.

"At least we have showers to look forward to back at the campground," I reminded her.

To assuage our lamentations we hit an upscale eatery. The French waiters were classic, standing off to one side — slightly aloof.

Having returned fashionably late from our Québec City reconnoitre we slept in, enjoying the serenity of not being discovered in a wild camping spot ... and trying to get value for our princely-summed plot of scabby ground. Sharon finally coaxed me into rising. "One night in a cottage, and we're spoiled," she yawned.

"Race you to the shower!" I said. We grabbed our towels and headed off in search of luscious showers.

But, instead of finding a well-appointed bathroom, I stumbled down broken concrete steps into a moulded and mildewed cinder-block cubicle. A single low-wattage incandescent bulb hung from a chain, casting a yellowish pall over the drab and dismal scene.

A mingy little grimace etched my lips. The distasteful place turned my stomach. It reminded me of a gulag where prisoners were taken to be hosed down after a delousing session. It was the sort of public shower so filthy and disgusting that one walks on his heels — while wearing Tevas. "Talk about the black hole of Calcutta," I muttered.

Nauseous, but unwilling to pass up an opportunity to shower, I hastily disrobed and squeamishly waded in. Twisting on the taps, greyish water swirled about my ankles. The drain, somewhere beneath the murky depths, burbled portentously, then let out a gurgle, gasping like the Titanic headed straight for the bottom. Talk about my shortest shower ever.

"I hope I didn't catch anything," I spluttered upon exiting. Sharon hadn't fared much better. We had a hard time believing that holidayers would tolerate such atrocious unsanitary conditions when even we hardened "my-kingdom-for-a-shower" cycle tourists found it abysmal beyond belief. Vowing to be more selective in the future, we abandoned the grungy campground to less fortunates.

Across the river in Lévis, a half-starved Sharon hustled into a grocery store. Emerging half an hour later, she strained under the weight of three bulging grocery sacks.

"Where are we going to put all that?" I groaned, gawking at the chock full bags of milk, cheeses, baguettes, muffins, tomatoes, cucumbers, sub sandwiches, and assorted mini chocolate cakes filled with puffy cream.

"Never send a hungry biker into a food store," Sharon said, grinning impishly.

"Yeah," I agreed, "from now on you're going to have to have adult supervision."

We cached as much of the horde as possible in our panniers, then strapped the remainder on top of our rear racks. Burdened like two pack mules, we wobbled off in search of the nearest picnic table.

Thankfully, we found a park a short shuffle away. The picnic tables had flown south for the winter. We hunkered down on the grass and feasted amidst stunning autumn leaves of fiery tomato reds, ripe oranges, and bright egg yolk yellows.

After an hour-long feeding frenzy, we progressed from starving Ethiopian dogs to overstuffed fat cats. We patted our bellies, and curled up together, grinning like Cheshires. Sharing a saffron sunbeam, we watched bloated clouds pussyfoot past overhead.

"Look over there...," Sharon said, pointing, "that one looks like Garfield."

"Yeah," I agreed. "Eating lasagna."

"Ohhh," Sharon groaned. "Don't mention food."

After an entertaining hour of cloud watching and guffawing over a sailboat crew's unsuccessful attempt to free themselves from a sandbar, we got back on our bikes and rode until dusk.

At a rest area, as daylight faded, we slipped over a bank and concealed ourselves amongst shadows. Lounging back on the grass, we stargazed. The Big Dipper already shone low in the northwest. While we watched, the pale moon rose — a thin silvery crescent — and hung in the star-studded sky like a glittery brooch on a sequined black satin gown.

As the vault of heaven wheeled overhead, a connectedness pervaded our beings. It felt as if we were two with the universe. A falling star suddenly streaked across the firmament, marbling a creamy path past the Big Dipper's rim. For an ever-so-brief moment it appeared as a cascading slip of milk.

"See that?" I marvelled in hushed awe.

"Amazing!" came Sharon's breathy response.

"I wonder who else saw —?"

"No one," Sharon purred. "That was just for us."

"I'm glad we had the chance to share it," I murmured, holding her close.

"Isn't this what life should be about?" Sharon said. "For dreaming ... for sharing ... for being with the ones we love?"

I nodded, and hugged her closer. Spooned together, we drifted toward sleep beneath the stars; the Milky Way spread above us like an immense shining comforter.

Bridge Over Troubled Water

> **"We cross our bridges when we come to them and burn them behind us, with nothing to show for our progress except a memory of the smell of smoke, and a presumption that once our eyes watered."**
> ~ Tom Stoppard, *Rosencrantz and Guildenstern are Dead*

An early start, coupled with an assisting tailwind and flat terrain, enabled us to crank out over 200 kilometres. (The strong wind at our backs reminded me of when we toured Newfoundland. From Gros Morne National Park, a brutish tailwind had pushed us north, past windswept vistas, past rocky fishing villages, past unhappy cyclists struggling haplessly in the opposite direction. We had clung to our handlebars for dear life, eventually covering 330 kilometres [over 200 miles] in a single day — still our personal record for fully loaded touring. We could have gone farther, but on Newfoundland's northern tip, at Saint Anthony, we ran out of road.)

Our windy Québec breakfast was beside a church, its massive stone walls sheltering us from the blasting wind. Sharon decided hot chocolate, café au lait-style, in our soup bowls, would be just the thing to warm us. It was, being both the right size for our morning thirst, and the perfect solution to cold weather blues.

A church caretaker spread maple branches along the church walls, making a splendid colourful autumn display. Upon finishing, he padded over proudly and asked us something. Of course, we didn't understand him. *"C'est bon! C'est bon! (It's good!),"* we said, then I quickly added, *"Je ne parler pas français"* — I don't speak French. (I was getting a lot of mileage out of that line, along with my favourite: "Une poulet barbecue.")

"It's really too bad I didn't pay more attention in French class," I lamented to Sharon after the chap gave up and wandered away to another part of the yard. "Madame Currie always said she'd have the last laugh."

We waved so long to the caretaker and cycled northeast toward Gaspé. The mighty Saint Lawrence grew ever wider, smelling sharply of salt and mud — more like a sea than a river. It even had a tide. And when it ebbed, it left a slick of black mud, like some sticky Valdez oil spill. Fishing nets hung stranded, row upon row, high and dry, awaiting the great river's return.

Flocks of southward-bound snow geese honked overhead like traffic jams of pearly white Hondas, wings beating the air in perfect synchronization. Farmers' fields, crowded with squadrons of wooden decoys, and hunters imitating bird calls, did their best to lure the big birds into landing. "Hmmm," I muttered, riding past the legions of mighty hunters, swathed head to toe in the latest camouflage gear, lying in silent wait. "Scientists think the shortening daylight hours stir the migration instinct. But, seeing this, I'll bet it's the start of hunting season that triggers migration. After all, it doesn't take much of a genius to figure out that if someone is shooting at you, it's time you went somewhere else."

"Sure," Sharon said. "Let's make like the birds and flock off."

Hunters notwithstanding, folks in Québec were peaceful and friendly. They spoke French first, then, discovering I was lacking in the communication ability department, they quickly switched to English — even when they didn't know much of the language themselves.

"Big wine today," one fella said.

"Yes," I agreed, nodding. "It is windy."

"Oh, yes ... 'wind,'" he corrected himself, a trifle self-conscious at his error. Still, his attempt was better than I could have done (and a big mug of hot mulled wine right about then didn't sound half bad). Besides the language, other differences in the belle province had struck us as well. Church steeples replaced the ubiquitous grain elevators we had seen everywhere on our march across the prairies. Québec's predominantly Roman Catholic population liked big churches — some even sported *double* steeples. Large white crosses, statues of Mary, statues of Jesus, statues of Mary and Jesus, and other religious artifacts were unabashedly displayed on people's front lawns.

Québec towns supported far more flower shops than other provinces. And lingerie boutiques! Even the smallest villages usually boasted at least one flower and lingerie shop on main street. *Ooh la la! Vive la difference!*

Traffic was intermittent until our secondary route ended in Rivière-du-Loup. Freight trucks became a grating reality again. They plagued us all the way to Trois-Pistoles, blowing us off the road on several occasions.

"Trois-Pistoles [Three Pistols]," Sharon grumbled, "no doubt inherited its name from irate bikers."

"Huh?" I said, intrigued. "What do you mean?"

"Cyclists, weary of bonehead drivers, packed three guns." I screwed up my lips, nodded, and she continued. "A machine gun, mounted on their handlebars to pick off head-on passing imbeciles; a revolver, pointed sideways under their seat, to keep cars a respectable distance when overtaking; and a third, a double barrel shotgun, bungeed to the rear rack, to deter smart aleck motorists from honking their horns at cyclists to get off their God-given road."

"No repeat offenders," I observed wryly. Sharon grinned. Her outburst had cheered her.

Back on the road, ignoring a detour sign, I blithely pedalled past the orange caution markers as if I knew what I was doing. Traffic worries became a non-issue. I smiled at my cycle logic.

"Um, what are you doing?" Sharon asked.

"What?" I replied. "You don't suppose there's a bridge out, or something, do you?"

Sharon shook her head at my illogic.

After a few kilometres, we learned the reason for the detour. A bridge was out. Or, at least, it wasn't open for normal traffic. And what it spanned was no little stream. Fording was definitely out of the question.

The under construction bridge deck had no approach. It stood above our heads like an illusory mirage. A lone worker toiled away, mid-span. With his back to us, he hadn't heard our approach. We waited, wondering if we were going to have to pedal back, or if the worker would allow us to cross the almost finished bridge.

A couple of minutes later, we were still standing there, unnoticed. "What do you think we should do?" I asked in a loud voice. The fella turned around and saw us. He smiled, waved, and dropped his tools. Striding to us, his well-muscled arms reached down and hoisted our bikes onto the bridge. Portage!

At the other end of the bridge deck, the worker propped a piece of plywood against the ledge. We eased our bikes down the incline, and gave our helpful friend two thumbs-up.

Traffic was non-existent for quite some way. "We should take detours more often," I grinned, relishing our traffic-free environs.

"You have no idea how lucky you are sometimes."

"Hey," I replied, "living life as an adventure requires the odd detour now and then."

"I think 'odd' is the key word there," Sharon said.

It was late afternoon by the time we pulled into a roadside picnic area to eat. I noticed it sported all the necessary amenities: running water and flush toilets. What else does one require?

"This looks like a perfect spot to spend the night," I said. "And the facilities will be close at hand in the morning."

"Do you think anyone will mind?" Sharon wondered.

"I can't see why they would," I said, attempting to allay her fears. "We can set up behind the shelter."

"You don't suppose this place gets used as a party spot, do you?" she asked hesitantly.

"Naw," I sniffled. There was no broken glass or even any burnt up picnic tables in sight. Since we arrived in Québec, the usual partying platoons of roving Canadian and American youths, bent on vandalizing everything in sight, hadn't plagued us as they had elsewhere. Even weekends had been bastions of relative calm.

"Maybe it's too cold?" Sharon asked, still wondering.

"I prefer to think that Québec's young adults have better things to do." (Nothing like praising teenagers to tempt the party gods.) We set our tent behind the picnic shelter and went to sleep.

Around midnight, two carloads of uninvited guests interrupted our peaceful slumber. Hidden behind the shelter, they couldn't see us. But we could hear them just fine. Although we couldn't understand most of what they said, the tone was jovial. The good-natured adolescents joked and laughed for a few minutes, then piled back into their vehicles and motored off without the usual screeching tires and tooting horns.

"Hmmm, how about that?" I said to a wide-awake Sharon. "No cursing. No smashed bottles. No kicked in garbage cans."

Québec youth were still Number 1 in my book.

The Ghosts That Haunt Me

"Make haste slowly."
~ embroidered on a towel at Margot's

Gaspé was still 260 kilometres away, a good two days' ride. A westerly wind blew, pushing us, providing an easy pedal over undulating terrain. Sunshine cascaded over our shoulders. For the first time in days, we removed our fleece pullovers, enjoying the warm temperature. Carload after carload of Sunday cruisers passed us, admiring tawny autumn leaves and pastel reflections.

In Rimouski, we came face-to-face with the realization that we had ventured far from English-speaking Canada ... locals no longer spoke our language. The harsh reality surfaced when Sharon bought a large bottle of pop I disliked (if it doesn't feel as though it's ripping my throat out, I don't like it). I ventured back inside to exchange it.

"Bonjour," I sang out in my best French accent. *"Échange?"* I twittered, holding the bottle aloft for the girl on the till to see.

"Un moment," came the cashier's reply. *"Je ne parle pas anglais."* Huh? She didn't speak English? Hey, wait a minute, dearie. I *was* speaking French!

Another clerk appeared. He understood enough English to facilitate the replacement. Barely.

Conversing became increasingly difficult. Accent, coupled with our poor grasp of the romantic language, made understanding nearly impossible. Feeling like one-year-olds, we struggled to comprehend the gist of the simplest conversations.

After one caustic encounter — more akin to a shouting match than a conversation — Sharon muttered, "I wish people would realize that sticking their face in mine and yelling louder isn't going to help."

"Yeah," I grinned. "Don't they know that only works for English?"

By the time we hit Matane dusk had overtaken us. I tried to find someone who would give us a spot to spend the night. All we needed was a little chunk of grass. A fellow cutting his lawn called "hullo" as we rode toward him.

I pulled to a stop. "Would it be all right if we camped overnight in your yard?"

"I don't think so," came his curt reply.

Refusal was a new experience for me. Taken aback, I stood there dumbly, mute, confused, rejected. Was it because I didn't speak French? I wondered. Or maybe the guy didn't trust the *Anglais?* The acrimonious taste of discrimination rose in my mouth. On a very tiny scale, I empathized with what some people encountered daily. Mulling his words, I thanked him and pushed off into the biting wind and gathering gloom.

A few kilometres down the road, in nearly total blackness, we approached a cemetery.

"There's a quiet place," Sharon said, pointing, too weary to care she was suggesting we sleep in a graveyard. Then she upped the ante. "You don't believe in ghosts, do you?"

"Nope," I gulped. (I'm a bit like the little old lady who said, 'I don't believe in ghosts. But I'm afraid of them.') "I wouldn't be able to understand them anyway."

The night was as fresh as a tomb. A heavy earthiness permeated the moist air. Between graves, near a crooked fence, we found a flat spot. Using the fence to block the haunting wind, I erected our mausoleum in haste. Stabbing the metal tent stakes into the soft ground, I couldn't help wonder if they should perhaps be wooden instead?

Crisp stars dotted a ribbon of darkness. "No need to put the fly on," I said. "The wind will just snap it and keep us awake all night." We tossed sleeping accouterments inside the cave, then, like a pair of myopic bats, fluttered in after them.

The wind lashed our tiny abode, whipping it one way, then another, threatening to flatten the whole shebang. In a futile attempt to keep the fabric structure from totally imploding, Sharon sat, gargoyle-like, hunched in the centre of the tent, her arms outstretched.

"Can't get much worse than this," I yelled above the din. The wind howled, as if in disagreement, and ratcheted up a notch.

"My, gosh!" Sharon snorted. "It's like being inside a wind tunnel!"

Shimmy. Shake. Rattle. I hoped there would be no roll. The tent collapsed inwards, sides nearly touching, then billowed out frenetically, like Dracula furling and unfurling his cape before takeoff.

"I always wondered what it would be like to sleep in a wind sock," I hollered. The tempest seized the words from my throat and flung them off into a dark corner. "The only consolation," I yelled, "if we liftoff, we'll probably get snagged on a tombstone!"

Sharon grimaced. "That's a consolation?"

By leaving the fly off, I had, of course, angered the weather gods. I watched the night sky through the tent's screen roof. Stars blotted out one by one. They winked out, like an invisible hand of Bill Gates removing light bulbs, and declaring darkness the new standard.

A sudden squall hit, spitting chilly spatters through the mesh. "Oh, bother!" I hissed, and bolted outside, sans coat, intent on quickly fastening on the fly — and learned firsthand that haste does indeed make waste. So absorbed in using the fence as a windbreak, I had placed the tent too close to it. Unable to stake the fly I cursed, and wondered what to do. Gobs of rain, cold as stone, drooled down the nape of my neck. Shivering like an Eskimo locked outside his igloo without a parka; my numb fingers awkwardly tied the wildly palpitating fabric to the picket fence. "Man," I shuddered, diving back inside the tent and cloaking a sleeping bag around my shaking shoulders. "I'm so cold, I could pee ice cubes."

It didn't take long for the fly to rip loose. The suddenly free end snapped in the frenzied wind like a madman's whip intent on shaping up neophyte slaves. The doors' zipper pulls jangled like a jailer's ring of keys. The frantic air reached a feverous pitch, screeching like a tormented soul enduring the burning coals of Hell.

"This is going to be one interesting night," I muttered, shoving in earplugs. I pulled my sleeping bag over my head. In the complete blackness, I punched the light button on my watch. Its face glowed copper green: 12:03. Whoooooo!

Thanksgiving

> **"On Thanksgiving Day all over America, families sit down to dinner at the same moment — halftime."**
> ~ Unknown

The sun forgot to get up in the morning. We woke from our cemetery sleep frazzled, feeling a bit dead ourselves. A pool of water, large enough to drown the average sewer rat, lay puddled in one corner of the tent. I recalled the advertising copy on the tent's box.

"Desert dry," I scoffed.

"Maybe it only applies if we camp in the desert?" Sharon grinned. It was heartening to see that someone hadn't lost her sense of humour.

I clambered out of our coffin-like sagging and drooping wet tent. *"Holy cow!"* I exploded. "Watch your step!" I cautioned my exiting partner. We were all of ten feet from a freshly dug grave. "Stumbling around in the dark last night...," I mumbled, peering wide-eyed into the muddy hole. "I have no idea how I didn't fall in."

Sharon lobbed me a taut smile. "I guess it wasn't your time."

"Yeah," I agreed. "I guess that's true. Besides," I kidded, "I'm way too young to take an extended dirt nap."

"And too handsome," Sharon responded, playing along.

"Why, thank you, dear," I replied. "Like Mother says, 'Live fast, die young, and leave a good-looking corpse.'"

Humming a happy tune, we packed our soggy tent-casket and pedalled off in rayless grey dimness, searching for a restaurant to buoy our spirits.

But, rather than a cheerful environment with petite French maidens scurrying about to care for our every whim, chagrin and disappointment met us instead. Nothing was open in Petite-Matane. All the shops in the next four towns were closed, too. *Is it because they're so small?* I wondered. We arrived in the larger settlement of Cap-Chat. Every business there was closed as well. "Huh?" I said, mystified. I was beginning to suspect we had overlooked something. "Is today a holiday by any chance?"

Sharon shrugged.

"It's not Thanksgiving, is it?"

"Hmmm," Sharon said, nodding. "That would explain all the hunters we saw yesterday. They must have been out trying to bag goose dinners."

"You know," I said, frowning, "I'm a wee bit worried we're beginning to lose touch with the real world. That's the first time I've ever missed a holiday! Especially Thanksgiving! With all that food, it's one of my favourites."

"All holidays have lots of food," Sharon reminded me.

She was right, but still, it was depressing. The inclement weather, our unknown overseas departure, deadlines looming for getting out of Canada before the snows came to stay. I needed some warm reassuring. And who, I wondered, would help my brothers-in-law eat all those lemon squares? We pedalled on, heads down, feeling homesick, missing loved ones.

The Saint Lawrence River became so wide we couldn't see the opposite bank. The river looked like an ocean. Breakers smashed against a rock retaining wall, splashing up and over the road — and onto us. Sharon's new Gore-Tex jacket did a fabulous job of keeping her dry. Soaked and miserable, I wished I would have parted with a few dollars and bought one, too.

An arctic wind howled from behind, pushing us, speeding us along at 40 kilometres an hour. The quick pace warmed us. The sun came out and our malaise lifted. Life became wonderful again ... even if we weren't gobbling hot roast turkey and savoury pumpkin pie.

A level road swept us along until 20 kilometres before Grande-Vallée. Then our route reared like a snorting stallion on hind legs. "Hey!" Sharon exclaimed. "Who paved this cliff?"

"Understatement," I grunted, and shifted onto my smallest front cog. "I should have gotten a smaller granny gear," I whimpered, my legs feeling like they were about 90-years-old.

Eighteen kilometres of knee-popping, thigh-burning inclines followed. My lungs felt as though a gorilla's hairy arm was down my throat trying to rip the pink wonders out. Then it got worse.

We spent two hours sweating up 15 percent grades, wheezing and panting like a pair of old cart horses with bronchitis. The exertion soaked us. "Look at me," I gasped. "I'm sweatin' like Mike Tyson at a spelling bee."

We pulled off the road into a closed rest area and, with difficulty, dismounted. Hypothermia became a definite possibility — the wind chill pegged the temperature below freezing. I unbungeed a two-litre plastic Coke bottle from my rear rack — I had lugged it 200 kilometres and up 4,880 vertical feet, nearly a mile straight up. "At least it's cold!" I puffed, taking a long chug.

"I think I'm colder," Sharon said. Our feet dragged behind us like frozen clods of dirt. We found a hidden spot to pitch our tent and assembled it with slow uncoordinated fingers. Shivering, we dove inside, fleeing the bitter wind, and pulled our sleeping bags around our shoulders. For 20 minutes we huddled together without speaking — but thinking warm thoughts — until we thawed enough to take out our stove. We lit the WhisperLite cooker inside our tent — actually hoping the fire would increase the air temperature (no danger of asphyxiation with the wind snapping through our much-screened abode). Sharon tore open a box of macaroni and poured it into the boiling water.

"Hey, Thanksgiving dinner in bed," I spouted.

"How romantic."

Lost Showers

> **"It does not matter how slowly you go so long as you do not stop."**
> ~ Confucius

Ice pellets tapped the rigid tent roof. It tinkled on our metal bike frames like faint strains of Aeolian music. Asininely, we ventured forth. At 83 kilometres an hour we zoomed down a steep hill, ice crystals stinging our faces like sandblasting grit, wind biting our tender cheeks. Tears streaming, we blew into Grande-Vallée — fingers so deadened I could barely squeeze my brake levers.

We entered a restaurant, chose the warmest looking location (by the kitchen) and ordered a round of hot chocolates. When my mug came, I just wanted to hold its hot frothy goodness to my frozen cheeks. After more hot chocolate, and fingers and toes thawed, we headed back out into the frosty world. Conditions had not improved. In fact, they may have deteriorated. Snowflakes fluttered through the air, as light as feathers, tickling my nostrils.

"Oh, this is something I *always* wanted to do," Sharon said. "Ride in a snowstorm. I could have done that in Edmonton!"

"Do I note sarcasm?" I asked. "Ice bikers!" I shouted into the wind. "Mount your sleds." We dejectedly pedalled out of Grande-Vallée, a lot slower than we had entered.

Hills on our route varied between 10 and 15 percent. Toiling up the grades, we sweated profusely, lathering like old plow horses; then, on descents, rivulets of perspiration froze into icy tributaries. Each climb started at river level. We ground up, slowly, slowly, conquering the knee-busting inclines, thighs threatening to cave in ... only to shoot back to river level and lose all precious elevation we had laboured in vain so hard to attain.

In 100 kilometres, we climbed a mile vertical. "My aching patella," Sharon lamented, massaging her swollen knees. "This is a masochist exercise in sadism," she declared, her teeth chattering after our umpteenth roller coaster descent.

"Yeah," I agreed. "If it's true that suffering builds character, we have a pretty good shot at becoming protagonists in the next Steven Spielberg blockbuster."

Pointe-à-la-Frégate registered a bone-chilling four degrees Celsius — and that was before the wind chill. Our feet had morphed into lumps of ice. My fingers registered no feeling at all. "Is this what frostbite looks like?" I asked, showing Sharon my whitened fingertips. "I think we better get inside and thaw out."

A warm bistro lured us in. I could have stayed forever.

"Mexico is sounding really good," Sharon said, only half-kidding. I think she was about ready to exchange her bicycle helmet for a sombrero. But, before she could do so, she discovered the clean rest room and its accompanying hot-air hand dryers. Sharon camped out beneath the hot stream (dreaming of warm tropical breezes, no doubt) until both she, and her clothes, became dry and toasty. She eventually returned. Reluctantly. A nebulous smile, like misty smoke from a wet wood fire, curled from her lips. I was happy to see she still had facial expressions.

In due time, we pried ourselves away from the salubrious environs, and continued on. In late afternoon, we arrived at Forillon National Park. It was closed. "Perfect," I sighed as we cycled around the barricade to find the best overnight spot and ran smack-dab into two workers. So much for best-laid plans.

"Is it okay to camp here?" I enquired, hoping they'd say "Sure! Pick any spot you like! They're all empty." No such luck.

"Not possible!" they both replied in unison in that French tone comprised of half-mockery, half-derision. "The park closed yesterday," one stated. Great. The dang place even had showers! Under the workers' scrutiny, we exited the park and rode away.

A hiking trail intersected the road. We scouted a ways up it. Finding a flattish spot, we dragged our bikes 30 feet up a steep incline and into concealing bush.

"This is great," Sharon marveled, gazing at the commanding view of distant mountains. An eye-arresting sunset caused us to forget the lost showers — at least momentarily.

Three cars swooped around the corner, spied the intoxicating sunset, and stopped. Thankfully, no one ventured up the trail. Maybe our luck hadn't completely run out, after all?

Quest for Percé Rock

> **"The major difference between a thing that might go wrong and a thing that cannot possibly go wrong is that when a thing that cannot possibly go wrong goes wrong it usually turns out to be impossible to get at or repair."**
> ~ Douglas Adams

The night passed peacefully: traffic-free and calm. Upon arising, my thermometer read a cool four degrees Celsius. "Have you noticed I've lost my craving for ice cream?" I said, rubbing my hands together briskly.

Our day's ride began with another frost-nipped downhill. Just when we were beginning to warm up, we came across road construction. A flagman stopped us. An oil truck coated the right lane in black muck. "They'll let us go after they finish the lane," I said. "They just don't want to splash us."

At the end of the row, the driver turned, and drenched the left lane in a mass of sticky gunk. I was still optimistic. "We can ride down the middle," I said, noting the still-free centre strip.

Oh, to be wrong twice — and so early in the morning, too. The oil truck turned 180 degrees again, and sprayed the centre. When he had finished, the entire road was one mass of oozing oily scum. I winced, half-expecting *The Monster from the Black Lagoon* to rise from its midst.

A pickup truck stopped behind us. "Hey," I said to Sharon, half-joking, "ask if we can throw our bikes into the back of his pick-me-up."

Sharon wasted no time. She whipped her bike around on a dime and pulled up to the driver's window.

"Hey!" Sharon called. "He says, 'No problem.' Hurry up and throw your bike in the back!"

"I like that a lot better than 'I think not,'" I said. Smiling, I tossed my bike into the back of the friendly Québecer's pickup. Our bikes safely stowed, the driver, instead of making us ride in the back truck box like a couple of unwanted French poodles, motioned for us to join him in the cab.

With the truck's heater on high, and the sun shining warmly through the windshield, a wave of tranquility washed over us. Warm and serene, Sharon and I nearly dozed.

"What a difference a windshield makes," I yawned.

"And a heater," Sharon said, closing her eyes and moaning. "Since I left Plumtree, down in Tennessee, it's the first time I've been warm," she said, quoting *The Cremation of Sam McGee.*

Far too soon we passed the oil, tar, and gravel construction. Our driver pulled over and let us out (had he continued down the road with us, I'd bet neither Sharon nor I would have protested). We wrestled our bikes out of the truck and onto a shoulder strewn with shards of broken glass. “Looks like we’ve arrived on the *Glasspé* Peninsula,” I joked.

In the town of Gaspé, at the Jacques Cartier shopping centre, we filled our panniers with fresh goods: eggs, milk, cereal, rye bread, muffins and doughnuts. (Never mind the pedalling! We required a huge number of calories just to keep warm.)

Sharon spied knitted gloves at the check-out counter and bought two pair. They’d make a fine addition to our infamous “stormless-shelter” gloves. “Anything to take the bite off,” Sharon said, pulling on her newest acquisition.

We filled our water bottles at a nearby marina. A worn path led us to picnic tables. The sun shone impotently. Even so, it was great to see old Sol finally making an appearance.

Apparently I was a mite hungry. I scarfed down nine eggs, six glazed doughnuts, three banana chocolate-chip muffins, and a couple of bowls of steaming hot chocolate. I suspected that if there had been a partridge in a pear tree, I would have chomped that down too.

“Talk about eating oneself into a coma!” Sharon grinned.

“Just a little fuel for my internal combustion engine,” I said, patting my stomach.

Sharon stretched back against the picnic table, not fazed by my gargantuan appetite. She had seen me eat more. Instead of staring at me in wonder and admiration, she was peering at my bike. I hated when she did that. “Bloody hell!” she suddenly exploded. I wasn’t surprised. “When’s the last time you cleaned your chain?”

Hmmm. I thought hard, but couldn’t recall. *Was it before leaving home?* Then I recollected. *“You* cleaned it last,” I informed her. “Remember that day my tire went *kablooie* (a technical term) and I went to buy a new one and had left you unsupervised with my bike?”

Sharon squinted at me like I was a bike abuser of the lowest kind. She whisked a rag off her rack, and bent to wipe my bike’s grimy rear rim. Polishing a two-inch section to gleaming chrome, she attempted to spin the tire to a new section. *“What?”* she sputtered, barely able to turn the wheel. “You’ve been riding like *this?* Your brakes are stuck on!”

“You know,” I said, rubbing my chin, “my legs have been feeling a tad tired.” Even tiny hills had been feeling akin to monster Ozark grades.

“Look here,” Sharon scolded, shaking her head and pointing a greasy index finger toward my rim. “You’ve got a broken spoke!” I looked, and sure enough, there was. *When had that happened?* I wondered. Then I recalled: the previous day, going up a steep pitch, my rear tire had jerked sideways for an instant. I figured a pebble had squirted from beneath the tire and never gave it another moment’s thought. “But you’re lucky.”

"Huh?" I interrupted. "How is a broken spoke *lucky?*"

"It's on your non-freewheel side," Sharon explained. "We won't have to remove your cluster to replace it."

"Ooh," I nodded, pursing my lips. "That *is* lucky!" Clusters can be notoriously difficult to remove in the field. (And even sometimes in a shop with the proper tools — as Arran and I discovered one sad day in Germany.)

Sharon searched the collection of spokes taped to her bike's down tube. She found one the correct length. I threaded it through, then Sharon got the tough part, truing the rim.

"Whew! Truly an art." I whistled in admiration after she completed the task 20 minutes later. "Watching you made me hungry!"

I grabbed a box of Mueslix cereal. On a side panel, the manufacture thought it prudent to caution: USE LESS THAN YOUR REGULAR CEREAL. "Harrumph," I smirked, tearing open the foil package and pouring the entire contents into my mixing bowl-sized trough. Then I added a litre of milk and four bananas. "Ah, heaven," I grinned, scooping up a mouthful. I finished the heap in record time and looked around for more. Two more banana chocolate-chip muffins and another six doughnuts disappeared down the old hatch. Eating frenzy completed I declared, "Let's ride!"

We hit the road, and were soon reminded that October daylight hours were short. We had planned on making it to Percé Rock before nightfall. (I wanted to take a photo of the morning sun rising behind it.) But, as the sun set, we were still 42 kilometres short of our goal.

We rounded a corner. In the distance, Percé Rock with its famous pierced hole loomed, rising ship-like out of the choppy grey Atlantic. We stopped to admire it and remnants of a sunset over Saint George's Bay. It was nearly dark by the time the lingering sunset faded. I went over to a house to ask if we could camp on their property. A geriatric couple, staring at me through a picture window, studied my approach. They opened the door on my first knock and peered out at me.

"Bonjour," I greeted in lilting French.

"I don't speak English," the old woman said in perfect English.

"Camping," I tried, and pointed to a swatch of land behind their house. "Tent? *Votre terre?"*

At my massacre of the French language, the old woman's husband stepped to the fore. His English was marvellous.

"You can camp by those trees," he said, gesturing to a nearby hill. "No one will mind."

I thanked them and turned to leave. The old man cleared his throat. "You can stay in the house across the road if you want," he said. "The fella who owns it lives in the States. He hasn't been here for ten years ... the last time was his 65th birthday."

"Maybe he's dead," I twirped.

"There's no electricity," the wrinkled chap continued, ignoring my capricious remark. "But the door around back is open." He craned his wattled turkey neck upwards, taking a gander at the clear sky. "Might get cold in the open tonight," he reckoned.

I thanked him, and turned to leave. The old man cleared his throat.

"The fella who owns the house used to have souvenirs inside," the old gent said. "But a gang of bikers from Toronto broke in one summer and stole them." He paused as if remembering. The old fellow cleared his throat again and pointed to the ditch. "They burned his Fleur-de-Lys flag over there." The old man raised a hand and wiped his eyes.

I shook my head. What kind of senseless act was that? And people wonder why some French dislike the English?

It was dark by the time I pried myself from their yard. I found Sharon on the grass beside our bikes, reading a book by flashlight. She had adapted to my one minute questions turning into half-hour-long ordeals. I told her about the old man's suggestion of staying in the abandoned house.

Sharon snapped her book shut. "I don't feel right about staying in someone's house without permission."

"I'm fairly sure the owner isn't going to show up tonight," I rebutted. "And we do have permission ... sort of."

But Sharon was adamant. We bypassed the "biker" house, opting instead for a little patch of ground with an expansive view of the bay. The view was indeed grand, but we needed protection from the elements. The chilly air gnawed our fingertips and licked our Popsicle toes. We assembled the tent and jumped into our sleeping bags.

I lit the candle lantern. It cast a warm buttery glow throughout the tent. We broke out milk and chomped down chocolate wafers. "Another fine dinner by candlelight," I grinned, taking a big swig of cold milk to wash down the crumbs.

"It's not exactly what I had in mind for a romantic candlelight dinner," Sharon replied. I glanced over and noticed she was so cold she was eating her portion while wearing gloves. Maybe it would be a good idea to change the subject?

"We sure are getting good value out of our candle lantern," I said. "It throws off a surprising amount of light. And candles are a lot cheaper than batteries." Like my other camping 'technology' purchases, Sharon hadn't been keen on the idea. "It'll get busted," she had said, fingering the glass enclosure when I had shown it to her. But, when the lantern isn't in use, the glass slides down into an ingenious protective metal covering. And, so far, it had survived the rigors of bouncing in my panniers.

"I'd say," Sharon said, "out of all the gadgets you've bought, this is your best." She reached her hands toward the flickering flame. "It even gives off some heat!"

Hang in There

> **"Happiness isn't good enough for me!**
> **I demand euphoria!"**
> ~ Calvin (Bill Watterson)

I peeked out the tent door. A thick coating of frost covered the grass. Icicles clung to our tent poles. I shoved my hands into wool socks and prepared to watch the lazy sunrise as rosy morning light irradiated Percé Rock. Sharon sat up, sleeping bag bunched around her shoulders.

We gazed out into the bay. A beluga whale's white bulbous head and hump appeared. It swam around the bay in tight circles, round and round. "Must be doing laps to warm up," Sharon joked. She got up and began performing jumping jacks.

We dismantled the tent, and struck off for Percé Rock without eating breakfast. The rock didn't look all that far away, and pedalling was sure to warm us.

It took an extra long time to complete those final few kilometres to Percé Rock. The fault was not just with the terrain. *Glasspé* finally did us in. Sharon's tires became enamored with the shiny stuff. As rocker Rod Stewart once crooned in his just-swallowed-a-beer-can voice, "The first cut's the deepest." Sharon suffered two flats in two kilometres. As if that weren't enough, we met with the cyclists' double bugbear: road construction and steep climbs.

The final hill into Percé was a smoking 17 percent. But it was downhill! I zoomed down like a rocket sled on rails. I could have set a new personal land speed record. But the highway emptied onto main street. As pedestrians and cars turned into the street, I envisioned my bicycle becoming a two-wheeled human rocket launcher. So, at 88 kilometres per hour, polar wind tugging at my watering eyeballs and teeth a rattling whine, I hauled on the brakes, saving life and limb — and speed record — for another day. After all our tribulations on the way to Percé Rock, I had no intention of making it my final resting place.

I cruised along the main drag and spotted a shop advertising postcards. "Just a quick stop," I said. Sharon's empty stomach protested. We still hadn't eaten a thing. "I'll be right back," I promised. Tipping my bike against the building, I dashed inside, intent on making a quick purchase.

Once inside, I became trapped by Frances, the shop's talkative owner. A full-fledged history accompanied each postcard I selected. And, since we were in Percé, she felt obligated to fill me in on the rock. The tourist attraction rose 290 feet, sheer out of the Atlantic. "And it's 300 feet wide and over a quarter-mile long," she informed me. "Its name, 'Percé,' comes from the big 50-foot arch at its seaward end — that means 'pierced,'" she explained helpfully. Even though she must have delivered the same information countless times before, her genuine affection for the area — and her fellow humans — was undeniable.

When I hadn't returned after 15 minutes, Sharon abandoned the bikes and came in to look for me. When Frances saw my riding partner, she repeated over and over how worried she was about "poor Sharon" riding her "little bicycle" out there in the big bad world "all by herself." Apparently she had forgotten I was there, too.

An hour later — tummies snarling like a starving wildcat — we extricated ourselves from the matronly owner. But before allowing us to leave, Frances handed Sharon her address and insisted we notify her when we made it home safely. It never failed to amaze us how concerned some folks were about the well-being of complete strangers. Bless their hearts.

I opened the shop door. A blast of cold air gusted in around my ankles. I shivered. "Next time," Frances advised, "come in the summer."

We bought sub sandwiches and headed to windy Ile-de Bonaventure Park. We had seen the rock from afar for so long it felt strange to be so close to it. A strong attraction drew me, like some unseen force, compelling me toward the rock. I needed to touch it.

The tide ebbed. We strolled along a shale sandbar to the rock. Standing next to the rock took me by surprise. From afar, sunlight striking its chiseled surface, Percé Rock seemed indefatigable. Herculean. Majestic. But up close, cracks fissured its surface like so much abused earthen pottery. Shards of shale perched precariously on its sides like old fish scales.

I took a deep breath, closed my eyes, and wended my palm over the rock's surface. "Tired. Tired. Tired," it seemed to whisper.

"So am I, my friend," I muttered. "So am I."

Think Heavy

> **"Now is no time to think of what you do not have. Think of what you can do with what there is."**
> ~ Ernest Hemingway

We headed toward New Brunswick, 288 kilometres distant, where we planned to exit Québec.

Rolling along a dead flat road, a slight headwind hampered our progress. A greater population peppered the Gaspé Peninsula's south side. "I hope that's because the winds are less," Sharon muttered.

In Pabos-Mills, a sign for a gym caught our eye. We needed showers. "I'm not sure I can say that French word for shower."

"Force yourself," came Sharon's reply.

I entered and asked the attendant in English if we could shower. She didn't understand. I gulped, and forced myself to say the *d-d-D* word. *"Douche."* I couldn't believe I said it. But the simple utterance opened a whole new world for me. I was soon splashing in hot, soapy delight.

"I feel like a new man," I said, exiting my refreshing *douche.* "Er, *nouveau homme,"* I sputtered to the amused clerk.

We had frolicked so long it was dark by the time we reemerged. A nearby school with a protected recess around back provided shelter.

All was well till 3 AM. Then the wind hit, yowling like a poltergeist tripping on bad acid. It blew into our alcove, ripping out tent stakes. The vestibule flapped about like a wounded albatross. A huge gust lifted one side of the tent off the ground. "Think heavy," Sharon advised. She groped out an arm and grabbed the flailing vestibule. A steady stream of biting air flowed into the tent. Wearing all our clothes we were still cold.

For the past two weeks, we had pushed our equipment's limit. My thermometer read zero Celsius. "My feet are so cold I can't sleep," Sharon griped. (On prior occasions, she had stuffed her frozen tootsies into my wool socks ... while I was wearing them. I didn't think her tactics accomplished much, other than keeping me awake.)

"Misery loves company," I muttered as she tried it again. "Would you like my wool s—." Before my sentence was fully formed, Sharon had whipped my foot coverings off. I laid there, wondering how on earth it was possible for socks to come off so fast. A snore jolted my pondering. My thoughts shifted to: *How can anyone fall asleep that fast?*

Wrapped in cold, I meditated mysteries — content in the knowledge that at least one of us was sleeping.

In the morning, I complained: "I was awake half the night with frozen feet." Then I added, "And I spent the other three-quarters of the night restraining the stupid fly."

"New math?" Sharon squinted.

"See?" I snarled (not unlike a mean-spirited wolverine). "I told you I didn't sleep at all!"

Unwisely, she pressed the matter. "So, what was all the snoring about then?"

"See?" I growled again. "You know I never sleep well when I snore." (Just call me Mr Wonderful.)

"Yeah," Sharon blinked. "Neither do I."

We packed and got underway in hopes that the pedalling would warm our bodies and spirits. But the frigid wind snorted straight into us. Frequent gusts brought us to a near standstill. Suddenly, a freak, doubly strong, gust hit me. I skittered into the middle of the lane before wrestling my bike under control.

I took back my comments about the south side of the peninsula being calmer. "Amazing anyone has any hair left!" I yelled, the wind practically ripping my lips back and forth. It was then that I realized why our former French-Canadian prime minister spoke out of the side of his mouth (a perfect trait for a politician). That horrendous Québec wind! Yep, whenever I tried to speak — the crosswind blew my lips like Jean's. And I sounded just like *dat.*

"Plenty scary!" I shouted as speeding freight trucks and autos bulled past our unsteady forms, a hair away.

"Maybe we should look for alternative transportation," Sharon suggested. "It's so cold, we're not having any fun. Maybe it would be different if you weren't so cheap and we stayed in bed and breakfasts or motels once in a while. And," she added, "we could at least eat in restaurants to warm up."

But my frugality was heavily ingrained. We stopped to eat, huddling against the leeward side of a building, ingesting a modest few hundred calories. Sharon nodded toward an approaching cyclist. "See how Québec bikers deal with drivers that come too close?" The fellow was clad in hunters' orange with a shotgun slung over his shoulder.

We cycled the windiest, dustiest, most rock strewn construction area ever. Jolted to bits, spitting sand, we could not resist the lure of a Port-Daniel train station. The grit and hissing wind had taken its toll. We were ready to be whisked away from the infernal peninsula. Sharon checked the possibility of hopping a train to Toronto. Upon learning how much it would cost to transport us and our bicycles, she changed her mind. "No wonder so few people use the train in Canada," she complained.

Half-frozen, we locomoted ourselves back outside, swung a creaky leg over our ice cars, and shivered our cabooses down more grueling kilometres.

In Shigawake, at lunch time, I bought my old standby: barbecued chicken. "Our ride in Québec should be named *'Tour du Poulet,'"* Sharon chuckled as we emerged from the grocery store. Outside, on the sidewalk, Mrs Malapropos with "the only yellow house in town" immediately accosted us.

"My daughter cycle tours," she said. My ears perked up. Someone sympathetic to our frosty plight? "I saw you two go by." I smiled. "You looked half-froze," she said warmly. I shivered on cue. "I almost invited you in."

"Uh, thanks," I said, any feeling of warmness evaporating.

"But the last time I invited cyclists in they didn't even write to thank me."

My smile vanished. *Cripes,* I thought. *If I ever meet them, I'll give them a piece of my mind!* "We'll write," I promised.

But no invitation was forthcoming. Fortunately, the more we spoke with Mrs Malapropos, the more we realized that the non-writing cyclists had done us a favour. The woman was wound tighter than a cheap wristwatch.

Thinking thoughts about the coming ice age, we pedalled away from Mrs Malapropos and Shigawake. At a nearby rest stop, we hunkered down behind a building to escape the glacial wind. The sun shone warmly upon our faces. Whitecapped Baie des Chaleurs (Bay of Warmth) sparkled in the distance.

Basking in the sunshine I took a bite of hot chicken. "I'm glad Mrs Malapropos didn't invite us in."

"Me too," Sharon sighed contentedly.

New Low

> **"I've found out why people laugh. They laugh because it hurts so much ... "**
>
> ~ Robert A. Heinlein, *Stranger in a Strange Land*

Bucking a stiff headwind, we averaged a miserly 11 kilometres per hour to Bonaventure and arrived just before sunset. We hung around outside the front doors of a grocery store, trying to look cute and adoptable, in hopes someone would offer us a place for the night. The sky was clear. Camping in the open promised to be another frigid one.

But no one offered us a bed and breakfast or even a "come and camp on my grass." The only thing we accomplished was having a lot of folks tell us what we already knew: *"Il fait froid!"* No kidding, Sherlock. Cold, indeed!

"Maybe we should write on a cardboard and hold it up: *CAMPER. VOTRE TERRE?"* I suggested.

"How about: CYCLISTS FOR ADOPTION," Sharon asked.

"That's way beyond my basic French."

Having stood around long enough in the miserable wind, trying to appear cheery and adoptable, we gave up and headed for a church. When we arrived, no one was around to ask permission. There wasn't much grass, anyway.

"Remember the municipal camp sign on the way into town?" Sharon asked. We turned around and went back to find it.

The cold wind blew us into a campground near a marina. Both were closed. Our bikes slipped deftly around the entrance posts. "Practically an invitation," I said.

Inside the compound, a collection of lavatory buildings called our names. I checked the *hommes* door and three shower doors — all locked tighter than a pickle jar lid. Around back, where the *femmes* washrooms were, I found Sharon inside the facilities.

"The door was locked, but the latch doesn't fit properly," Sharon told me. "When I pushed on the door — it popped open." She paused. "That's not breaking and entering, is it?"

"Well, you didn't break anything," I answered, not sure of the legalities when the washroom held nothing to steal ... not even a roll of toilet paper. The washroom was clean and freshly painted, all ready for the next season.

"Wow, plush," I said.

"Best of all," Sharon grinned, "it's odourless. How about if we cook supper in here? We'll be out of the wind."

"Sounds good to me."

We bounced out (making sure the door didn't latch behind us), rounded up our bikes, and carried them inside. Leaning our rides carefully against a bare wall, we hauled out our food. The countertop between sinks made a superb surface for heating our beef stew.

We ate our meal without being deafened for a change. "It sure is great being out of the wind," Sharon sighed. That's when I formulated the plan that we could stay in the john overnight. Physically and mentally exhausted from battling the nonstop gale all day, I grabbed my sleeping bag and pad. Sharon wasn't so sure about camping in a women's bathroom. But, dead-tired, I didn't give a crap that I was about to bed down in a lavatory.

I snuggled in, ready for a good night's stupor. Out of the darkness came Sharon's quizzical voice. "What's the purpose of our trip?" she asked. I was still pondering a suitable response when more questions burst forth. "What expectations do we have? Why are we doing this anyway? What do we hope to prove? What do we hope to find? Why are we inflicting these hardships on ourselves? Why did we leave so late? How could we be so foolish to think that cycling in October — even with the beautiful colours — was a good idea? My gosh!" she gibbered. "Look at us! We're sleeping in a women's toilet!"

"Potty-mouth!" I cried. "Sorry," I quickly apologized, "couldn't resist." I paused, considering, but I was way too tired to formulate a proper response to her excellent questions. Instead, I kidded, "I prefer to think of it as a small house with three bathrooms."

"Oh, brother!" Sharon muttered, clearly not smitten with my analogy. "Create your own reality! We're sleeping in a women's toilet, and you're marvelling over it?"

Apparently the journey had lost its allure. Combined with the cold weather and my cheapness about not getting motels, or even eating in restaurants, I was subjecting Sharon to an unrewarding experience that wasn't providing her with a great deal of personal satisfaction. "When I was slaving away at work," she said, "at least I was warm."

There was a long pause. Then Sharon's voice again shot from the blackness: "If this trip doesn't start getting fun real soon, I'm going home."

Princess For A Day

"Respect yourself most of all."
~ Pythagoras

I awoke with the horrible realization we had camped inside a toilet ... and I had slept like a log. My face flushed with embarrassment.

Outside, a savage cold wind howled. Instead of complaining, I should have been thanking my lucky stars for my good fortune. Without shelter I'd have suffered another sleepless night, frozen like a cow turd in January ... and tired and cranky the next day. At least it hadn't snowed, as the charming Mrs Malapropos had predicted.

Sharon, being so close to the emotional edge of calling it quits, was dubbed "Princess-for-a-day." I agreed to do anything, and everything, her little heart desired.

"Let's have breakfast at a restaurant," she said, testing her new powers.

"Certainly, my dear."

"I like this!" Sharon exclaimed. Her smile popped out for the first time in two days. We bid our commode home farewell, and rode into town to find a restaurant with a blazing fire.

Heat and piping hot food regaled us. Unfortunately, when we emerged from the restaurant's snug interior an hour later, the hostile wind felt twice as nasty. "Gosh," I said, holding my hands over my ears. "Amazing how soft I become in such a short time." We left town — straight into the horrendous headwind.

Sharon usually let me ride in front to break the diabolical wind. But, every five kilometres, she spelled me off, taking the lead on several occasions. *Hey,* I thought, *maybe I should take her to restaurants more often!* Whatever the reason, I was glad for it. Sharon had been much too spry the previous evening — peppering me with questions I didn't have the stamina to think about. When cycle touring, I found 12 hours of sack time barely enough to survive on. (If someone says a person needs an average of eight hours sleep a night, and you're only getting four, hey, I've got you covered.)

In New Richmond, attempting to solve the cold-as-ice dilemma, Princess Sharon bought fleece mitts, and two pairs of 'Chilli Willie' socks, reputed (by their own advertising) to be "the best thing for cold toes since sitting in front of a roaring fire."

She donned her new attire, and we headed out. Immediately, a mean headwind slapped us in the face. Sheer willpower and dogged determination kept us going. Have you ever been so far behind you could see yourself up ahead? We crept along, slower than sludge. Eventually, we attained a distance we usually covered in half the time. "The sooner we're off this peninsula," I whined, "the sooner we'll have less wind."

Grinding along at a laggard snail's pace, my stomach turned queasy. I had trouble pedalling. Something I ate? Or maybe from exerting myself near maximum for so long?

I spied a corner store. Reaching it (barely), I dropped my bike in the gravel. Clutching my belly, I made it inside (barely). A small sound, involuntary and wordless, broke from me. The clerk pointed to a washroom.

"Crap," I said on my re-emergence, "cycling and being sick don't mix." I climbed back aboard and pedalled for another six hours.

Early evening, near Pointe-à-la-Garde, we spotted a school playground and swung in to see if it presented any possible overnight spots. Teetering behind the school, we found an alcove surrounded on three sides.

"Looks like our best bet," I said. A ferocious gust suddenly drove into me, flapping my ears, and curling my toenails.

"Oh, I see a restful sleep with the fly flapping all night!"

"Wait," I sputtered, blinking grit. "I'll check around and see if there's anything else."

I traversed the schoolyard, scouting the area for a more sheltered site. Across a field, I spied a skating rink. Its bleached boards harboured three-foot-high weeds, but maybe the enclosure would offer better protection.

Then I spotted a shack. It didn't seem occupied. At least no smoke curled from its chimney. *Maybe it's a change house?* I suddenly realized. I slogged through the weeds and peered in a window. What I saw heartened me: a row of wooden benches for use while putting on skates. Surely no one would mind if we stayed there. And, if someone did discover us, I'd just say we were a little early for skating.

I tried the door. Locked. Loping around to the back, I found a second door. Saying a silent prayer, I jiggled the knob. The door creaked open!

I went back and told Sharon the good news. "I guess your Princess status is still in effect."

"We must be living right," Sharon sighed.

"Either that or the guardian angel pin that Pat gave you is working overtime."

We hauled our bikes inside the change house. The wind continued to rant, rattling the window panes. Handfuls of grit peppered the old glass. The wind, disgruntled that we had found sanctuary from its energy-sapping howls, was throwing a monumental temper tantrum.

Leaving the wind to beat the door, we discovered a kitchen. I flipped a light switch. "No electricity," I reported. I twisted a tap over the sink. "No water, either."

"Oh, well," Sharon said. "Beggars can't be choosers," she said. "I'm just glad we're inside."

She was right. Rather than complaining, I should have been counting my blessings. I put on a happy face and helped whip up noodle soup, tuna sandwiches, and hot chocolate. For the first time in a long while, we sat on real chairs, at a real table. Luxury! Who needed electricity?

"What's the forecast?" Sharon asked between bites. I turned on our battery-operated radio. The weatherman was calling for a daytime *high* of four degrees Celsius, accompanied by a meteorological cocktail of precipitation: freezing rain mixed with flurries, ice pellets, and a chance of rain later in the day.

"Oh, it just keeps getting better and better," Sharon grimaced. "We'd better get overseas and head south. Fast. Before we freeze to death. Almost all the leaves have blown off the trees, anyway."

"Yeah," I sniffed. "Seeing how strong the wind is I'm surprised trees are still standing."

Roger and Suzanne

> **"Friendship improves happiness and abates misery by doubling our joys and dividing our grief."**
> ~ Joseph Addison

A crisp Sunday morning welcomed us across the Restigouche River from Pointe-à-la-Croix, Québec, to Campbellton, New Brunswick. Throwing our hands into the air, we high-fived one another. Cheers all around! We had survived the Gaspé's debilitating headwinds.

"Let's find a breakfast buffet and celebrate!" We cruised Campbellton's main drag, up one side and down the other. No luck. In a scant two minutes, we were on our way out of town.

"Campbellton's not as big as I had hoped," I whined. In nearby Atholville, we pulled into a small corner grocery store. I went in and asked the lone clerk if he knew of a place that served extra large breakfasts.

Upon my exit, I had only sad news to report. Seeing my long face, Sharon suspected the answer. Straddling our bikes on the gravel shoulder, I lamented our plight. A VW van puttered alongside. The passenger window rolled down. In a sing-song French-Canadian lilt, a woman enquired, "Where are you two headed on such a fine day?"

"Around the world," Sharon replied. "That is, if we can find somewhere to eat."

Suzanne, a petite blonde with green eyes, introduced herself, and then the smiling driver as her husband, Roger. "We're on our way to church," Suzanne said. "Our daughter, France, plays the organ there. We'll be home in about an hour and we'd be delighted if you'd join us for lunch."

"Woo-hoo!" I said. "Who needs buffets when friendly New Brunswickers are out and about?" We quickly accepted, got directions, and waved them on their way. Talk about getting the sweet end of the lollipop for a change.

"So," Sharon grinned as the van puttered off, "what do you want to do for an hour?"

"Eat!" came my immediate reply.

We rolled on to Tidehead where we indulged in a quick snack to tide us over before lunch. A sign explained that Tidehead was the point where the surge stopped becoming a bore. I chuckled. "Is this where it quits talking about itself?"

Just before noon, we pedalled off in search of Roger and Suzanne's house. We found their two-storey home overlooking the Restigouche River. (According to legend, a Micmac chief named the river. A rival band of Mohawk were poaching salmon. The Micmac designed a hasty battle plan; the chief expressed his opposition over the ill-conceived details. When his son and the entire Micmac party were slain on the river bank, the distraught chief named the river: "He who disobeys his father.")

Picture windows on Roger and Suzanne's house gazed toward Québec and its few remaining sienna and burnt orange-coloured leaves. As we pulled into the yard, Roger tumbled out of the house.

"Quite the view!" I commented.

"The leaves are nearly finished," Roger said, waving casually. "You should see them at their height. Spectacular! We never tire of the scenery ... it's constantly changing."

"I'd like to live beside a river someday," I said.

"You should see it in the summer," Roger said enthusiastically. "It's a World Heritage River. Thousands canoe it. Avid fishermen recognize it as one of the best rivers in the world for salmon and trout fishing."

"Thousands canoe it?" I said. "That must be quite a sight."

"Oh, it is," Roger assured me. "You'll have to do it some time," he said. "I did it one summer with our girls and it was a party I'll never forget. Some people had entire canoes filled with beer!

"We'll store your bikes in the garage," Roger said, steering us toward a separate structure. We didn't plan on being there *that* long. I wondered if they had a high crime rate and our new friend was just being extra cautious. But our lucky streak was still rolling.

"You folks are invited to spend the night," Roger said. "Our eldest daughter, Sonia, is away at uni in France. You're welcome to use her room."

We parked our bikes, grabbed clean clothes, and followed Roger as he ushered us downstairs.

The "room" turned out to be an entire suite. A kitchen area held stove, fridge, table, chairs, and a television set. There was a separate bathroom. And a bedroom, complete with feather duvet and cozy flannel sheets, looked more than inviting.

"Wow! Deluxe digs," I said, looking around and marvelling. We dropped our kits on the bed and followed Roger upstairs.

While Suzanne fried eggs for sesame seed Kaiser bun sandwiches, Roger gave us a quick tour of the house. Extensive wood, brick, and tile complemented the main living area. "I did it myself," Roger said, when we remarked on its wonderful blend of textures. "There's an upper suite, too," he added. "We rent it out. It's a great way to pay the mortgage."

Suzanne called that everything was ready. Sharon and I, grinning like a pair of hyenas invited to a zebra kill, slid onto comfy seats around an oak table. Large windows overlooked white and yellow birch, trembling aspen, balsam poplar and the "river out of Eden," as one American writer saw fit to term the Restigouche.

Roger worked as a psychiatric nurse at a local hospital. Suzanne was a nurse as well, but she had taken a fall on some ice and had broken her wrist. She was on leave. "I don't miss work one bit," she said.

"Me neither," I concurred.

"Yeah, work is somewhat overrated," Sharon summed up.

"It certainly takes up a lot of one's free time," I added.

"Free time," Roger said, mulling the words, turning them over slowly in his mouth as he chewed his sandwich. "If I had more time," he finally decided, "I think I'd travel more."

We hit it off immediately with Roger and Suzanne. Adventurers at heart, they entertained us with stories of their past camping and canoeing escapades. In a couple of hours, we felt as if we'd known them all our lives. After a round of ice cream and apple pie, we all hopped in their VW van and motored off to watch France and her dance group practice.

A guided tour of the picturesque area ensued. We zipped to see Sugarloaf, a local ski hill, intended, perhaps, to impress us prairie flatlanders. But in comparison to the Rocky Mountains, we found it little more than a bump. Folks tend to forget that Alberta, along with its vast plains, is also home to some of the highest peaks in the Canadian Rockies. (Mount Columbia, in Alberta's Jasper-Banff National Park, rises 3747 metres. In comparison, New Brunswick's highest point of land, Mount Carleton, stands a more modest 820 metres.)

Painted on a rock face, Roger pointed out two red and white crosses. "That's where a mother and daughter died, trying to scale the bluff," Roger said. "I climbed it once," he recounted, "when I was 16. But I only did it once." He paused, recollecting. "In one spot, I remember being a bit concerned. I couldn't go up or down...."

All that talk about climbing made me hungry. We returned home in time for supper. Suzanne had set the oven timer and roasted a large farm chicken. Generous quantities of mashed potatoes, squash, carrots, red and yellow tomatoes, and corn on the cob, complemented the meal.

"All homegrown," Roger stated, his voice edged with pride.

Dessert was delicious, too — more of Suzanne's scrumptious pie made from a neighbour's apples. "How do you manage to get the crust so flaky?" I asked.

"It's my secret recipe," she teased.

"What's the secret ingredient?" I kidded.

"7-Up," she confided.

"It's not a secret any more," I said.

While Suzanne rustled up tea and biscuits, Roger strolled Sharon and me through their vegetable garden.

"What's this?" I asked, puzzled at a profusion of greenery.

Roger laughed. "In the spring, I plant three seeds together: corn, squash, and string bean. The beans climb the corn. They tangle together and help keep the wind from blowing down the stalks. The squash covers the ground and helps retain moisture while preventing weeds."

"Brilliant!" I said. "How did you ever think of that?"

"Oh, it wasn't too difficult," Roger replied, smiling. "The ancient Inca and Maya civilizations devised the gardening strategy long before the birth of Christ."

"I learn something new every day," I said.

"Those ancients are always stealing our good ideas," Sharon joked.

"Sounds like we should celebrate the idea," I decided.

We returned inside for more apple pie and multiple cups of Red Rose tea. Over many refills, we shared our cycling tales with Roger and Suzanne.

"Do you ever have trouble finding washrooms?" Suzanne asked as I suddenly excused myself to use theirs.

"Not usually," Sharon replied. "A couple of nights ago, we slept in a women's washroom."

"Holy crap!" Suzanne erupted, green eyes wide.

Well looked after, we savoured our time with our new friends. Often, when we were travelling, it seemed that whenever we were at our absolute lowest, someone (or something) came along and lifted our flagging spirits. Sharon had been resigned that she was destined to endure frozen hands and feet until southern Spain. Instead, Roger and Suzanne rescued us, warmed our fingers and toes — not to mention our souls — with their generous hospitality, easy and abundant laughs, and bottomless cups of scalding tea.

We headed off to our downstairs suite to get ready for bed. After a luxurious long steamy shower, we felt pampered indeed.

"Clean, warm, and dry," I said, towelling myself off. "Hard to think of anything better."

"And imagine," Sharon said, flashing me a wide smile, "all three at the same time."

We slipped into a warm and comfy bed. Fleece sheets caressed us. We tugged the comforter to our chins. The scent of spring meadow potpourri floated through the air.

"Sure beats mint deodorizers," Sharon murmured.

Trifle The Ticket Man

> "If you obey all of the rules,
> you miss all of the fun."
> ~ Katherine Hepburn

Following our night's blackout, we awakened refreshed for the first time in ages.

After breakfast, Roger bid us adieu and drove off to work. With Suzanne's help, we phoned several travel agents. Roger and Suzanne had convinced us that, rather than fly from Halifax or Toronto to Spain or Portugal, we would get a much better deal by flying from Montréal to Paris. And since their daughter Sonia had flown to Paris the previous month, they already knew some good places to check.

Airlines' price variance shocked me. A thousand dollar difference stood between the lowest and highest fares. Narrowing our choices to two, we wrestled with the final decision. Sharon's favourite: a Paris package consisting of three night's hotel, continental breakfasts, and airport transportation. (Transportation cost wasn't a trivial matter: Sonia's taxi ride had cost her big bucks ... when she found one that would take her. The first cabbie had brushed her off, "I don't have time to take you into the city." Huh? Wasn't that his job? She tried the train next. An agent told her, "Go back where you came from! Immigrant!" And that was how folks in France treated someone who spoke fluent French? Yikes. Sharon and I, true monoglots, were more than a little apprehensive about our foray into their territory.)

The other finalist was a one-way flight to Orly airport, south of Paris, for a paltry amount. The deal clincher came down to the fact that the three-night Paris package had a later flight date. Combined with the three nights in Paris, we would have six fewer days to reach Lisbon where we were to meet Sue and Vicky. It would be difficult enough without losing *any* riding days. Sharon conceded her Paris aspirations for the time.

We phoned to book the one-way tickets. The travel agent said he was sorry, but he couldn't accept a verbal confirmation.

"What?" I gasped. "For a credit card transaction?"

"We require a signature, sir."

Flummoxed, I blanked, then stammered, "Will you accept a fax confirmation?"

"Oh, yes, sir," he said. "As long as you sign it."

"I'll send a fax right away," I promised. I hung up the phone, and belly laughed. "He has no idea what my signature looks like."

"Certain rules make no sense," Sharon agreed when I explained why I had to send a fax.

Suzanne phoned Roger at work. Roger helpfully signed *my* signature and faxed the confirmation to the ticket agency.

A few minutes later, I rang the travel agent back. "Have you received the fax with my signature?"

"Yes, sir, everything is in order," the agent assured me. "Your tickets will be waiting for you at the airline counter."

I hung up the phone. Sharon smiled. "Now," she said, "all we have to do is get to the airport on time."

"Piece of cake," I prattled. Perhaps I was being just a tad over-confident?

Invitation

> **"People who accumulate lots of road rash over a lifetime have spent their lives happy."**
> ~ Tim Parker

Roger arrived home at noon. After lunch, we prepared to hit the road, our panniers stuffed with leftover chicken and apple pie. Saying goodbye, we learned our new friends had one more surprise in store for us. "We're planning on visiting our daughter, Sonia, in France at Christmas," Roger said. "We have two suites booked for a month on the French Riviera. We're inviting you to come and stay with us." Sharon and I stood in flabbergasted silence. I'm sure my mouth dropped open.

"There'll be plenty of room," Suzanne added. "We probably won't even be there much of the time," she said. "We want to explore the area and go to Paris for a week."

Still in shock, we assured them that if we were anywhere near the French Riviera at Christmas, we'd be there.

"If you decide to, just give us a call and we'll give you the details," Roger grinned.

We hugged them, and pedalled off, waving until we were out of sight, excited about the possibility of meeting up with them in two months.

The bright sun skipped its way across a cloudless denim blue sky. And, for the first time in days: no wind! Highway 17, lined by thick stands of evergreens, whisked us toward the New Brunswick - Maine border. Our plans had been slightly revised. Instead of meandering casually through Nova Scotia to Halifax we were now hustling in the opposite direction. We hoped to catch warmer temperatures and glorious hardwood autumn leaves by dipping south into Maine, heading west through New Hampshire, Vermont, and then north, back into Québec to catch our flight from Montréal's Mirabel airport.

With the great weather, it should have been a tranquil forest ride. But it wasn't. The narrow road, combined with weighty logging trucks, made for a tense journey. The trucks boomed past in both directions. In ten short kilometres, we were twice forced to ditch onto the shoulder or eat spruce.

"No matter how much ketchup I put on those wood chips, I'm sure they're going to taste lousy," I grumped. "Good thing I put on that knobby front tire," I said. "Sure handles better than skinny touring tires. More rolling resistance, but it beats picking gravel out of my palms."

Logging traffic diminished as the forest changed from conifers to groves of poplars. Branches barren, leaves already departed, skeletal trees waved long bony fingers in the slight breeze. With a ghost-like glide, we swept up a long hill into Robinsonville. (Hey, we did it! Roger had warned us we'd *never* pedal *all* the way up Robinsonville Hill. But, it was no problem. Pyrenees, here we come!)

Robinsonville townsfolk displayed a raunchy sense of Halloween gallows humour. Headless men, clad in red and blue plaid lumberjack shirts, sat on veranda rockers. Giant pumpkins, along with sinister depictions of black cats, witches, and ghosts, infested front yards. Tombstones leaned at crazy angles like a hag's crooked teeth. One headstone, bearing the current date, read: JASON RIP (did it stand for 'REST IN PIECES'?). A hand groped out of the still fresh grave. "I guess it's true," I said. "There is no rest for the wicked."

Grind

> **"I don't suffer from insomnia —**
> **I enjoy every minute of it.** ~ Unknown

Near nightfall, we came across a closed-for-the-season picnic area. "Looks like an ideal spot," Sharon said.

In the morning, we opened our eyes to a frosty wonderland. *Inside* the tent! The drop in temperature and our exhalations had sublimated into intricate lacy crystalline patterns.

The frost burned off, and we got underway. The terrain had altered significantly since we'd left the Gaspé Peninsula. Rolling hills replaced Gaspé's tormenting 17 percent grades. Sweeping water vistas changed to dense blocks of dark forest. The fir trees obstructed our views, but they also did a fine job of curtailing the dogged winds that had hounded us all along the peninsula.

Second-growth 40-foot-tall evergreens sprouted in tidy row upon row, like giant carrots planted by bunny people. Hemming us in both right and left, it felt akin to wearing enormous green blinders. We rode for miles through nothing but towering fir and spruce. (The soil may not be great for agriculture, but it knows how to grow trees. Forest covers 90 percent of New Brunswick.)

In Saint Quentin, weary of anything coniferous, we settled down to lunch beneath an apple tree. Its naked arms swayed under a deep cobalt sky; bright red apples clung tenaciously to leafless branches like fragile ornaments on a Charlie Brown Christmas tree.

At 5:30 PM, we arrived at Saint-Léonard Provincial Park. Unlike the height of tourist season, on this fine October day, we had the entire place to ourselves. No screaming kids like misbegotten banshees; no motorhome generators buzzing like angry bees. Even the wind in the trees seemed to whisper sweet lullabies in hushed tones.

Tucked into our sleeping bags by 7 PM, the night air clamped down with an icy breath. Teeth chattering, we realized we were in for another cold sleep.

"This routine is wearing me down," Sharon said, pulling her sleeping bag around her nose. "All we do is pack, ride, unpack," came the muffled grumble.

She was right. Our relaxed pace had turned into a race. And the short daylight hours weren't doing us any favours — little time remained for anything but riding. However, with our airline tickets booked, it was necessary to crank out a requisite number of kilometres each day to ensure we made it to Montréal in time.

"When we get to Europe, we'll slow down," I said, happily ignoring that once there we had to cover two thousand kilometres in three weeks to meet Sue and Vicky in Portugal by our appointed date.

"Yeah, right," Sharon mumbled.

Not So Smart Aleck

> **"Never be bullied into silence. Never allow yourself to be made a victim."**
> ~ Harvey Fierstein

"What is your purpose in the US?" a border guard enquired brusquely at Maine's Van Buren crossing.

I want to see if you're cutting trees as fast as New Brunswick, I thought. But I answered, "We want to check out your autumn colours."

Eyes narrowed, he rephrased his question, and stated it slowly — like I was a titch daft. (Or maybe he thought I was French, and if he spoke deliberately enough, I would understand?)

Nope. Not me. *I haven't seen enough disposable diapers in the ditch lately,* I thought. But I answered, "We want to see New England's fall foliage."

All border guards — I know now — are trained in mental telepathy. He read my smart aleck mind, and figured we were two plumb crazy Canucks, shy a few eggs of a full carton. Who else but someone certifiably insane would be riding in such seriously cold weather? To see leaves? Give me a break.

"Take your bikes around the corner," he said, pointing to the side of the building.

I turned to Sharon. "Did I win a prize?"

"I don't think so," she mumbled.

"Maybe you should take care of the questions from now on."

"Gee, ya think?"

We wheeled our little bicycles to the side of the building as instructed. A sullen officer met us near an area of narrow bench-like tables. Before I even leaned my bike over, he unzipped a rear pannier and began groping about the dank interior. I hoped he didn't discover any long-forgotten banana corpses.

"Any switchblades?"

"Aren't those illegal?"

He frowned. "Do you carry a gun?"

"Nope," I responded. "Too heavy."

"Any ammunition?"

"For the gun I don't carry?" I said, then sighed, remembering whom I was speaking to. "Sorry," I apologized. "Nope. No gun. No ammunition."

"Go inside!" he barked, sending me for an attitude adjustment. Being a comedian quick with answers wasn't always the best when dealing with border crossing guards. In the future I would try to remember to engage brain before opening mouth.

Leaving the officer to probe touring cyclists' curiosities, Sharon and I began the long march to the office. Jeez. I hoped a strip search wasn't next on our list of pleasantries.

"Know what the queer guy said when officers conducted a rectum search for drugs and didn't find anything?" I whispered to Sharon. "I'd like a second opinion."

"Shaddup, already," Sharon grinned.

"Passports," an agent demanded as we approached the counter. (His request was unusual — Canadians required only a driver's license or birth certificate to enter the States.) But, because Sharon and I planned on heading overseas, we indeed possessed passports.

The officer, taken aback slightly when we handed him passports, flipped open the shiny new booklets. Scanning the personal information, he punched some data into a computer.

"You're a teacher?" he sniffed, eyeing my unkempt hair. I sort of had the Don King thing going that morning. Sharon had been bugging me for the past month to get a haircut. *Good thing I cut off my ponytail,* I thought.

"And you're a *Chartered Accountant?"* he practically snorted at Sharon. The disheveled female presence before him appeared markedly different from the passport image with coiffed hairdo and natty business suit. I nodded my condolences.

When the officer finished his questions, I quizzed him. Might as well not make our unscheduled stop a total wash, I figured. "Where's the best place in Van Buren to eat?" I asked. "Well, not the *best,"* I corrected myself. "Where can I get the most food for the least amount of money?"

"That would be John's on main street."

Not finding anything amiss, the agent surrendered our documents and returned us to retrieve our bikes and their contents. Or rather, what was left of them. Eight panniers worth of goods lay scattered along the tables, zippers yawning wide, innards strewn about like so many discarded pig entrails.

"Maybe they wanted to know what to take on their next bike tour?" Sharon laughed, shoving items back into her bike bags.

I took the opportunity to re-organize my packs. "Hey, look!" I spouted, holding up my long-lost Swiss army knife. "Thought I'd lost this puppy somewhere back in Saskatchewan."

We saddled up, and, humming a happy tune, waved to the guards as we pedalled past. "Thanks, guys!" I called. A thinly veiled smirk rewarded my effort.

In Van Buren, we spotted John's café. "Lunch time! Might as well see if that guard knows what he's talking about." We parked, entered, and sat at a window booth where we could keep an eye on our bikes. I overheard a clique of old-timers at a table in the rear speaking in French. Maybe the border guard hadn't been trying to be condescending after all (about half of New Brunswick's population speaks French).

I ordered the lunch special. "I hope it's big," I remarked to the efficient waitress. "I'm fairly hungry."

"Oh, it's plenty big," she assured me.

She was right. A few minutes later, two turkey-sized serving platters, laden beneath multiple slabs of roast beef, arrived. A sea of dark brown gravy lapped at the shores of a pair of Double-D-sized hills of mashed potatoes. "Dolly!" I spouted. Heaps of bright orange carrots, yellow turnips, and green beans added a colourful touch. "Not bad," I said with a smile, calculating the calories on my enormous plate, "especially considering the price is what we usually pay for a slice of pie."

"I hope I can still pedal," I moaned, waddling forth nearly an hour later. I mounted up. My knees hit my stomach with each pedal revolution. We rode due south under a faultless blue sky.

Surrounded by trees that were no longer naked, we basked in windless mid-20 degree Celsius temperatures. When was the last time we had seen such fine conditions?

The terrain slipped past. "Cycling is fun again," Sharon said with a wide grin, sun splashing off her dappled cheeks.

Near dusk, at a turnoff to the local Monticello campground, we met two teens who had been drinking by the river.

"Are you guys party animals?" the cinder-eyed one asked.

"Not really," Sharon answered in a weary tone. "After pedalling all day, we don't have enough energy left to poop, let alone party."

"I guess you'd call us party-poopers," I said.

"Well," the other continued, ignoring me, "we left a fire burning that you're welcome to use."

We descended to the riverside, and found the pleasurable flames as promised. After warming ourselves to a toasty glow, Sharon reconnoitered for a camping spot. She discovered an unlocked cookhouse door. "Life is good," she smiled. We pushed our bikes inside and set up our tent. Observing our protected confines, Sharon grinned again. "We're going to be warm tonight."

I laughed at how content she seemed to be. "It's wonderful to see that it doesn't take much to make you happy these days. Some food, a little fire, a place to lay your head ... talk about getting back to the basics."

"Like they say," Sharon murmured, unrolling her sleeping bag, "happiness isn't having what you want; happiness is wanting what you have."

Keag's Hospitality

> "Estimated amount of glucose used by an adult human brain each day, expressed in M&Ms: 250."
> ~ *Harper's Index*

Rain trip-trapped across the cookhouse roof like small billy-goat hoofs on a wooden bridge. But, instead of hunkering down, and waiting out the drizzle — enjoying our dry refuge — the two trolls packed up and hit the road.

"If we're going to catch Sue and Vicky in Portugal, we'd better get a move on," I prodded.

The lashing rain sapped our energy reserves. Near Houlton, we pulled in to a rest stop and consumed a dozen doughnuts. Strictly medicinal, of course. Blood glucose level zoomed into the hyper zone. Under the influence of a sugar buzz, I listened to a busload of giddy seniors ("recycled teenagers," Sharon called them).

"*Where* are we going again?" a blue-haired woman with a jutting jaw questioned. "Nova-*what?*" she intoned upon hearing they were on their way to Nova Scotia. "How do you spell that?" she asked, thrusting her jaw even more forward. While motion may not necessarily constitute progress, apparently the most important thing was that one was going. We got underway ourselves, back into the grey mist and drizzle.

The rain in Maine turned into an all-day pain. By evening, in Mattawamkeag, I was past drenched. We donned dry clothing, and entered Keag's café, seeking warmth and respite from the horrid outdoor conditions. The folks treated us well, feeding us, joking with us, warming our bodies and spirits. They even suggested we could find a camp spot behind their café.

So, after supper, in sulky light, we explored the area, searching for high ground. Each step squelched deep into sodden grass. Squish. Squash. Sploosh. "So much for dry socks!" I lamented.

But our search was not in vain. Amongst the swings and teeter-totters, we found a playhouse on a raised platform. In the murky dimness, even though I couldn't see Sharon's expression, I knew she had hit upon the same idea. High. Roof. Perfect. Being suspended five-feet above the ground suited us just fine. Bring on the rain!

In near blackout — no moon or stars to aid us — we pitched our tent on the tiny wooden platform, poles dangling off into mid-air.

"Swiss Family Robinson-style," Sharon concluded.

"Yeah," I muttered, sleepily. "If you go out tonight, remember that first step's a doozy."

Home Sweet Cabin

"We knew it would rain, for all the morn
A spirit on slender ropes of mist
Was lowering its golden buckets down
Into the vapory amethyst."
~ Thomas Bailey Aldrich, *Before the Rain*

We slept the night like jungle cats perched in a secure tree. Upon arising, a child's round face peered out at us from a house across the lane. While we decamped, I'm sure every member of the household took a wide-eyed turn at the window to gawk at us. "Jeez," Sharon commented, "the way they're staring, you'd swear they'd never seen anyone camped on their playground equipment before."

Past East Corinth, in the hosing rain, we pedalled by acres of oak, maple, and birch. The autumnal colours almost made the wet weather worth enduring. Almost. Luckily the riding was easy. On downhills, we coasted — wind ringing through our spokes like wind chimes. It would have been downright pleasant if it hadn't been for the foul weather.

We passed a house. Three pink-nosed kids and a dog stared out a rain spattered window pane at us. "Too wet to play," I said.

"I wonder what they're thinking?" Sharon asked.

A spackle of cold rain pinged the nape of my neck. "I'd rather not know," I replied as the raindrop slid down my back.

Wet and cold, somewhere west of Canaan, we arrived at deserted George Lake Park. A lone duck landed, emanating concentric ripples across the dusk-lit pond. A row of rustic cabins graced the waterfront. A quick check revealed two unlocked cabins. Sharon grinned. "How are we ever going to choose?"

"The largest," I suggested.

Inside a spacious one-room cabin, we scattered our equipment. "I hope this stuff dries before we fly to Europe," I said.

With wet synthetic and natural fibres draped everywhere, we laid out our sleeping bags on the floor (at least they were still dry — thank heaven for plastic bags). Lying in the dark — listening to rain patter the cabin roof and waiting for sleep to overtake us — we suddenly heard voices.

"I wonder how you rent a cabin?" one said.

"Should I yell 'the far one's open'?"

"Shhh," Sharon shushed me. "I hope they don't discover us."

They didn't (although if they had, I'm not sure who would have been more surprised). After they departed, we weren't disturbed again. We arose refreshed and in good spirits — even though our musty gear was still damp.

Beaver Tales

"Life is not measured by the number of breaths we take, but the moments that take our breath away."
~ George Carlin

At the aptly named Pleasant View rest stop, a golden sun finally broke through depressing cloud cover. Streams of buttery-yellow light coddled us in warmth. Sharon even removed her rain pants!

"Your legs are looking fit," I commented, glimpsing sight of her gams for the first time in days.

"Thanks," she allowed. "But they're tired ... like the rest of me." We were still feeling the effects of our deadline drive.

We pushed westward. The landscape around us became drier. Papery leaves scrunched under our treads. Beneath an arched bridge, Androscoggin River reflected hues of shimmery autumn crimsons and golds.

"Ah, fall in New England!" I exclaimed, breathing in the pungent, yet pleasant, fragrance of burning leaves. A cool breeze waltzed through stands of oaks and maples. Leaves drifted downward in their final, silent, earthbound dance, swirling, sailing, pirouetting on unseen eddies.

"This is exactly what I hoped to see," Sharon said, a radiant smile stretching across her face. "When the sun is shining it's perfect."

But perfection is not of this world, and it began to rain.

In late afternoon, skies clearing near Bethel, we stopped at a rest area to refuel. Cumulus clouds, flecked with pink underbellies, dramatized the sky. We were still oohing and aahing when darkness fell.

Oof. The air drained from me like a well-placed kick to the solar plexus. We hadn't planned on staying overnight at the rest area. Near us, a prominent NO CAMPING sign waggled in the breeze. We debated. Which was worse? Riding in the dark? Or breaking a rest area's no-camping rule?

"Let's ignore the sign," I suggested, not at all eager to ride in the dark. Staying at the rest area was the healthier of the two evils. Sharon wasn't keen, but she agreed that riding in daylight hours was hazardous enough.

We pushed our bikes along a riverbank trail. Small woodland creatures scurried through the underbrush creating a tense calm — their tiny footfalls cracking like shotgun blasts.

A small clearing, ten feet from the river's edge, came into sight. "This'll do," Sharon whispered. We pitched the tent in near blackness and total silence, worried that someone might see or hear us. A beaver's tail suddenly smacked the water, breaking the forest's dark tranquility, and echoing through the woods like a jealous lover's slap. A small gasp broke from me.

Sharon laughed. "A little jumpy are we?"

"I always jump when a female cracks the whip," I joked, quickly regaining my composure.

"And how, may I ask, do you know it's a female?"

"Well ... it's a beaver, isn't it?"

"Ohhh," Sharon groaned. "I'm way too tired for your asinine jokes."

"Ooh, baby, I love it when you talk dirty." In the dark, I couldn't see her eyes, but I knew they were rolling.

Embarrassing

> **"Climb the mountains and get their good tidings. Nature's peace will flow into you as sunshine flows into trees. The winds will blow their own freshness into you, and the storms their energy, while cares will drop away from you like the leaves of Autumn."**
>
> ~ John Muir

Dismantling our tent in pre-sunrise glow, we reversed our previous night's footsteps along the river to the rest area. Near the parking lot, a truck's backup beeper sounded. We didn't give it any thought ... until we materialized from the bush and into the stark parking area.

A maintenance crew stared. We felt about as inconspicuous as Shaquille O'Neal at a midget convention. Sharon, still harbouring pangs of guilt about our unlawful overnight stay, visibly cringed.

However, rather than lecture us about the feloniousness of rest area camping, the workers ignored us and went about their business. Sharon's eyebrows rose. I could tell that, like a juvenile delinquent who realized her crime held no consequence, she changed from feeling guilty to planning future rest area camping!

Covered Bridge

"Who has never tasted bitter does not know what is sweet."
~ German Proverb

Near the town of Newry, Sunday River flowed unruffled and limpid beneath a covered bridge known as Artist's Bridge (in the state of Maine it is the bridge most painted by artists). This magnificent structure — an 1872 Paddleford truss — spans 87-feet. We stopped for breakfast under its cover, marvelling at its wooden peg construction. I dropped bits of cheese into the river, and watched as a dozen finger-sized fish darted in from all directions to nibble the offering.

Upon entering New Hampshire, a state sign greeted us: COLLISIONS WITH MOOSE IN NEW HAMPSHIRE: 211.

"Wow!" I exclaimed. "That's a whole lot of moose!"

"What do drivers think they are?" Sharon wondered. "Speed bumps?"

"Only in Newfoundland," I replied.

"Never a good idea to slap a moose."

The Appalachian Trail intersected our route. "Want to check it out?" Sharon asked. "Maybe we'll see a moose."

"Sure," I answered. "My legs could use a stretch." (Being chased by a moose does that.)

We hid our bikes behind bushes, and struck out on the famed trail. Our brief portion presented us with a series of hummocks cloaked in immense stands of ghost-white birch. Devoid of leaves except for a puffy yellow crown, they imitated burning candles at a centenarian's celebration.

After too short a distance, we forced ourselves to turn back. Just as in cycle touring, we'd found ourselves wondering: "What's around that next corner?" But lunch called — the mysteries of the Appalachian Trail would have to wait another day.

"Let's eat at a nice restaurant today," Sharon said.

"Aw, gee," I whined, backpedalling. "Do we have to?"

"Yes, we do," Sharon declared. "We're out of stove fuel, anyway," she added.

"Aw," I whined again. "Do I at least get to see what it looks like first?" My dislike of going into upscale eateries — and Sharon's insistence on them — was a source of friction. I didn't enjoy the restaurants because I felt grubby. (Worse, fancy-schmancy restaurants usually didn't serve biker-size portions and I often left hungry and feeling taken advantage of.)

Sharon liked restaurants because she could relax, be out of the elements, and enjoy an appetizing meal we couldn't easily prepare for ourselves (cheese soufflés, even with Sharon's masterful culinary skills, were beyond the capabilities of a blowtorch stove). I suspect clean washrooms held an attraction, as well.

I rode along, head down, not in a cheery mood. In Gorham, Sharon spotted a mamby-pamby restaurant. I groaned. Just by the outside, I could tell it was one of *those* places.

Sharon cajoled. Still not happy, I reluctantly entered niminy-piminy and took a cushy seat, feeling as though I had to sit on the edge so as to not smirch the flowery fabric.

With a frowny face I gaped around. The decor was much too posh for my taste. "Obviously," I griped, "they're spending my dollars on amenities other than food." (I preferred something similar to Coalmont's Heartbreak Hotel — where I knew the only things they spent money on were the basics. I tried to follow two time-tested observations when choosing eating establishments. One: Never eat at a place called 'Mom's.' Was she really that great a cook? Two: Never eat at a place that employs the word "grub" when describing their fare. Sorry, but 'pub grub,' or even 'good grub,' doesn't cut it for palatable chow.)

A winsome lass appeared. I ordered the lunch special: 'American Chop Suey,' in hopes of a respectably large serving.

When my meal arrived, I complained (after the waitress left, of course, like a good Canadian).

Sharon squinted. "You're ruining my appetite."

"That's a *good* thing," I shot back. "Look at the piddly size of this!" I pointed to my minuscule entrée. "American Chop Suey! Phooey! For plain old macaroni and hamburger, I'd think they could at least serve up a decent amount."

I shoveled in my dainty portion in record time, then sat grumbling, complaining almost as cantankerously as my stomach. "When the waitress comes back," I whispered to Sharon, "and asks how I found my meal, I'm going to say, 'I lifted a mushroom, and there it was!'"

"Don't you dare!" Sharon hissed.

The waitress, wise beyond her years, never did come back. After 20 minutes, I rose and treaded to the till, paid and exited, my stomach still protesting its emptiness.

Across the street, I spied a bakery with a promising name: LOAFING AROUND. I strolled over and checked out their wares. They were more to my tastes. After inhaling half a dozen luscious cream-filled pastries I began to feel half-human again.

"I hope you're satisfied," Sharon chided, still teed off about my boorish restaurant behaviour.

Wiping confectioner's sugar from my lips, I muttered an apology. Hunger often elicited my less genteel qualities.

We moved on to a hardware store, searching for Coleman fuel. When the fellow there discovered we were on bikes, and didn't need a whole gallon of fuel, he offered to fill our bottles for a buck each. Apparently I was still in my foul mood.

"I'll think about it," I said.

Sharon nearly died.

"That's a good price," the proprietor said. "Go ahead ... look around. But most places won't even fill bottles." That was true. And it was a good deal.

We left the good proprietor's premises. I thought about it for a full two seconds — realized the guy was right — and tried to send Sharon back in to do the transaction. "Oh, no," she said, shaking her head emphatically. *"You're* going back in there. By yourself."

The owner was gracious enough to make good on his original offer (it would have served me right if he'd refused or upped his price).

So, with two full fuel bottles — and my mood returning to a more normal level — we struck out toward Lancaster where we'd cross the yawning Connecticut River into Vermont.

Cresting a long hill, a panorama of New Hampshire's Presidential Range in the White Mountains spread below us, rewarding our efforts.

"Are you happy now?" Sharon enquired. "The view is free."

I grinned. "Indeed priceless."

Centre of the Universe

> **"The world is a book, and those who do not travel, read only a page."**
> ~ Saint Augustine

We pushed our bikes up a steep bank and through brush, away from our overnight camping spot. Huffing along Highway 2, our breath hung in the dawn air like thick cotton mist. "Sure hope we hit a hill soon," I said, shivering, "so I can warm up." And, being in Vermont, we didn't have long to wait.

At a roadside gas station, morning constitution calling, I rushed in, and hastily selected a drink and chocolate bars (I had learned that workers treated me better if I was a customer). While paying, I asked the young woman with big teeth if I could use the facilities. A response frostier than a snowman's willy met my request.

Bowlegged and scowling, I waddled back outside. "Can't she see I'm on a bike?" I whined. "Sheesh, it's not like I can hop in my car and drive another 30 kilometres down the road in a couple of minutes."

"More people should travel," Sharon decided. "Then they'd know what being denied washroom privileges was like."

I felt like taking a dump on their stoop. Instead, in considerable pain, I got my sorry rump back on my bike and rode 30 kilometres down the road to North Concord.

"Gives a whole new meaning to 'brown bagging' it," I said, lumbering into a corner grocery store before getting too log-jammed. I asked if I could use their facilities.

"Go right ahead," the friendly woman said, pointing the way.

I was so grateful that upon my return I tried to buy out half the store — including a gallon of milk. The woman glanced out at our bikes leaning against the railing. "*Where* are you going to put a gallon of milk on those things?" she asked, incredulity straining her voice.

I smiled. "Just balancing the load, ma'am." I didn't have the heart to tell her I already had a gallon jug of milk shoved inside a rear pannier. (At the time, I was unaware I would lug two gallons of milk over Cold Hollow Mountains.)

Sharon assumed that after my buying spree we would be eating right away to help lighten the load. But, instead of enquiring if there was a park nearby, I surprised her by asking: "Can you tell me if there are any good restaurants near here?" (Still feeling guilty about my previous day's loutish behaviour?)

"The Wagon Wheel," the clerk replied. She proceeded to give me directions. When I asked her how far it was from the store, she replied, "It's about a car mile down the road." Hmmm. One might reasonably assume that miles are miles — the *exact* same distance no matter what one's mode of transport. But you would be wrong. We had learned that 'car miles' are *not* the same as 'bike miles.' Oh, no, they're not even close. A bike mile invariably turns out to be *at least twice* as far as a car mile! And, if someone utters, "It's a *good* car mile...." May the good Lord be with you — a *'good'* car mile means your destination is anywhere from five to twenty-five miles down the road.

In six (!) miles we arrived at the restaurant.

"Worked up an appetite on that mile," I grinned, sliding into a booth. "I think I'll have a mushroom and cheese omelette," I said, without even picking up a menu.

"You're over the last one?" Sharon asked.

"Nearly."

Just about every patron stopped to chat with us either on their way in or out of the restaurant. "Where are you going?" was at the top of their list. And our answer: "Around the world" always resulted in hoisted eyebrows. We interpreted their looks as, "Come on, quit pulling my leg. I'm nobody's fool, ya know."

"How are you getting across the ocean?" one befuddled woman stammered.

"Pontoons," came Sharon's immediate facetious reply. I guess the poor woman figured we weren't cycling around the world if we didn't pedal across the ocean, too.

"Yep," I concurred, "we're going to paddle instead of pedal."

Another customer, learning of our cycling ambitions, cried, "And here you are! In the centre of the universe! Concord!" (Huh? I thought that was Toronto.)

Leaving Concord, we spotted a shoe store. Sharon pulled to a stop, and gave her shoes a perambulatory glance. Our footwear had taken on a ragged demeanour. Cycle touring puts shoes to a severe test, exposing footgear to all the natural elements, in addition to long hours of sweat and toil. "We should buy new shoes before heading to Europe," Sharon said. "At least we'll look somewhat presentable on our entry."

We entered the shoe store. A saleswoman approached. She looked down. Her jaw dropped. "I can't believe how battered those shoes are!" she said, taking a step back to get a better angle. A frown stamped her dimpled cheeks. She stared and stared. Feeling like an octopus with eight bad ankles, I shifted nervously from foot to foot. Finally, the saleswoman stammered, "How ... how much do you wear them?"

"A lot," Sharon answered. "We're cycle touring," she added, as if that explained everything.

The woman nodded slowly and put a hand to her chin. "So ... so, you wear them a few hours, two or three times a week?"

"Actually," Sharon answered, "we wear them seven days a week, all day, every day."

"I take them off when I go to bed," I said. Then I laughed. That wasn't entirely truthful. "At least sometimes," I corrected myself. With that revelation, I thought I saw a tiny night light illuminate a dark cranial cavity in the sale clerk's brain somewhere between *'Hmmm?'* and *'Aha!'*

"We don't have anything like that," she said finally. "Maybe our hiking boot section?" she suggested.

We pored over their boot selection. But the models appeared too big and heavy to wear cycling all day. We eventually tramped out the door — still clad in our faithful, but tattered, Shimano and Specialized cycling shoes.

Kissing Bridge

"Drink to me only with thine eyes,
And I will pledge with mine;
Or leave a kiss but in the cup,
And I'll not look for wine."
~ Benjamin Jonson, *Song to Celia*

Somewhere after Saint Johnsbury, we were cycling merrily along when we bumped into a BICYCLES PROHIBITED sign. We stopped. We pondered the sign, wondering what best to do. While pondering, we watched in shock and horror as a slate grey van careered down the four lane highway — speeding the wrong way.

"He must have had the grey matter removal operation," Sharon mused, shaking her head as the vehicle disappeared over a rise in the road.

We had little choice but to pedal on the out-of-bounds road — one eye on the lookout for patrol cars and the other watching for misdirected vans. In a short distance, a small road shunted us off the forbidden highway to North Danville and then past Joe's Pond. Our new route proved hilly, but traffic was sparse. Sleepers River slumbered on our right, walking over rocks. Tree branches swayed in the breeze, applauding our efforts. Best of all, no vans plied our scenic course.

Six kilometres past Hardwick (home of America's studs?), we came upon the old Fischer railway bridge. "This must be one of the last remaining covered wooden railroad bridges in America," I said. Built back in 1908 when coal was king, a high open-sided cupola allowed smoke to escape. The bridge spanned lazy Lamoille River. I traipsed across. Hazardous gaps — wide enough for a horse to fall through — threatened to plunge me into the sluggish river gurgling 20 feet below.

Upon returning to my starting point, we followed along the Lamoille River to Waterville. The town, rich in history, boasted three covered bridges.

Sharon and my favourite was Kissing Bridge. We kissed, of course, then rode onto the one-lane bridge. When we were halfway across, a car approached from the opposite end at high speed. The driver spotted us at the last minute, and slammed on his brakes, laying down a lengthy patch of black rubber on the bridge's wooden deck.

"Hmmm," Sharon said, reconsidering. "I have another theory as to the bridge's name. Cars don't see each other until it's too late, and then they kiss together in the middle."

Hero's Welcome

> **"My wife Mary and I have been married for forty-seven years and not once have we had an argument serious enough to consider divorce; murder, yes, but divorce, never."**
> ~ Jack Benny

Past Grande Isle and the town of Hero and not far before the border to head back into Québec, we happened upon a road crew. Warning signs dotted the roadside: WORKERS IN TREES. We pedalled slowly, scanning overhead for labourers leaning on shovels. But we couldn't even spot a branch manager. "Maybe they wear camouflage?" Sharon giggled.

"Or maybe we're so close to Québec," I said, "it's that French accent and means 'Workers in Threes.'"

Remembering our last crossing, we approached the border with some trepidation ... and just when I had my pannier contents figured out, too. But our worries were for naught. We crossed back into Canada without any problems.

We cycled to Hemmingford, Québec, and got ready to camp at a ball field. Setting up our tent behind the stands, we were just about ready to crawl inside when two guys rambled around the corner and stopped short, giving us quizzical looks.

"We're cycling across Canada," I explained.

"Sorry," they murmured, and walked away, leaving us in peace.

"Gee," Sharon said, "it's sure great to be back in Canada."

"Yep," I agreed. "What does a Canadian say when you bump into him?"

"Excuse me."

"Man," I complained, "we've been together too much. You know all my jokes."

Before hitting the sack, Sharon and I discussed what would be the best route to the airport. We had two days. My plan: make a wide sweep around Montréal, and through the native village of Oka — thereby getting a ferry ride and missing Montréal's traffic. (And I had a hidden agenda: I had a joke that I wanted to pull off in Oka — don't tell Sharon.)

Montréal's city lights glowed a mere 50 kilometres away. Sharon contended a direct route, straight through Montréal, best. She insisted my route, long and meandering, was a recipe for disaster. "We'll miss our flight!"

"It doesn't matter if we get there sooner," I squawked, "if we get run over by a lead-footed driver on the way." (It's difficult to argue with illogic.)

We both went to bed in a huff.

Dirty Laundry

> **"Silently, one by one, in the infinite meadows of heaven**
> **Blossomed the lovely stars, the forget-me-nots of angels."**
> ~ Henry Wadsworth Longfellow, *Evangeline*

At 2 AM, I arose, still unable to sleep after my tiff with Sharon. I exited the tent. The sky was clear, speckled with winking stars. I watched in cold fascination as ice slowly encased our aluminum tent poles. Then, frost descended — everywhere — forming even on the shoulders of my fleece jacket.

Six-thirty. It was still dark, but I chomped at the bit to get going like a race horse waiting for the starting gate to open. There was hardly any traffic. Sharon slept on.

When she arose at the lordly hour of 7 AM, she was still mad at me for insisting we take "the long route" around Montréal. By the time we packed up and hit the road, we still weren't on speaking terms.

At a corner in Hemmingford, I made a right turn and cycled a couple of blocks. At Louie's motel (where we had stopped the previous night to check out the price and had offered $10 less than the asking price but were rebuffed), I noted the parking lot was devoid of vehicles. "Looks like Louie rented them all," I chuckled, and glanced to see if Sharon's face betrayed a smile. To my amazement, Sharon was nowhere to be seen.

I pulled to a stop and waited. I waited some more. After ten minutes, I figured she must have gotten a flat. I retraced my route and found her waiting on the corner where I had turned.

"Wrong direction, Scout," she blinked. "That'll take us directly into Montréal." She pointed straight ahead. Following her finger, I silently pedalled off in the new direction.

I whipped along, churning past farmyards of cows, not caring if I worked up a lather: we planned on finding showers before our flight.

Sharon was not impressed with my pace. She lagged behind. Far behind. (When we weren't getting along we tended to cycle farther apart. I don't know what folks on tandems do! Maybe they're more compatible?)

Hunger ground me to a halt. Sharon eventually puffed alongside, panting and complaining. "I'm tired," she said. "Maybe I'm low on iron."

"I'd settle for a banana."

Sharon reached into a pannier, extracted a banana, and threw it at me. The yellow fruit bounced off my chest and on to the ground. As I bent to pick it up, Sharon determined the law of averages to drop me were on her side. She powered away, a strong wind at her back.

What a woman! I inhaled the banana, and pounded off in hot pursuit.

I doubt I would have caught her, but road construction forced her to stop. I halted alongside her, gasping. Offering a peace pipe, I apologized, and hugged her. Wind-at-Back reluctantly accepted Banana-in-Face back into tribe.

A barge, towed by a powerboat, transported us across the river to Oka. A priest, on his day off he told us, was out for a hike. High on the hillside, he pointed out three churches hidden in the trees. "That's where I'm headed," he said. "There's a Trappist monastery up there. They make great cheese."

When we arrived in Oka, cheese was not on my mind. Partway down main street, I saw it — a barber shop. Sharon had been bugging me the past few weeks to get a haircut. And, I figured, if there's anywhere in Canada that knows how to do a Mohawk haircut, it's gotta be Oka. After all, Oka is home to a band of Mohawk Indians. (In 1990 an armed confrontation arose between Oka's Mohawk warriors, the Québec Provincial Police, and the Canadian Armed Forces. The problem began when Oka's town council planned to expand their nine-hole golf course into an 18-holer (a rather insensitive decision considering the expansion was slated for construction on a tract of sacred native land that included a centuries-old cemetery). Not being avid golfers themselves apparently, the Mohawks took exception. They slapped on some war paint and set up an armed road block. The Canadian government sent in the army. After a tense 77-day standoff, the Mohawks, despite being outnumbered by thousands of army troops, emerged triumphant.)

We approached the barber shop. "Hey!" I shouted. "I should get a haircut."

"Good idea!" Sharon replied. "I'm glad you've finally seen the light." She wanted me to make a good impression on my entrance into France. And, oh, what an impression I would make!

Leaving Sharon with our bikes, I traipsed inside the barber shop. "Most people need parental permission to get one of these," the barber told me. Fifteen minutes later, I sauntered out with my new Mohawk haircut.

Sharon groaned. "I can't believe I didn't see this coming." As I suspected might be the case, she wasn't all that impressed with my new hairstyle. Banana-in-Face was once again in danger of being booted out of tribe.

"Maybe you *are* low on iron," I said. "You're getting a little slow." I paused, then asked, "How do you like it?"

"Looks a little odd with glasses."

"Think of all the shampoo I'll save," I said, rubbing my mostly bald pate before strapping on my suddenly larger helmet.

"Yeah," Sharon mumbled. "I hope your head sunburns." Perhaps she thought it'd bake some sense into it?

That went well, I thought, saddling up and following Sharon's rapidly departing form. She gamely pulled to a stop in front of a WELCOME TO OKA town sign and took my picture.

In Saint-Eustache, at a junior high school, I went in and asked a teacher if he knew where I could get a shower.

"Sportif," he responded.

His directions sent us to Sportif's parking lot. Just looking at the parking area I could tell we were way out of our league. Numerous snazzy BMWs, Porsches, and Mercedes lined the parking stalls. We leaned our overloaded bikes against a railing (praying they wouldn't topple over and scratch a paint job on a car that cost more than our house). Sportif was a tad greater on the ritzy side than we had first imagined.

I approached the sparkling clean double-glass doors, fully expecting to be given the heave-ho before I even had a chance to lay one foot inside. But, a pert aerobics instructor took interest in me (my new haircut?) and invited us in.

The showers were deluxe. The whirlpool wasn't half bad either. The white collar clientele, however, wasn't altogether sure about what to make of my new flying wedge hairdo. As I soaked in the spa, they stared and stared, and then stared some more. I'll bet they mistook me for a lawyer right off.

After a long soaking, scrubbing, lathering hot shower, we reluctantly bid Sportif farewell. We arrived at a launderette — just in time to have a worker lock the door in our faces. With six minutes to closing, there was not a chance we were setting even one foot inside. "Oh, well," I said, "two out of three ain't bad."

"You're not counting your haircut as a *good* thing, are you?" Sharon asked.

We rode off, planning to camp at the same church we had a month earlier. No doubt the vast improvement of our French would impress the monsignor! I forgot I had unbungeed my bag of dirty clothes at the laundry. When we stopped a few blocks later to check directions, I discovered the still open bag clinging to my rear rack. "Wow, that's amazing," I marvelled, wondering how on earth it hadn't toppled off. "Must be my lucky day."

"Or not," Sharon laughed. "If you'd been lucky, it'd have fallen off." (She's always in a better mood when she's clean.)

I snorted, and checked the bag's contents. One Chilli Willie sock wasn't there. I convinced Sharon we should backtrack to look for it. Following the smell, we found it — right beside the laundry door.

"Still dirty!" I exclaimed, plucking the dank bundle off the sidewalk.

"I'm sure no one dared touch it," Sharon said. "No doubt it's radioactive."

We set off once more. In the dark we cycled a bike path, keeping a keen eye out for the "you-can't-miss-it" church.

At the edge of town we realized we had somehow missed the church. I recognized the spot we were — it was well past our intended camping spot.

It was late. Rather than backtracking again we cycled into a nearby residential area and discovered a quiet park. A next door neighbour dog announced our presence, yapping hysterically without relent. "Mangy mutt," Sharon mumbled, pulling her sleeping bag over her head.

Bagged

> **"The difference between fiction and reality? Fiction has to make sense."**
> ~ Tom Clancy

The day dawned a grim green. "I hope that's not an omen of things to come," I said, peeking out the tent door.

We slipped onto the still-sleeping streets and headed for Mirabel airport, a mere 14 kilometres away. We had plenty of time to catch our early evening flight. Or so we thought.

In the next town, I spied a sign on a restaurant promoting a 99¢ breakfast special. "Wow!" I yelped. "We've gotta stop. When's the last time you had breakfast for under a buck?"

"Never," came the reply.

I tried the door. Locked. No lights. No hours posted. It was 7:30 AM. "Hmmm, no wonder they have such a cheap breakfast special. They don't open till noon," I joked. "Sorry, Monsieur, the breakfast special ended at 11:00."

"Do you think we should wait?" Sharon asked, fidgeting, anxious to get to the airport.

"Oh, sure," I answered casually. "They probably open at 8."

A large woman, bundled in an even larger coat to ward off the early morning chill, strode purposefully down the sidewalk. Upon reaching the restaurant she riffled through her purse, pulled out a key, and unlocked the door.

"What time do you open?" I asked.

"Seven," she admitted sheepishly.

We followed her in. "Sit anywhere you like," she said, flipping a switch and illuminating the empty restaurant. The smell of fresh-perked coffee floated through the air. "Thank goodness for timers," she sighed, slipping off her jacket and hanging it on a tree rack by the front door. I hoped the lack of patrons didn't indicate lack of quality. Sharon and I settled into the best seats in the house as the waitress-chief-cook and bottle washer brought over a coffee pot and filled our mugs.

"What's your breakfast special?" I asked.

"Two eggs any style, bacon, hash browns, toast, and coffee."

"Make mine over easy, please," Sharon said.

"May I order two?" I asked.

"Certainly," came the reply.

"What a country!" I said. Little did I know it would be our last good thing of the day.

When my plate arrived with its four eggs, mountain of grease-fried potatoes, and strips of bacon, Sharon took one look and announced, "Looks like a coronary on a plate."

After our filling breakfast, we followed a recommended bike route to the airport, pedalling at no more than ten kilometres per hour — we had plenty of time and we didn't want to work up a sweat. "Nothing worse than sitting on a six-hour flight next to someone with stinky underarms," Sharon said.

"Yeah," I agreed. "It's even worse when they're not mine."

We rode and we rode, but we didn't get any closer to the elusive airport. It was so tantalizingly close — and yet so far! The bike route led us in a lazy loop around the entire airport. "I'm sure we've seen it from all four sides," Sharon groused.

When we arrived at noon, our day-trip meter registered an astounding 38 kilometres! But even with our circuitous route, we still had plenty of time before our scheduled 6:40 PM flight.

"We're finally here!" Sharon shouted, pulling to a stop in front of the entrance. She glanced at her odometer. "After 8,179 kilometres," she said, "we're about to embark on our first overseas adventure."

"France, ready or not, here we come!" I shouted. We were about to discover that France was not ready.

We entered the terminal and approached the airline desk to get our on-hold tickets. "You can't pick them up until 3:30 PM," a belle brunette informed us. "Over there," she added, pointing to a check-in counter across the terminal.

"We have bikes," I mentioned. "Do you have bike bags?"

"We have them," she answered. "If you want bike bags, just ask when you check-in."

I thanked her. Sharon and I went and sat down in sculpted plastic chairs to relax a minute. No sense getting ready too soon, I figured. When the clerk we had spoken to went on break a half-hour later, I approached the new clerk and double-checked on the status of our tickets. The new clerk happily echoed the first, stating that we picked up our tickets at the check-in counter at 3:30.

We strolled outside the terminal for fresh air, waiting for our appointed hour to roll around so we could find out whether we actually had tickets or not. I sat on a bench and read. Sharon determined it an opportune time to clean her bike. An old T-shirt she had liberated from a roadside ditch was perfect for the task. She worked the rag around and around her wheels, polishing rims and spokes until their chrome surfaces gleamed in the sun. I could have done the same, but why bother, I figured. They would just get dirty again.

For the next two hours, Sharon worked diligently. The airport was as quiet as a ghost town on a Sunday afternoon. It seemed that we and employees were the only ones around. An officious white-haired crossing guard paced back and forth at a pedestrian crosswalk — definitely the Maytag man of crossing guards. He had nothing to do. When an infrequent pedestrian made an appearance, he raised his arm and held out his sign with extravagant gusto — signalling for all traffic to stop — except there wasn't a single vehicle in sight for a country mile.

It was so quiet I wondered if we had failed to hear about an airline strike (we joked that while cycle touring we were sometimes so out of touch with world events that WWIII could have broken out and we wouldn't have known it).

Without warning, at 3:25 PM, mayhem broke loose. Several fully loaded buses roared to a halt in front of us. Hordes of passengers disgorged onto the sidewalk, grabbed their neat and tidy luggage, and formed a long queue for Paris. "Hmmm," I frowned. "Maybe we should get ready?" I hadn't expected such an abrupt change of milieu.

We got out our six-inch crescent wrench and Allen keys to prepare our bikes. The handlebars turned sideways without any problem. But that was the end of our good fortunes. When I attempted to remove the pedals, they wouldn't budge. Sharon liberally squirted lubricant onto the recalcitrant joints.

After waiting a few minutes for the oil to penetrate, Sharon's pedals loosened without much difficulty. Mine, however, were another story. I placed our little six-inch wrench on the connection, and applied pressure. Nothing. The threads were frozen more solidly than an Inuit's tongue on a metal slide in the dead of winter. I placed a foot solidly on the wrench, and — worried something might snap — gave a sharp push downward. Nada. It hadn't budged. Sharon stood on the pedal opposite while I jumped on the wrench — literally. There was an ear-wrenching screech, reminiscent of a rusty barn door creaking open after half a century of non-use, but the pedal loosened. Yahoo! After celebrating with a little happy dance, we attempted the same technique on the second pedal. But when I jumped on the wrench, Sharon popped into the air like some aspiring trampoline artist. And still, the pedal refused to budge. "This isn't going to work, is it?" I admitted after Sharon's fourth or fifth tumbling maneuver.

"We're going to have to figure out a different way," Sharon said. She glanced around. "How about that?" she asked, pointing to a nearby iron railing. "Stick the pedal under there. That'll keep it from moving." What did I have to lose? Besides busting a crank arm, that was. I jammed the pedal beneath the railing. It fit like a glove on OJ Simpson. While I held the rear rack, steadying the bike upright, Sharon got into position to jump on the wrench. "Geronimo!" I yelled, as she leaped into the air and onto the wrench. A sound — like Arnold Schwarzenegger breaking his knuckles on some bad dude's face — shattered the stillness. The wrench winged off the pedal and skittered across the sidewalk. I was afraid to look. Had my crank arm survived? I peeked down with one eye closed. Whew! Everything looked all right. Best of all, the stubborn pedal had loosened. Ah, travel. The art of ingenuity and getting to exercise new brain cells. "Um, remind me to put extra grease on the threads when we put them back on," I grinned.

The airline had a two-piece luggage limit per passenger. With our bikes counting as one piece, the challenge was to assemble all our remaining gear into two packages. We set to work, combining tent, sleeping bags, sleeping pads, and eight panniers (our handlebar bags would be carry-on) into two largish bundles — all strapped together with an assortment of straining bungees, packing tape, sweat and spit. My finest efforts culminated in an absurd bulky conglomeration. Sharon mused over my handiwork. "They look like inflatable rafts in bondage."

I grimaced and hefted my dinghy. "Ugh," I grunted as it squirmed from my grasp. "Sort of like wrestling Jell-O."

The airline's weight limit was 60 pounds. We figured it'd be close. I trundled over to a weigh scale for passenger use, and thumped my prodigious package onto the metal table. It tipped the scales at 58 pounds. Sharon's tilted in at a more svelte 55. I chuckled. "Hey," I said, "we could have bought that extra jar of peanut butter, after all."

Confident our luggage wasn't overweight I snagged an airport pushcart. It possessed the prerequisite wonky wheel. No matter how I maneuvered the thing, it insisted on venturing only south. (Maybe it was trying to tell me something.) With great difficulty, we shimmied over and stood at the very end of a very long check-in line. Sharon held our bikes while I balanced the precarious jerry-built skyscraper of panniers.

After what seemed like hours, a few paces before the check-in counter, an impish lad in front of us groped out and, with the lightness of a feather, touched my helter-skelter load. Like the infamous straw that broke the camel's back, our ragtag collection of panniers, sleeping bags and tent, clattered to the tile floor. Fortunately, no one was injured — at least not permanently.

I reloaded our hazardous cargo and succeeded in making it the final ten feet to the counter. Once there, a conundrum confronted me: Why do airlines insist on hiring personnel that weigh less than allowable luggage? A check-in elf with a waist size rivalling an HB pencil dragged one of my slipshod messes onto the official weigh scale. Wrestling the unwieldy package, she scowled, and pointed to a shrinkwrap machine across the terminal. She was suggesting I have them plastic wrapped. Good idea! But before doing so, I asked about our tickets. Alas, they weren't at the counter. The wispy brownie pointed a slender finger toward the desk where I had enquired, twice, hours prior.

Leaving Sharon in line at the check-in counter, I dashed to the ticket desk. The clerk — the same one whom hours earlier had told me she didn't have our tickets — slid open a drawer and handed me an envelope. I sighed, thanked her politely, and thought our problems were solved. But I was wrong.

I sprinted back over to the check-in counter and handed the airline pixie our tickets. "May I get two bike bags?" I asked. My idea — rather than shrinkwrapping — was to stick our lopsided bundles into the bike bags, thereby effectively containing them. It would be brilliant, saving me the convoluted and risky trip over to the distant shrinkwrap station. I'd send our bikes sans bags — I had faith the airline would scratch and dent our rides regardless of them being bagged, boxed, or securely crated and encased in multiple layers of foam.

"We don't have any," came the curt reply.

"But...," I stammered. "The woman over there told me the airline had them and to ask for them here." The petite clerk pulled an extremely frowny face, like someone who had just bitten an extremely distasteful lemon. She sputtered something in French to the assistant beside her that I didn't understand. The helper disappeared into the back. The check-in clerk sucked in her cheeks and stood mutely, staring off into space while absently tapping a blue and gold airline pen on the countertop. I couldn't read the pen's inscription, but I was quite certain it didn't say: SERVICE IS OUR MIDDLE NAME.

Maybe this was a good opportunity to practice my French? But before I could ask her what the time was, two bike bags magically appeared.

I began to stuff our panniers inside. In a frequency best-suited for shattering glass, the clerk shrieked, "For bikes only!" I could tell she was restraining herself from throwing both hands in the air as she pointed to the shrinkwrap machine again. Maybe she got a commission?

I returned the bike bags, checked our bikes through, then wheeled my tottering load through a maze of pedestrians to the shrinkwrap attendant. He did a fantastic job, even fashioning handles, which helped marvelously in the manageability department. I wheeled back to the check-in counter with a smug expression.

"You *must* purchase bags for your bikes," the clerk huffily declared as I plunked down our tidy parcels. Huh? Hadn't she been the one whom — only minutes before — stated they didn't have any bags? It was my turn to stare off into space. I returned to earth and gazed at Sharon with a distant look of perplexity. Atlas shrugged. "Pay for them over there," the clerk proclaimed, snapping me out of my reverie, and pointing to yet another counter. "Come back here and show me the receipt," she instructed. "I will return your bikes, you will put the bag on, then you will hand them back to me." A not unpleasant picture of a certain clerk shrinkwrapped arose in my mind's eye.

Being a neophyte air-traveler, I hadn't realized I had broken the cardinal rule: Thou shalt not hassle thy check-in clerk. They have surprising powers. Somewhat dazed, I hobbled over to the cashier's counter. A wan smile creased my lips as I recognized the cashier. She was the one who originally told me bike bags were optional.

"This doesn't make sense," I whimpered. "What's going on?"

"They're better for your bike, sir," she answered.

"No, they're not," I blurted. "I've flown before with a bike bag and my bike still got scratched and dented."

"You don't want them?"

"No," I said, shaking my head. "I don't want them."

"Okay," she said.

I turned and slouched away, still befuddled as to why this was so difficult. *Perhaps my new Mohawk haircut is having an adverse affect? Maybe I should consider a ball cap?*

The cashier caught up to me ten paces before I reached the check-in counter. "You *have* to take them," she said, in an almost pleading tone. "They keep other people's luggage from being damaged."

"Then you should provide them for free."

"You don't want them?"

"No!" I said.

"Fine," she said.

"Good," I said.

"Then I won't send your bikes!"

"Two bags," I whimpered, perilously close to a sob.

I followed her back to the cashier's counter. I paid for two bike bags. I trotted back to the check-in counter and presented the receipt to the frosty clerk. We waltzed through the afore agreed upon exchange. The clerk accepted our bagged bikes, then presented me with a release form, absolving the airline of any responsibility "in case there happens to be damage to your bikes."

Terrific. I had to sign a paper agreeing that the airline's baggage gorillas were free to smash our bikes to smithereens. "When are they going to build that bridge across the Atlantic?" I asked Sharon.

Our bikes signed away, we proceeded to the boarding area. "I'm sure glad we rarely fly," I grumped. "What a rigmarole."

After all that, the flight was delayed. "Time to spare, go by air," Sharon rhymed.

We were boarding-area captives. We took seats near the X-ray machine and watched people check through. After observing a succession of suspect males, I whispered to my partner, "I think French men are more effeminate than men in general."

"And I think you have an overactive imagination," Sharon replied. She turned just in time to see a fellow run past on tippy-toes.

An hour later, we received our boarding call and collapsed into padded airliner seats. Jet engines roared. We were off!

My exhausted mind refused to fathom that in three short weeks — with 2,000 kilometres to pedal through France, Spain, and Portugal — we were to rendezvous with our cycling buddies in Lisbon.

"I hope that's the end of our troubles," I sighed, and gave Sharon's leg a pat.

"Moi ossi," Sharon replied, already practicing her French. "But somehow I doubt it."

Little did I know at the time, she was right. I closed my eyes and thought back to how our trip had begun.

The Big Inning

> **"We are not rich by what we possess but rather by what we can do without."**
> ~ Immanuel Kant

A thud sounded at the back door. Crossing the carpeted entryway, I yarded open a heavy metal storm door, and peered out into all-encompassing blackness. A blast of January air smacked my T-shirted torso like a *Polar Express* freight train loaded with ice blocks.

"Hello?" I called out.

The greeting vanished, snatched from my windpipe into a maelstrom of whirling snow pellets. A lump of whiteness, unobtrusively blown against the doorsill, rose, pushed past me, and staggered four steps inside before collapsing.

"What do we have here?" I grimaced, recognizing a scrap of multi-coloured scarf peeking forth from beneath a corner of the white mound. Having struggled three blocks from the nearest bus stop through a paralyzing whiteout, my wife appeared more akin to an abominable snowman than I dared mention.

"Yeti!" I exulted, throwing caution to the wind. "Welcome home!" No response. "Ah, life on the edge of the frozen prairie," I muttered, slamming the door.

"Frosty the Snowman?" I guessed.

Silence.

"Icicles for sale?"

The slumped figure stared at me through ice-rimmed eyes, casting tiny daggers my way.

"Why did the snowman have a grin on his face?" Cold silence met my question. "He heard the snowblower was coming." Did I detect a faint smile from the snowdrift?

"Hoo boy," I said, surveying the mostly motionless heap of melting snow. "Lucky *I* have a car." Another unblinking glacial glare from behind frozen lashes telegraphed I was not endearing myself to her.

"Guess what?" I intoned, ignoring the wise adage: When one is in a hole, the first thing to do is stop digging. "We received a wonderful letter from the Sidewalk Police today. They're threatening to fine us severely if the snow's not removed from our sidewalk within 48 hours. I phoned and informed a Gestapo that I had already swept the sidewalk ... should I vacuum it too?"

Sharon rolled her eyes. "You know," she said, finally thawed enough to move her lips, "maybe the rat race isn't all it's cracked up to be ... after all, even if you win, you're still a rat."

I twisted my lips, nodding, and concluded that frozen brains were short on insight. "Maybe," she continued, "we should do something while we're both still young and healthy."

"Like what?"

"I don't know ..." Her voice trailed off. She summoned strength and picked herself off the floor. She struggled, removed her sodden woolen overcoat, and draped its dripping bulk on a peg over the boot tray. "How about cycling around the world?" she asked. "Now's our chance. No kids. No mortgage."

"Hmmm," I heard myself reply. "Sounds good." Warm tropical breezes sashaying amongst palm fronds already danced through my mind like pernicious nymphs. "Anything has to be better than this," I murmured, gazing out at a frozen white world and envisioning turquoise as a perfectly delightful colour for water. "Will there be hills?"

"Of course not," came the sweet reply.

Galloping Emotions

> **"There is no time like the present, for postponing what you ought to be doing, and go bicycling instead ... "**
> ~ Moni

A few weeks later — as fate would have it — the provincial government axed new teachers' contracts on the budgetary chopping block. Mine was one of them.

When Sharon, a Chartered Accountant, arrived home at midnight after cleaning up a box job [a year's receipts in a shoe box], I told her the news.

Rather than whine about budget cuts and temporary setbacks, she suggested it was our big opportunity to get away from it all.

"I've been thinking that I'm not cut out for the dog-eat-dog business world anyway," Sharon said. "I'd like to pack in this *fabulous* career and its 100-hour work weeks." She paused. "Maybe this is our chance to get out of the rat race and make a fresh start. Besides," she cooed, flinging her arms around my neck, "you always said you would take me on a honeymoon."

Her presentation was difficult to resist. Maybe the universe was trying to tell me something? Perhaps I just needed to be quiet and listen. Maybe we really could make a new beginning ... escape the concrete jungle ... take that world cycling trip and honeymoon Sharon had dreamed of for so long....

As she pointed out, when was there going to be a better time? Were we destined to live passionless existences, too afraid to take a risk and live? Subsisting instead on drudgery, dead to the core, working day in and day out, hanging on for the day we could retire so we could live? I had heard that clergy, administering last rites, said: "People on their death beds never regret what they've done ... they only regret what they haven't." Purportedly, not many were heard to utter the popular phrase, "I wish I'd spent more time at the office."

"Well," I declared, "the only difference between a rut and a grave is its depth." *Live life large! Bold! Daring, even. Make the most of the short time we're allotted.* As my mother was fond of saying: "There's always a reason not to do something. But it's just an excuse. Figure out what you want to do ... then do it."

"Why not?" I heard myself say. "No regrets."

Our decision to embark on a cycling tour of the world required us to change our planned summer trip of cycling to Alaska. No problem — except for the fact that we had already invited two friends, Sue and Vicky. What would they think about our change in plans?

Sharon thought it'd be a neat idea to make our round-the-world trip a doorstep to doorstep endeavour: ride home, to a new beginning — the long route. We would cycle southeast out of Edmonton to Cypress Hills — the highest elevation in Canada between the Rockies and Labrador — then east across Canada to Halifax, hop a plane to Spain, tour around Europe, India, Australia, New Zealand, then over to Alaska and bike from Anchorage down to Vancouver and back to Edmonton. The orange highlighter lines I drew on our world map looked so neat and tidy. It all seemed so easy.

We presented the new plans to our cycling buddies. Vicky, who had been eager to take on the Alaskan adventure (and had spent considerable time researching and route planning), was devastated. "There goes my summer cycling," she grumbled.

"Why don't you come with us when we set out from Edmonton?" I suggested.

"No, thanks," Vicky replied. "I can cycle out of Edmonton any time." She paused, brightening. "But maybe I'll join you somewhere in Europe. Or New Zealand. Or Australia!" The twinkle returned to her eyes. I chewed my lip. I knew how difficult it could be to meet someone parachuting in.

Sue, living in Victoria, had already booked three weeks of vacation and a flight to Edmonton that would be difficult to change. Fortunately she was keen on the change in plans. "We even have a bonus," she informed us cheerily. "My mom and dad are on our route. We can hit them up for hospitality."

Things were looking good indeed!

On prior trips, we'd usually depart the same day I finished classes. However, touring for one or two months is not the same as touring for two years. At first, we entertained the idea of renting our little home. But, being absentee landlords seemed fraught with problems. And, unless we rented it fully furnished, we still had to find somewhere to store our belongings. Better to sell the house we finally concluded. Not only would it rid us of possible future headaches, but we'd reap a tidy sum for the trip.

Besides the usual necessities of getting our bikes and ourselves prepared, we had a myriad of other tasks and complexities to deal with ... all within a few days.

What to sell? What to put into storage? Indeed, where to store it? Sharon's brothers and sisters (she has eight) helped us by offering to take bits and pieces. One obtained a bed, another a barbecue, and still another a greenhouse. Our friends, Heide and Ryan, inherited an aquarium complete with fishy inhabitants. Sharon's mom and dad were kind enough to relieve us of our living room furniture. (I even got one feel-good experience from the getting-rid-of-material-items effort: after I sold our television set, I donated the entire proceeds to a local church. Who said nothing good ever came from television?)

Our remaining household items got squirreled away in a spare bedroom at a house Sharon's dad owned. My vehicles — a black and gold Firebird Formula 400, and two antique oval window Volkswagen Beetles — found storage space in a dusty corner of a quonset hut at Sharon's mom and dad's farm in Morinville.

Sharon's sister, Faye, arranged to receive our mail. Faye also agreed to be our Power of Attorney and attend to matters for us when we were thousands of kilometres from home.

We visited banks, signed forms, transferred accounts, and signed more forms. We asked pertinent questions about Visa and MasterCard PINs to ensure the cards would work in overseas banking machines. Trying to obtain a telephone calling card, we discovered it near impossible once we didn't have our own phone number. Sharon's mom and dad came to the rescue by allowing us to use their phone card.

We trooped several times to the health unit, receiving boosters and vaccinations for various countries on our itinerary. Along with typhoid pills, we endured many pokes and prods from health professionals: tetanus shots, yellow fever shots, polio shots, meningococcal shots, diphtheria shots, measles, mumps, and rubella shots. (I hadn't realized how jostling Grade Twos could be until after a round of needle jabbing at the local health unit. "Ouch! Please don't touch my arm!" Maybe that needled them to bump me even more? Isn't it fun watching Teacher grimace!)

Medical and dental coverage through our respective employers would end. We contacted Alberta Health and secured information concerning citizens who planned on being absent from Canada for an extended period. "You're not covered after three months," the efficient clerk informed us. "You must arrange for alternate private coverage."

At the end of June, my teaching contract concluded. Sharon resigned her Chartered Accountant position. Sue flew in to accompany us on our grand start.

With all our running around — and working till the very last minute — we'd had no time to train or even get our bikes in order. When Sue arrived, we still hadn't finished packing all our household contents.

Sharon, even though she had 'officially' finished work, trooped into the office two extra days and completed files. Talk about professionalism. Meanwhile, Sue and I threw possessions into boxes and transported them to the designated storage area.

Four days later, our to-do list was still incomplete. Sue's precious holiday time was ticking away. Past midnight, Sharon and I freaked, frazzled by details still not complete ... drained from tearful goodbyes with family and friends ... debilitated from overwork and lack of sleep. So tired, we couldn't think straight.

Our galloping emotions reached the breaking point. Sharon and I argued. Over what to do. Over what not to do. Over whose fault it was. Over whose fanciful idea this whole trip was in the first place. We threw our hands up in frustration. When Sharon's face rained tears, I grabbed her and hugged her tight.

Then it dawned on me. Why not begin the trip as planned? Ride to Medicine Hat with Sue ... she could catch her return flight to Victoria ... and we would hop a bus back to Edmonton and finish loose ends. Brilliant! Past exhaustion, we fell into bed, wondering why we hadn't thought of it sooner.

On Our Way

> "**Far away there in the sunshine are my highest aspirations. I may not reach them but I can look up and see their beauty, believe in them and try to follow them.**
> ~ Louisa May Alcott

Wednesday, July 6th. We spent the day packing our panniers and twiddling with our neglected bikes. By the time we were ready, it was late afternoon. Sharon and I would have liked one more sleep in our bed. But since it was Sue's vacation time, we thought it only fair to ask her.

Not surprisingly, she voted to head out. We couldn't blame her. In the fun department, helping someone move on your vacation time is right up there with having a root canal.

I later read in Sharon's journal: "For years I anticipated, hoped for, dreamt about, a world tour cycling trip. In all my musings and daydreams, I visualized my departure a thousand times. Not one of those times did I come close to the reality of today."

In actuality, there were no grand send-offs, no tearful goodbyes, no ticker tape parades, no journalistic camera crews seeking interviews.

Instead, after frantic days of packing belongings — "our very lives" Sharon deemed it — into cardboard boxes and stashing them at various relatives' homes, we hit the road.

Rather than Sharon's grand visions of an early-morning sun-drenched parade route, a sultry July evening shooed us on our way. We slammed the door on our humble west end abode and wobbled away ... on ill-prepared bicycles powered by overtaxed bodies. We didn't even have the strength to shout "Yahoo! World here we come!" Never in the history of a world cycle tour had there been a more ignominious beginning.

Heading south out of Edmonton — the place we'd called home for the past 18 years — we soon lost our way in a convoluted maze of Millwoods' neighbourhood streets.

"Where are you folks headed?" a fellow in his front yard cutting grass called as we pedalled past.

"Around the world!" I shouted.

"Where are you from?"

"Edmonton!"

"Well, good luck!" he replied, as we cycled toward a dead end.

Ten-thirty PM, after three hours on the road (and lost an equal number of times), we struggled into Beaumont — a skimpy 42 kilometres from the back door we had so exuberantly slammed.

"We're barely out of the city," Sue trilled, "but it sure feels good to be underway!" I wasn't so sure. Caught up in lesson plans, report cards, parent-teacher interviews, and shifting households, I hadn't had time to train. Worse, I had totally forgotten that ancient instrument of torture — the bicycle seat. For the past two hours, my nether regions had jolted as if jostling atop an electric chair.

"The sparks are flying!" I discharged, parroting our friend Ryan, after he's spent too long on an exercise bike.

"All I want to do," Sharon wheezed, "is find a place for the night." She hadn't had time to train either.

"How about the church?" Sue asked, pointing to a distant hilltop. I sighed. That was the last thing I needed. I didn't want to get sweaty just before bed. And my chain was skipping. Without speaking, we pedalled toward the church.

Before reaching it, we lucked across an RV parking area. "I think we qualify," I panted. "We're loaded like pack mules."

Sharon spotted a porta-potty. "That settles it!" she said, swinging her steed into the gravel lot.

"We must be living right," I said, happy not to attempt the church hill. Not only did it save me from extra exertion, but on a slope ascending Edmonton's river valley, Sharon and I discovered our chains skipped like world jump rope champions. I had replaced our bike's worn chains, but in my pre-trip delirium I hadn't tested them. The old rear cogs' teeth no longer meshed with the new chain.

On one edge of the parking lot, after determining that late arriving motorhomes wouldn't trammel us, we found a grassy patch upwind from the porta-potty. Despite the darkness, we erected our tent in record time.

"Impressive," I allowed. "Considering it's by moonlight."

Sharon tossed in her sleeping bag. "I'm hitting the sack," she announced, exhausted from late nights and departure stresses.

Sue, a lithesome blonde with no fat reserves, protested, "I'm *starving!*" On cue, her stomach growled menacingly, punctuating her statement like a jungle cat about to stomp a zebra.

I sprang into action like a cheetah on a trampoline. "A true biker," I grinned. "Come to think of it, I'm hungry too."

Sue wasn't one to complain unduly — she hadn't even uttered cries of despair when we made her pack our household things on her cherished vacation time. A friend indeed.

"Let's go for a midnight snack," Sharon said, relenting. "My legs could use a stretch."

We hobbled down the road into Beaumont, on the lookout for an open establishment. Luscious odours wafted through the hushed night air. Our noses led us to a lighted doorway. Like three starving mice, we scurried inside the pizzeria and immediately placed an order for two extra large pizzas before they could tell us they were closed.

"Would you like it cut into 8 or 12 slices?"

"We're pretty hungry," I said. "Better make it 12."

"You're a goose," Sue laughed, shaking her head.

At the stroke of midnight, Basile Pizza presented us with two sensational piping-hot pizzas. We whisked the pies outside and plunked ourselves down on a bus bench. Sharon and Sue each balanced a toasty pizza box on their goosebumpled legs.

"This is great!" Sue raved. "My legs are freezing, but these boxes make great leg warmers!"

Camrose or Bust

> **"The only limit to our realization of tomorrow will be our doubts of today."**
> ~ Franklin D. Roosevelt

After polishing off the leg warmer contents, we returned to our campsite. Sharon handed Sue a pair of ear plugs. We shoved ours in too, entered the tent, and fainted into an unconsciousness so profound that apart from lazy heartbeats and languid circulation we could have been certifiably dead.

The first rays of new freedom shone into the darkest recesses of our tent around 5 AM. I groaned and pulled my sleeping bag over my head before slipping back into a coma. At 9 AM Sharon and I crawled forth like a pair of garden slugs. Sue was up, hunched on a nearby picnic table. We popped out our ear plugs to bid her good morning.

What a shock we received! Our perfect campsite sounded as though a hive of bees had invaded it. Five energetic park employees surrounded us, engaged in a buzzing arrhythmic symphony of clearing brush and small saplings. Armed with metal-bladed gas-powered weed eaters, and wearing black-rimmed safety goggles, they looked — and sounded — like a swarm of deranged bald-faced hornets. From her tabletop nest, Sue beelined us a look of dejection.

"They arrived shortly after 7 o'clock," she moaned.

"Didn't you use the ear plugs?" Sharon asked.

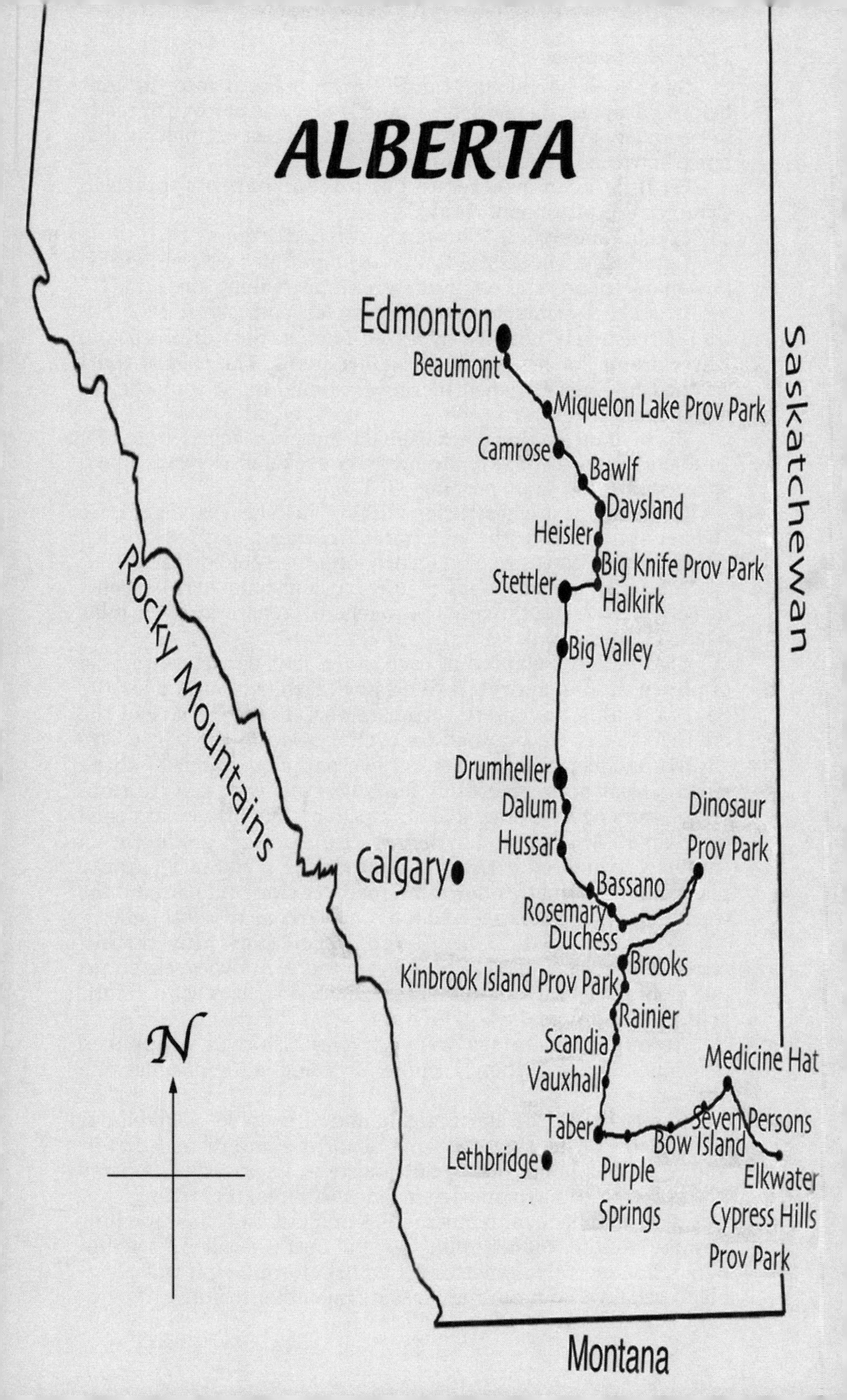
ALBERTA
Edmonton
Beaumont
Miquelon Lake Prov Park
Camrose
Bawlf
Daysland
Heisler
Big Knife Prov Park
Stettler
Halkirk
Big Valley
Drumheller
Dalum
Hussar
Dinosaur Prov Park
Calgary
Bassano
Rosemary
Duchess
Brooks
Kinbrook Island Prov Park
Rainier
Scandia
Vauxhall
Medicine Hat
Taber
Seven Persons
Bow Island
Lethbridge
Purple Springs
Elkwater
Cypress Hills Prov Park
Rocky Mountains
Saskatchewan
N
Montana

Sue shook her head. "I didn't even make it into the tent before I dropped them on the ground." She was more than ready to be underway. We dismantled our tent and set off, putting distance between us and the noisy contraptions.

"It'll be even sweeter to get to your parents' place in Camrose this afternoon," I said.

"Yeah," Sue sighed. "Showers ... soft bed ... quiet."

I smiled. A successful tour was sometimes determined by how many friends and relatives were situated along one's route.

In a short distance, my posterior felt as if astraddle a hot iron. Gruesomely hot. We bypassed Looma, then dribbled into New Sarepta for brunch and yogourt cones. The cold yogourt soothed my lips; I wished there was something it could do for my burning cheeks.

Back on the baking black asphalt, the sun reached its zenith. In a cloudless azure sky, the mercury rocketed skyward like a space shuttle intent on probing old Sol.

Churning past wheat fields glinting like sheaves of gold, we slabbered hot and frothy with a don't-bother-us attitude etched on our brows, into Miquelon Lake to order ice-cold drinks.

After a couple of rounds of juice, curious onlookers — seeing us refreshed — tentatively approached. "Where are you folks headed?" they asked.

Sharon and I glanced at each other. Our departure's initial euphoria had evaporated like fair-weather clouds over the Sahara. Unlike my giddy response on Day One, I lacked the courage to say we planned on cycling around the world. We shifted our feet. There we were, two pathetically out-of-shape clods, sweat pouring off our faces like our own private rainstorm, nursing sore rears and cramped legs, on bikes that belted out *Skip To My Lou* on anything over a 1 percent grade. Hell, I seriously wondered if I was going to make it to Sue's parents' place, a few kilometres down the road, let alone ride around the world. The whole idea seemed too preposterous to say aloud.

"Medicine Hat," I finally answered (anything farther sounded absurd — even to me). From there, in two weeks' time, Sue would board an aircraft and be whisked back to her comfortable, air-conditioned job in Victoria.

As our questioners strayed away, Sharon whispered hoarsely, "The only thing keeping me going is the promise of a shower tonight."

Barely out of the starting gate and already we doubted our lofty goal. Considering our lame departure and dismal performance on our home turf — flat prairie — I seriously wondered how we were going to manage in lands with real mountains.

We eased back onto our saddles and out onto the scorching tarmac. "Rollin', rollin', rollin', boy my butt is swollen," I whimpered. For several kilometres I tried to determine if it was possible to pedal without putting pressure on nether regions.

Sun. Pounded. Down. Sweat streamed off my forehead into burning bleary eyes. With each painful revolution, I questioned my sanity and good sense.

Seventy-five agonizing kilometres later we arrived in Camrose, our heads swimming in green fuzz and our ears ringing as though we'd been napping next to a gong.

We had just enough time for a cool shower before tackling the evening meal. Heaven! Sue's mother, bless her little domestic heart, had cooked up a festive meal: roast beef with all the trimmings. The *coup de grâce* was her delightful Yorkshire pudding with plenty of real gravy. None of that canned stuff for us!

Following bounteous scoops of chocolate-cherry ice cream, we phoned our longtime cycling buddy, Vicky, and invited her to join us for a weekend ride ... so long as she agreed to bring new gears for our ailing bikes. She consented. And, like a true friend, she even refrained from laughing.

At the crack of noon, not altogether ready to abandon feather pillows and multi-coil padded mattress, Sharon and I dozily shuffled forth from the cozy guest room. Evidenced by our belated rising, we had yet to recover from those late nights of work and frantic packing. Not only physically tired, we felt emotionally drained, too. We had yet to come to grips with the idea we would be absent from friends and family for two years.

Sue, ready and raring since daybreak, had spent her time in the back alley, practicing fly casting. Her father, an avid fisherman, patiently administered pointers. He never missed a chance to engage in his favourite hobby (and with Canada's over two million lakes and rivers, there is plenty of opportunity).

By 2 PM, we were ready to leave for another glorified bed and breakfast: Sue's brother and family in Daysland. (Have I already mentioned strategic alliances?)

Who said cycle touring had to be tough? Sue's mom and dad, kind souls they are, offered to *drive* us to our planned overnight stop. Maybe my newly acquired limp affected them? Or perhaps the anguished look that creased my face the previous evening as I set myself gingerly onto a dining-room chair?

Inanely, I declined. *What was I thinking?* I even went so far as to assure them we *liked* bicycle touring. (Who was I trying to convince? Myself?) As a strict matter of conscience, Sharon and I never accepted rides — we felt it akin to cheating. If we hadn't earned it, we didn't enjoy the accomplishment ... at least that was the theory. Besides, we never wanted to hear some friendly trucker (ensuring his place in heaven by giving cyclists a lift to a summit) as we pushed off for a free downhill glide, yelling at our backsides: "You're not real bikers! You didn't earn it, ya know!"

Sue rolled out of the driveway weighted down by extra goodies — not leftover roast beef and Yorkshire pudding as I had hoped — but rather, stocked with a snazzy new fly fishing rod, abundant tackle, and an eye-catching rainbow spectrum of wet and dry flies, preserved frogs, and tiny iridescent minnows. She was ready for anything. I looked forward to her successes. "You catch 'em; I'll clean 'em; Sharon'll cook 'em," was the deal I suggested.

Knowing that showers awaited us in Daysland, we pedalled hard. The time flew by and we arrived with plenty of light left to enjoy the hospitality of Sue's brother, Brian, his wife, Bev, and their three kids, David, Kenny, and Barbra. We took full advantage of it.

Brian barbecued thick steaks to perfection. While we were savouring them, and cobs of buttery corn, who should arrive in shining Lycra from Edmonton but our heroic friend Vicky. She flourished a George's bike bag, holding aloft two sets of gleaming new rear clusters.

"You're the best!" Sharon exclaimed.

"Wait till you see the delivery charge," Vicky teased.

Big Club in Big Knife

> **"The voyage of discovery lies not in finding new landscapes, but in having new eyes."**
> ~ Marcel Proust

We spent a second night in soft beds. "At this rate we'll never toughen up," Sharon pouted, pretending to complain. Before getting underway, we enjoyed more pampering at the hands of Bev. Breakfast was a feast. All was right with the world!

One of the clusters Vicky brought didn't fit. She drove us to Camrose. The bike shop there fixed us up with the correct type. With a special cluster removal tool that we carried in our tool bag (and that I thought we'd never use), Sharon and Vicky installed the new clusters.

"Bring on those hills," I smiled, surveying their handiwork.

Vicky unloaded her bike from her rooftop Thule rack, and joined us as we swept out of Daysland on a smooth backroad, assisted by a fine tailwind.

"We have to invite you more often!" Sue gushed, revelling in our first tailwind of the trip. For a change, fields of bright yellow canola were swaying in the same direction we were travelling.

Grinning, we cruised along. The only traffic we met were farm tractors, driven by grey-haired sodbusters who passed with bounteous waves. I glanced at my speedometer. Due to our tailwind good luck, pleasant sunshine, and non-slipping new gears, our pace was an easy 30 kilometres per hour. Gotta love those tailwinds!

Highway 855 swept us into the small backwater town of Heisler. In the noonday sun, we plunked ourselves down on a curb (almost as hard as a bike seat) and consumed Creamsicles. A fellow, picking up his mail, joked, "You guys riding across Canada?"

"Yep," I replied. His smile faded like a two-year-old prayer flag on a mountain top. I guess they didn't get many cross-country cyclists in Heisler. The fellow disappeared down the street.

"Did you get a look at his face?" I chuckled.

"Yeah," Sharon drawled. "I'm beginning to realize this is more than a jaunt around the block."

A strong southerly pushed us onward to our night's destination. The helpful tailwind and good company made the kilometres seem half the usual distance. We arrived at Big Knife Provincial Park in good spirits.

We cycled through the packed campsite, looking for a spot. The proximity of adjacent campsites took us by surprise. Surrounded by acres of vacant land, the powers that be had deemed it necessary to squish everyone together — closer even than neighbours in a city. It wasn't exactly what I'd call "getting away from it all."

Then I spied a sign: WALK-IN SITES. Maybe we could get away from the crushing humanity, after all? I dropped my bike to the dusty earth and ran down a path to check out the sites. Not a one was taken. "They're empty!" I called to my riding partners.

"That's the place for us," Sharon decided. "Not that we're anti-social or anything."

"We just like our privacy," Vicky finished for her.

Fortunately for me, few fellow campers were around to observe my inaugural lighting of our new WhisperLite stove. I pumped the plunger several times, pressurizing the canister. Hoping I remembered the convoluted directions correctly, I twisted the silver knob. Coleman fuel spurted, and flowed into a primer cup at the base of the little three-legged stove. I watched the primer cup fill to overflowing. That was my first mistake.

My second mistake was to hold a match to it. A little gas goes a long way. With a jet-on-final-approach roar, the fuel exploded. An orange flame leapt several feet into the air. Arm hair vaporized. Eyebrows disintegrated. Not only was the entire stove engulfed in an eerie ball of blue fire, but the picnic table was aflame as well.

"Cool!" Vicky inhaled, like someone who had just met her teen idol. I could tell she was impressed.

"I've gotta get longer matches," I exhaled.

Once the fireball quelled, we fried a pound of ground beef in record time. The stove blasted like a mighty blowtorch. If I ever needed any soldering done, it could surely handle the job.

We warmed our tortilla shells by merely waving them in the stove's general direction. Water boiled in the blink of an eye.

Simmer could be a problem, I realized, smoothing down the remnants of one eyebrow. (Maybe I could help Bob light the barbecue at the Teachers' Annual Corn Roast?)

Tents assembled, dishes cleared, table fire extinguished, I felt like a true outdoorsmen (albeit, one with thin eyebrows).

We strolled around the campsite, enjoying the tranquil evening, keeping a watchful eye out for folks lighting Coleman stoves. Other campers sat around campfires, chatting, toasting marshmallows — white goo stuck to their lips.

"There's one camping implement we failed to pack," Sharon said, nodding toward a redneck special.

The fellow was middle-aged, clad in Nike sweatpants, lumberjack shirt, and ball hat. I could tell right off he was a baseball fan. Not because of his attire, mind you. Nope, the dead giveaway wasn't the baseball cap, but rather the baseball bat. And he was wielding it in a most menacing manner.

We stopped to watch. By his own rules, he had devised a perverse game of 'Bash the Mole.' Legs spread wide, bat held high overhead, he stood rooted over a gopher hole waiting for the unsuspecting occupant to stick forth its furry little noggin. Ringside seats were sold out. Four family members sat on lawn chairs, encircling the spectacle, nursing cans of Budweiser.

"Saturday night entertainment on the lone prairie," Vicky cringed.

"I hope he has a couple of aspirin taped to the end of that," Sue winced.

"Must be a CritterVille Slugger," Sharon opined.

"Whack the brat with a baseball bat," I said, and decided that my strategy for travelling through strange lands would be to sharpen my powers of observation. Who knew what I might see?

Where We're Not From

"Sometimes I wake up grumpy; other times I let her sleep."
~ Sign at Jim Stolth's *Backroads Bike Shop*

Sunday morning, Sue, Vicky, and I sat around the picnic table examining scorch marks. Sharon was still sleeping, performing a remarkable feat of imitating Sleeping Beauty. At 8 AM, I woke her — not with a kiss, but by shaking her shoulder and explaining that an independent study revealed that 75 percent of all campers in walk-in site 1A were up.

"And you wish to make it unanimous?" she growled, rolling over. "Who says this is a majority rules, democratic campsite?"

I revised my tactic. Summoning my best officious Russian accent, I spouted: "Comrade! Time to get up!"

Sharon groaned and rolled over again. "Is it possible to wake up more tired than when I went to bed?"

We were still reeling from our lack of training and poor physical condition. Not only did we have to become accustomed to the demanding chore of pedalling a fully loaded eighty-five pound touring bike all day, but we were relearning how to sleep on the ground, as well. Usually, in the past, in preparation for trips, we'd spend a couple of hours a day on a stationary bike (except for my ill-fated first ever bicycle touring escapade). The exercise bike saddle time not only increased aerobic threshold and toned leg muscles, but, more important, it helped toughen the old heinie. We packed up and limped out of camp by 9 AM — a new record.

The road dipped into a valley. We approached a bridge spanning the Battle River. Silver mist spiraled off the water's surface. Morning fog enshrouded a canoe, floating around its bow, making it seem as though a spirit vessel was materializing from another dimension. Silvery coils swam across my vision like schools of surreal piranha. Abruptly, we climbed out of the valley, leaving the water and visions behind.

The hill leading out of the river valley provided a real-world test for our new gears. Not one skip. "Yeah!" I yelled. "Maybe I'll be able to pedal those Pyrenees after all!"

Passing a trout pond, I motioned to Sue. "I'm getting hungry. Maybe you should try that fancy rod of yours." I licked my lips in anticipation of a tasty fish fry.

Sue fished for half an hour getting nary a nibble. The only bites were from mosquitoes. (Her casting technique was flawless however.) The slippery creatures taunted us — leaping left, right, and centre, snapping up little airborne gnats.

"Did you see that one stick out its tongue and give us the fin?" Sharon asked.

Two boys fishing nearby nabbed a small fish. "Hey, what are you guys using for bait?" I called to them.

"Cheese!" they yelled back.

Drat. That was possibly the only thing not in Sue's bait box.

"Maybe we can make salad," Vicky said, watching Sue reel in some delectable-looking weeds.

When Sue tired of catching water cress, we hopped on our bikes and headed off in search of better odds for lunch. The fishing expedition's only good news: We didn't lose any bait.

At Paintearth Mines, along the banks of the Battle River, immense hydraulic shovels stood, sentinel-like, ready to chomp buckets of coal from the coarse open-pit mining area. Bumpy, lime-green hills, resembling dragon scales, constituted a reclaimed area. I gazed in lust at the machine operators' thickly padded ergonomic chairs. We pedalled on in silent contemplation, on the lookout for that elusive lunch spot, while not-so-silently cursing the sadist who invented the ill-shapen bicycle seat. Those folks who rode recumbents were sounding mighty intelligent to me.

An enormous black water tower on spindly legs, looking like some extraterrestrial invader from *War of the Worlds,* heralded our arrival into the windswept prairie settlement of Halkirk, population 131. Halkirk's claim to fame? One summer's afternoon, a deluge bucketed 175 mm of rain on the community and surrounding farmland *in a single hour* — fully half the region's normal *annual* precipitation. The resulting torrent swept away telephone poles, roads, crops, fences and anything else in its path.

In summer months, the old-time Prairie Steam Train makes a scheduled stop at Halkirk. Local service clubs serve up an abundant meal to the lucky train passengers. But on this day not even a fly stirred. It brought to mind those old cowboy movies where everything is so quiet just before the guns start blazing. The stores weren't quite all boarded up, but the place was about as close to a ghost town as one could get without going to a Casper and Friends convention.

"This is beginning to look like another fishing expedition," I said, grimacing as my stomach rumbled.

The only establishment showing any sign of life on this fine Sunday afternoon was the Halkirk Hotel tavern. We locked our bikes near a window and strode up the creaky wooden steps (spurs would have been a-chinking), and poked our noses into the dim and smoky interior. Not detecting any cooking odours, I wondered if they served food. Three regulars occupied a far table — they shifted round in their chairs and stared at us.

"We're closed," a gruff bartender polishing glasses over yonder in the dimness bluntly informed us. Sue clutched her abdomen. "Are you folks looking for something to eat?" he asked, his demeanour softening somewhat at seeing a maiden in distress.

"Most intuitive," I mumbled.

"Yes!" Sue exclaimed.

"I've got four roast beef subs left."

"Sold!" we shouted in unison.

We wended our way to a table next to the locals and flopped down on the tattered, overstuffed chairs, ready to be imparted with homegrown words of wisdom. The locals didn't disappoint. Not only were our beef sandwiches the best we had ever eaten, but a heaping helping of good ol' boy erudition accompanied our food as well.

"Where did you say you were from?" one patron asked for a third time.

"Edmonton," we replied yet again.

He shook his head. "That can't be where you're from," he finally stated flatly. "I saw youse ride up on them thar bicycles."

"What's your route?" another regular astutely cut in.

"Well," Sue sighed, "you know that place we're not from? We're cycling from there to Medicine Hat."

Everyone nodded.

Bellies sated, entertainment quota filled, we spilled out of the dim Halkirk Hotel into eye-piercing sunshine.

Vicky gazed at the sun's position. "Aw, gee," she griped. "Looks like I'll have to start heading back." She had to work the next day and still had a good three or four hours' ride back to Daysland to retrieve her car.

"Thanks for the new clusters," Sharon said.

"And the tailwind!" Sue added.

"How about joining us next weekend in Medicine Hat for a ride to Cypress Hills?" Sharon invited.

"Sounds good!" Vicky replied, swinging a leg over her bike.

I grinned. "I'll look forward to a ride back to Edmonton in your comfortable bucket seats."

"I'm sure you will," Vicky agreed. "Cheerio!" she called as she tootled off out of town, absconding with our tailwind.

Greek Sampler

> **"Life isn't a matter of milestones, but of moments."**
> ~ Rose Kennedy

Storm clouds massed on the horizon. Sharon, Sue, and I arrived in Stettler at 6:15 PM. Moments later, we discovered the town's grocery store had closed at six sharp.

"Plan B?" Sharon enquired.

We rode down main street and stopped in front of an unassuming Greek restaurant. A debate broke out on the merits of Greek food. Locked in a dead heat, the restaurant owner bounded forth to help break the impasse.

"Super bikes," he said. "Many people in my home country ride bikes." And with that as an introduction, he invited us inside his restaurant.

"Ah," I kidded, "since you own the restaurant, I guess I can't ask you what the food is like."

"If you don't like what's on the menu you may leave," he replied, and disappeared back inside the restaurant.

Who could turn down such a fair offer? We parked our bikes against the wall and were in the process of removing our helmets and padded gloves when the nimble owner reappeared, wife in tow.

In the proverbially inquisitive nature of the Greek people, they prompted us into talking about our camping gear, the contents of our bags, and, of course, what we ate while on tour.

"Everything and anything!" I replied, as the cold wind picked up a notch and hurled dust down the street.

"Cycling is good in my country," the restaurateur said, as I pulled on a fleece jacket. "It is always warm ... not like Alberta." A dust devil concurred with that pronouncement, forcefully whirling a handful of street grit straight into our sorry traps. More than happy to be ushered out of the elements, we blinked dust from our eyes and followed the owner and his wife inside.

A tiny oasis met us — a restful combination of giant plants and twittering parakeets. We found a table near the kitchen, hidden deep in almost impenetrable equatorial flora.

Mr Papadopoulos served us juicy tidbits straight from the kitchen. We learned he was a chef of some note. Plaques of distinction extolling his culinary preeminence from New York and Los Angeles restaurants adorned the walls.

Two hours later — after sampling a large portion of the menu — we waddled out. If the cycling in Greece was even half as good as Mr Papadopoulos's food had been, we would be in cyclists' heaven.

Big Valley Mud Wrestlers

> **"I loafe and invite my soul, I lean and loafe**
> **at my ease observing a spear of summer grass."**
> ~ Walt Whitman, *Leaves of Grass*

A black blizzard howled toward us. Main street Stettler was a dust bowl. We threw on rain gear, departed the friendly Greek restaurant and beelined to a campground. When we found it didn't have hot water — let alone showers — we turned around and headed back to set up on a school field.

In the morning, even with ear plugs firmly seated, a loud crash roused me. I glanced at my watch: 6 AM. Propping on one elbow, I peered through the tent's mesh. A garbage truck clanged huge steel bins overhead with a front-end forklift. Collection was probably only once a month, but this was the day.

I had been using my fleece jacket as a pillow; I bunched it over my head, trying to block the din and grab a few more winks. Not a chance. Shortly after the garbage truck departed, the school loudspeakers crackled to life, blaring forth resinous lounge music.

Sharon jabbed an elbow in my back. "Someone must have turned that music on," she said. "I think we should leave before someone finds us camped on school property."

"I hope they do," I squawked. "Maybe they'll invite us in for coffee and showers." But, alas, no one came out, or even showed up to do morning calisthenics. Sue demonstrated a few slow-motion Tai Chi movements from a class she was taking. "Sloths in motion," she termed it.

I wasn't moving any too fast myself. Sharon helped pack Sue's tent, then kicked me out of our tent. I crawled forth into the daylight. Inhabiting a tent doesn't come without a few bodily complaints. ("This lightweight tent sleeps three," the salesman had said. "Yeah," I quizzed, "but how many comfortably?" "None!" he had chirruped gleefully. "It's a *tent*.")

On the way out of Stettler we spotted a municipal swimming pool that stopped us dead in our tracks. Sharon and Sue sent me in to ask if we could use the showers.

"Certainly!" a cheery employee replied. *Must be a morning person,* I decided, looking through bleary eyes at the smiling face. "Come on in and help yourselves."

The hard stream of pulsating water massaged my cramped shoulders. I lathered and rinsed, lathered and rinsed, regaling in the delights of hot running water. After 15 glorious sudsy minutes, the smiling pool employee appeared. "Kids arriving in five minutes for swimming lessons," he said. "They're a little rambunctious," he warned.

If it hadn't been for the thought of 50 screaming little hellions invading my private spa, I could have drowned myself in the steamy shower all day. Instead, I exited the shower, slipped on clean clothes, rinsed my previous apparel, and departed the change room as a horde of screeching young 'uns ran in — swinging multi-coloured swim bags like tiny catapults before releasing them at the ceiling, the walls, the lockers, and, most importantly, each other.

I exited to the safe haven outside and waited for Sharon and Susan. The sun shone bright — and hot. *If it stays like this,* I thought, *it won't be long before I need another shower.*

"Ahhh," Sharon sighed as she emerged from the women's locker room fresh and clean. "Puts a whole new perspective on life!"

We slathered on sunscreen and followed Highway 56 south. Before long — necks scorched and tongues dragging in bicycle spokes — vultures began to circle (just kidding about the birds of prey; just me imagining I was near death). Pulling to a stop at an artesian well to regenerate our minds and bodies, we soaked bandannas, sopping up cold water, and draped them around our necks in hopes of evaporative coolness.

Back on the tarmac, in the blistering sun, it wasn't long before Sue called to me. "Hey, Mick." Sun, wind, and stress had combined to create a monumental cold sore on my lower lip. I guess Sue figured my lips rivalled Jagger's. Too bad I can't sing. I ignored her. "Want to stop at Big Valley for something to eat?"

That got my attention. Not one to refuse a chance to eat, I swung off the main highway into Big Valley. The village's façade appeared ripped straight from the tattered pages of a Louis L'Amour novel. Wooden boardwalks, false-front buildings, saloons, and chairs fashioned from old whiskey barrels lined the dusty streets.

On the edge of town, railway tracks loped past grain elevators; iron rails shimmered in the dry heat, running off into the horizon and fading to hazy parallax convergence.

An ancient mossy-trunked tree grew in the station's yard. Its full branches spread earthward, bending along a white picket fence, producing a tranquil, Mark Twain, back-in-time atmosphere. We lounged under the tree, enjoying the soft grass, while escaping the day's hottest rays, inhaling carrot cake and cinnamon buns as if there was no tomorrow.

Two boys snuck past on the other side of the fence. One pointed at Sharon and Sue. "They look like mud wrestlers," I overheard him blurt to his buddy. Unlike me, did he think muscles on women unattractive? Lucky for him, Sue and Sharon, deeply engrossed in conversation, didn't hear him. It'll be our little secret.

A strong southeasterly tossed us out of Big Valley and down the road toward Drumheller. Towering cottonwoods produced a swirling flurry of fluff as we swept along in a near whiteout. Propelled by the tailwind, we sped down the smooth flat pavement, legs spinning like windmills. Pedalling on the flat, in my top gear I easily hit 52 kilometres per hour. Tailwind high!

Sue found the wind uplifting in a different manner. Being in the lightweight category, gusts caught her and flung her willy-nilly across the lane. "This is the windiest I've ever ridden in," she confessed, her pale face the colour of birch ash. The wind picked up and howled at our backs, pushing us along at a rollicking 40 kilometres per hour.

Grape-purple thunderheads ripened in dusky globules overhead. Cloudbursts soaked us on three separate occasions. After each downpour, the sun reappeared, hot and bright. Our attempts to stay dry proved fruitless — we didn't know whether to put our raincoats on or leave them off.

Our smooth pavement ended abruptly at a construction zone. Worse, the downpours had succeeded in turning the entire site into a mud bath. Trucks passed us, big tires spraying fans of water and muck. For 15 kilometres, we slogged through a sticky black quagmire. Shoes, socks, and legs (along with bikes, packs, and backs) became coated in layers of waxy grime. The Big Valley boy's words proved prophetic: Sharon and Sue had become mud wrestlers after all.

The work zone ended. But our poor-surface ordeal didn't. We found ourselves deposited onto grooved pavement. The furrowed surface assailed our skinny bike tires, causing us to creep along, our rides hopping and wobbling like inebriated bullfrogs, threatening to dismount us.

"Preparation for cobblestones in Europe?" Sharon asked.

"Preparation for something," I replied, wondering how long the dead-genital syndrome would last.

I was still lamenting my lack of feeling when red necks in a rusty pickup passed too close for comfort, honking, scaring the blue blazes out of me. "Jeez!" Sue screeched, practically jumping out of her skin, too. "They have no idea how loud a horn is on the outside!"

"Just trying to be friendly, no doubt," I grimaced.

"Yeah, right!"

After 108 kilometres, a Drumheller campground popped into view. It even boasted hot showers!

We checked in, then waded into the shower room to scrub the muck from our arms and legs. From the amount of grime adhered to my shoes and socks, perhaps I should have worn them into the shower as well?

Warmed by the hot water, we searched for a suitable tent spot. Everything along the scenic Red Deer River was a trampled mass of muddy grass. We chose a site on higher ground, beneath a trio of sturdy (or so we hoped) cottonwood. Another downpour began. Our arboreal umbrella leaked.

We watched in silent horror as a torrent of water raced down the curb. "I don't think this is a usual summer storm," I said, seeing the water rise and climb onto the sidewalk. We huddled beneath our leaky umbrella trees, and watched in stark fascination as water rose all around us, stranding us on a small island like modern day Robinson Crusoe castaways.

"I think we better abandon ship!" Sharon declared as the ring of water encroached ever closer. "Let's swim for it, mates!" Dripping wet, we deserted our bikes. Doing our best to jump the swirling water we splashed through ankle-deep water (so much for dry socks), and bolted for a yellow-striped awning, emblazoned with one sweet word: BAKERY.

The enticing sign lured us in. However, once inside, we discovered it wasn't a bakery at all. It didn't even have day-old goodies for sale. A pimply-faced teenager behind the counter rubbed his eyes. He looked as though he had just woken up. "Looks like it might rain," he yawned.

"Yeah," Sharon grinned, as water trickled from our soaked shoes and clothing onto the floor. "If it keeps up like this it might."

I wondered if he was one of those people who thought pineapples grew on trees. I decided to hassle him, even though it's not entirely fair to have a duel of wits with an unarmed opponent. "That's a fake bakery sign on your awning ... ever heard of false advertising?"

"Well," he retorted in a tone somewhat less than 'the customer is always right,' "it came from a real bakery."

"I can tell," I said, rubbing my belly. "It still smells like doughnuts." My stomach growled. "Anywhere around here we can find something to eat?"

"If you're looking for something to eat," he said, sunnily, "Dinny's is, like, only a block away."

"How do we get there?" Sue asked, desperate for food.

"You don't know how to get to *Dinny's?*"

Sue glowered. The kid wisely continued. "Okay ... go...," he stammered, like he wasn't the most milk-filled coconut on the old palm tree, "a block out, turn right, and go, like, a block, and then, like, take the alley for a block."

"That's three blocks," Sue curtly informed the mathematically challenged youth. It's difficult to fool an accountant ... even when she's on vacation and doesn't have her trusty calculator.

We exited the falsely advertised bakery. "Kids these days," Sue muttered. I thought he was lucky she hadn't called him a blockhead.

Drumheller's Royal Tyrrell Museum

"Who bravely dares must sometimes risk a fall."
~ Tobias Smollett

Another unsolicited early morning wake-up call roused us. An electrical transformer on a telephone pole near our tent exploded reminiscent of a 6 AM cannon blast. We levitated.

Soon, a dozen workmen with heavy equipment crowded around the site. Backup warning Sonalerts beeped, backhoe buckets clanged, and dump truck boxes slammed. Men in hard hats, orange coveralls and reflective vests bellowed unintelligible instructions into the din. I peered out. "It's true," I moaned. "Canada has only two seasons: winter and construction."

Camped in the midst of a major destruction zone, any further attempt at sleep proved futile. We admitted defeat and got dressed in a daze; the humour of repeated early morning wake-ups somehow escaping us. A trifle less amiable than a grizzly awakening from hibernation, I scowled at the offending workers as they ripped the earth apart mere metres from our tent. "Can't get much worse than this," I roared to no one in particular.

Suddenly, slate grey clouds with engorged bellies slit open; water gushed forth like so many slaughtered swine intestines. To our amusement the backhoe mired down in its just-created slippery muck hole. Talk about digging one's own grave. Only the very tops of its tires showed above the mud.

With no abatement in sight from either rain or noisy workmen, we folded our soggy tents. Other camp inhabitants — snug (and smug) within motorhomes' dry confines (whose sizes rivalled our house) — pointed and sniggered. "Wretched weather brings out the best in folks," I grouched.

Deciding the best course of action would be to spend the day inside, we headed for the Royal Tyrrell Museum of Paleontology — a world-class dinosaur and archeological artifacts museum. Once there, we met other cyclists traipsing around in rain gear. I guess we all had the same good idea. Warm, dry, and comfortable, we spent the entire day enjoying the spectacle of enormous dinosaur bones wired together like immense 3D jigsaw puzzles.

Hours later, still not having seen everything, we exited. The outside world was no drier. Rain continued to hose down; roadside ditches brimmed with rushing water.

Foregoing another night at the construction zone campsite, we braved the elements for five kilometres to another campground. At Dinosaur Park RV Resort, the woman in the check-in office tried to console us. "This is the poopiest day we've had in a long time," she understated. We laughed at her remark, but her assessment didn't make us feel a whole lot drier.

For a hefty fee we acquired a site downwind from the biffies. "Oh, joy," Sue said, noting our less than bucolic location.

"Look at the bright side," I ventured. "You can drink all you want without worrying about not making it to the washroom."

"With all this rain," Sue said, "I doubt I'll ever be thirsty again."

The only good thing about the campground was a group of Tour du Canada cross-country cyclists (Tour du Canada is a non-profit corporation that offers the longest annual bike ride in the world — from Vancouver to Saint John's). Tom, one of its 40 group members, told us they had 64 days to cycle across Canada.

His bravery encouraged us. Not because he was cycling across Canada in slightly over two months, but rather, four days earlier, Tom had crashed and burned — knocked from his bicycle by a wayward travel trailer awning. When the trailer had passed him, its dangling sunshade had mowed him off at the ankles. A souvenir row of jagged red stitches marched up the length of his left calf.

"You should get lots of sympathy riding like that," I said.

"Well, the attending cop was less than sympathetic," Tom related.

"Huh?" I asked. "What do you mean?"

"The cop said to me: 'You guys shouldn't be on the road anyway.'"

"No kidding!" I exclaimed, shaking my head in disbelief.

Tom smiled. "The Tour du Canada tour operators lodged a formal complaint at the cop shop."

I shook my head again, amazed that even the authorities seemed unaware of cyclists' road rights.

Food for Thought

"You got to be careful if you don't know where you're going, because you might not get there."
~ Yogi Berra

"Is it my imagination, or is everyone in camp wearing high heels this morning?" Sharon grumbled, rubbing the sleep from her eyes. Our record for longest streak of noisy campgrounds continued. Unchallenged. Unequaled.

The sleep thief on this particular occasion was the washrooms' raised platform. As each camper entered, footsteps crescendoed, reverberating on the wooden deck. Then, the grand finale: two doors slammed together, cracking like a pair of giant wooden cymbals.

After a brief rest, the process began in reverse. Even ear plugs failed to block the constantly repeated movement.

The musical campers (and sunshine!) prompted us to get a move on.

"Want to get anything?" Sharon asked as we passed a food store on our way out of Drumheller.

"Nope," I replied. "We'll just have to lug it up that steep hill out of town." My snap decision would prove to be a mistake we would all pay for later.

Pedalling past our old campsite, a familiar beeping caught my attention. The backhoe! They were still working on repairing the transformer. Behemoth motorhomes sat trapped, mud up to their axles. Ha! It was my turn to laugh and point.

We warmed quickly as we pedalled the kilometre-long hill out of Drumheller. A herd of pronghorn antelope grazed peacefully on the hillside as we ground our way slowly upward. The males in the group were particularly attractive with black cheek patches and foot-long pronged horns. Natives called the little animals 'Prairie Ghosts' — perhaps because of their camouflage, or perhaps because of the little animal's uncanny ability to disappear so quickly. Pronghorns can reach a zippy hundred kilometres per hour. Their velocity easily outdistances any predator audacious enough to try to catch one for its dinner.

We attained the top. Our reward was a sweeping panoramic view of the surrounding valley and farmland. On a distant crest, we spied the old Rosedale Suspension Bridge from bygone coal mining glory days. (At one time, more than 120 coal mines were active in the area.)

Riding past field after field of butter-yellow canola, rolling to the distant horizon and beyond, we arrived in Dalum shortly before noon. The entire place consisted of one ramshackle gas station, a clapboard church, and two dilapidated houses.

The gas station didn't appear too busy. Its grey-haired proprietor dozed — arms folded across his chest — roosting on a scuffed wooden chair just outside the doorway. Like a bored school kid, he had the chair tipped back. It balanced precariously on its two hind legs like a trained circus dog.

"Got any pop?" I asked, as we pulled to a stop near him. He opened one eye and surveyed our sudden appearance.

"Sure," he drawled after squirting a stream of brown tobacco juice the length of his arm. He jerked an oil-stained thumb toward an antiquated Coke machine inside the station.

Leaving him on his recliner, we entered and discovered the machine's money slot taped over. "Owner-operated," he called as his chair thumped down onto all four legs. He rose and hobbled inside like someone who had sat too long on a wooden bicycle seat. "What's your flavour?" he asked.

Satisfied with our choices, he plumbed the depths of a greasy overall pocket, and fished forth a shiny silver key. Twisting the machine open, he extracted our dusty effervescent selections.

I passed the old gent a fiver, took the change in chocolate bars, and sauntered back out into the sun. On the church's sun-bleached steps we flumped down and popped open our drinks. Imbibing the cold liquid in warm sunshine, we extolled the virtues of bicycle touring.

At 12:01, a resounding clang, not unlike a large pipe wrench being thrown on metal, echoed from the gas station. The station owner sallied forth, studiously locked the station's front door, hopped in a faded red pickup, fired up the vintage beast in a trembling belch of grey exhaust, revved 'er twice ... and drove to a house 30 feet yonder. Didn't even get out of first gear.

"Must be time for lunch," Sharon mused.

"World's shortest commute!" I guffawed.

"Nice to see some folks don't spend long fighting traffic," Sue chimed in with a belly laugh. She paused. "Do you think there's a washroom?" she asked. "I need a washroom."

"Looks like a fine spot over there," I suggested, waving toward the adjacent graveyard.

Sharon reproved me dourly. "That's *not* what's meant by 'paying one's last respects.'"

"Has anyone tried the church door?" Sue wondered aloud. I watched in amusement as the Lycra-clad cyclist got up and knocked on the old wooden church door. She waited. Then, when there was no answer, she tried the knob. Like magic, it silently glided open.

"My God! It's true!" I exclaimed. "Knock, and it shall be opened unto you." We traipsed inside the church. Its dim interior was a cool and welcome respite from the soaring outside temperature. Kaleidoscopes of stained glass lined exterior walls. Thick tan ropes drooped from steeple bells in the loft overhead.

"Bells!" I cried. "I wonder what they sound like?"

"Restrain yourself," Sharon said, cautioning me with a look similar to the one I reserved for misbehaving children.

Hells bells. All the fun taken out of my church explorations, I slouched back outside to sulk in the sunlight. "Too cold in there anyway," I shivered.

Before long, strains of *Amazing Grace* were resonating from the church piano, spilling out into the peaceful afternoon, washing like a tonic over the sleepy countryside, raising my spirits. When the two maestros had exhausted their combined repertoire they rejoined me on the church steps.

"Did you find a washroom?" I enquired.

"Yep," Sharon answered. "No showers, though."

"I guess we'd better go look for some then," I said. I stood and rubbed my stomach. "I'm beginning to feel a little peckish, too." We struck out for the gas station where we had abandoned our bikes. They were still there: in the exact spot we had leaned them against the rust-stained and peeling beige wall.

Thirty-two kilometres later, we rolled into Hussar, past hungry, on the lookout for a grocery store. A row of grain elevators stood off to one side. But there was little else.

"Not exactly on the mainstream tourist route," Sharon noted, glancing at the lack of habitation and amenities.

A lone cowpoke earnestly studied our arrival. "You folks lost?" he called.

Grinning, we flung him two wraps and a hooey, and reined to a halt in front of Tom's General Store — the only store in town.

"Looks like this is our choice of eating establishments," I said, laying my bike curbside and striding ten feet to push open the door. Somewhat rudely my nose squished against the glass. "Must be out," I said, stepping back, bemused.

"By any chance," Sue asked slowly, "is this Wednesday? Because if it is," she said, surveying the posted hours, "they closed at 1 PM."

"Oh. Terrific," I managed, consulting my digital watch, and confirming the time was indeed later than 1 PM and the little black triangle was pointing to 'W' for the day of the week.

"Maybe the post office knows where we can get some food," Sharon suggested. "If they're not closed too."

We trundled into the post office feeling like starving hoboes. A woman behind the counter smiled kindly. I enquired about food places. The woman sadly shook her head.

"Tom's is the only place in town."

Oh, my. We stood transfixed, the postal clerk's portentous words sinking in like fire on ice. Sue cursed under her breath.

We must have looked about to cry. The postal worker spouted, "If I was home right now, I'd fix you bunch a sandwich."

"I can man the post office while you run home and fix us something," I said, only half-kidding.

"Hang on a minute," she said, not taking me up on my offer. I guess she didn't think I was serious. "I'll phone Tom and see if he can open up for you."

She dialed as we looked on hopefully. Alas, Tom didn't answer. The postal clerk, looking ruminative, thumped the receiver back onto its cradle. "You know," she said, "I usually have cheese and crackers here. But today I don't have any."

The invisible offering made us feel no less hungry. Maybe more so. "I'm starving," Sue whined, clutching her bare midriff. "I've cycled over 50 kilometres and all I've eaten is some crappy cereal, a pop, and a stale chocolate bar." Hunger brings out the best in one.

"Hey!" the postal woman said, beaming. "The gas station sells pop." Then her face twisted, as though remembering something wonderfully sinful. "I shouldn't tell you this," she said, giggling like a prepubescent school girl, "but just before you came in here, I ate a chocolate bar."

At that confession, something inside the postal worker snapped. Unable to contain her mirth, she broke into fits of laughter. She came perilously close to toppling off her stool.

"She doesn't realize how serious food is to famished cyclists," I whispered to Sharon.

"We best get Sue out of here before she tampers with a mail clerk," Sharon whispered back. "No doubt, that's a federal offence."

Leaving the mail lady alternately holding her sides and wiping tears, we escorted Sue outside onto Hussar's main street. "Before she goes postal," Sharon grimaced. "It may put Hussar on the map, but not in a good way. I can see the headline: HUSSAR HUNGER. CRAZED CYCLIST STAMPS POSTAL WORKER."

Not having the strength to get back on our bikes, we pushed them to the gas station. No chocolate bars, no chips, no junk food of any kind greeted us. "What kind of country is this?" I whined. Only a few soft drinks were available.

I snickered when Sue selected a diet variety. "I'm sorry," I apologized, "but that's hardly the boost you need. I think we'd better find somewhere to cook our emergency rations."

Dejected — and bellies growling — we rode to the town's fairgrounds. One lone picnic table squatted in the weeds. Waiting for the water to boil, we lamented our 'luck' of arriving late on the only day the only store in town closed early.

Sue guzzled her allotted portion of noodles. "That was a good appetizer," she said. I noted the sharp look of hunger still haunting her eyes. I scoured deep into my panniers and discovered a forgotten packet of oatmeal.

Sue devoured the steaming porridge. I hoped its carbohydrates would tide her over until we found an open food store.

Over 40 kilometres stood between us and the next town of any size on our route.

Two hours later we arrived in Bassano. We besieged the nearest dairy bar and inhaled double mozza-bacon burgers, double chocolate-banana milkshakes, and double-scoop chocolate ice cream cones.

Finishing our feeding frenzy, I proposed we hit the IGA for groceries before they closed for the day.

We prowled IGA's well-stocked aisles, buying packages of pasta and glass jars of tomato and mushroom sauce. Hang the weight! We never wanted to feel hungry again.

After forking over our money for the multiple bags of grocers, we treated ourselves to the city campground and its opulent hot showers. Our Shangri-La was disturbed only by passing freight trains that rumbled past every hour.

Intolerance

> **"We don't see things as they are,**
> **we see them as we are."**
> ~ Anaïs Nin

An earthshaking clatter rattled us out of our sleeping bags. Train derailment? No, it was from the leaden sky. Odd. A thunderstorm in the morning? But something had to keep our early morning wake-up streak alive.

The main part of the storm ran to the north. A few wind-blown drops sprinkled us before the wind cleared the clouds off, then blew them back in to sprinkle us again.

"I have zero desire to spend the day cycling in the rain," I said. "Maybe we should stay and stock up on hot showers."

My riding partners needed no convincing.

We breakfasted on stacks of golden pancakes topped with fresh strawberries and mounds of whipped cream.

When I approached the trash barrel after breakfast to discard rubbish, an old gent from a motorhome sidled over.

"I saw a hobo picking through the garbage the other night," he grumped. "I'd a blasted him if I had my shotgun with me!"

Yikes! This citizen's intolerance frightened me. I returned to our campsite ... wouldn't want to linger near the garbage bins too long.

"Sure glad we have gun control laws in Canada," I declared, before repeating the old man's story to Sharon and Sue.

"You know," Sharon said, shaking her head, "the older I get, the less I can stand intolerant people."

Dinosaur Park

> **"Laughing stock: cattle with a sense of humor."**
> ~ Bumper Sticker

Near the village of Rosemary, on a tabletop-flat road, we passed a road warning sign: STEEP DOWNHILL.

"Get a load of that!" I chuckled at the absurdity. "Cripes, there's not even a hill in the vicinity, let alone a steep one!"

"I think they mean that dip," Sharon said, motioning to a barely perceptible undulation in the road surface. "It's darn flat around this part of the prairies," she contended, gazing out at the horizon in all four directions. "Refreshing when the road ripples now and then."

"Even a corner is cause for celebration," Sue laughed.

The sun bristled in a hot blue sky. We stopped in Rosemary outside Harry's General Store. I bought a root beer Popsicle, and asked Craig, the owner of Harry's General Store: "What's with the 'steep hill' sign back there?"

"Ah," Craig responded, "some highway worker spilled his coffee one morning when he hit the dip. 'Jeez,' he said, 'we better put a sign up.'"

"Ah, ha, that explains it," I said, and shuffled outside. Sitting curbside, opposite Harry's General Store, we felt as if we were in a sauna as the temperature approached broil. Lucky for us, Harry's had a sale on Popsicles. I did my best to consume the entire lot myself. With Sharon and Sue's help, we polished off Craig's complete inventory. Time to move on to Fudgesicles! We trooped back inside the general store.

"When's your next delivery of ice cream products?" Sue asked, noticing with alarm that we were nearing the bottom of the bin.

"Oh, probably in a day or two," Craig figured, glancing outside at the glaring sun. "Don't worry about it though ... eat as many as you like."

While I paid for the last remaining Fudgesicle, a cowpuncher waltzed in on the heels of his scuffed cowboy boots. He picked out a pair of new leather work gloves, waved them at Craig, and strode toward the door. "Add them to my tab," he spat in a crisp tone as he passed the till without paying.

Amazing! A place in the world that still ran tabs?

"How do I get a tab?" I asked. "I'm planning on eating your entire stock of Revels next."

"All you have to do is ask," Craig said. "It's been a tradition at Harry's General Store for over 50 years now ... from when my dad, Harry, owned the store." He paused with a wide smile. "It's rather hard to break the habit. People seem to like it — a lot."

Impressive. A bastion still existed where folks trusted each other? What would we discover next?

"Is there somewhere I can fill my water bottle?" Sharon asked in a rather sticky voice. Craig whipped the bottle from her hand and flitted to a sink at the rear of the store ... leaving his cash register wide open, money visible. Being a hardened urbanite, his naïveté shocked me.

I mentioned it to Craig on his return. "I wasn't too worried," he responded with a wink. "Just how far ahead of me on a bike do you think you could have made it, anyway?"

Okay, he had a point. It still boggled my mind though.

Sharon, Sue, and I moved outdoors to a bench to enjoy the heat — and another round of Revels.

Craig swished out the door. "I'm off to the post office," he sang out. "Answer the phone if it rings, will ya?"

"Sure!" we chorused.

"Where do you hide your washrooms?" I asked Craig when he returned from the post office.

"At the bakery," he replied. "Two doors down."

"What!" we gasped. "There's a bakery in town?" We had been upwind the entire time.

"Uh, excuse us," Sharon said, abdicating our phone answering duties. "I think it's time we moved on to our second course."

"Is it okay if we leave our bikes here?" I asked.

"No problem," Craig replied. "If anyone wants to buy them I'll just deduct the amount from your tab."

Still chuckling at Craig's sense of humour we entered Rosemary's scrumptious-smelling bakery. Lynn, the afternoon counter person, laughed when I requested "one of everything." As she filled my order, I asked her how the town got its name.

"Rosemary is named after the Queen's cousin," she said.

"Really? The Queen has a cousin named Rosemary?"

"Oh, yes," Lynn replied. "Other towns in the area are named for Royalty too ... Patricia, Duchess, Countess...."

Hmmm. Maybe that accounted for the royal treatment we were receiving in Rosemary?

After taste-testing at least one of each baked goodie, we ambled back to Harry's General Store and resumed our positions on the bench. We were beginning to feel like regulars with our tab and all.

A gritty elderly farmer pulled up to the store's gas pump. He sprang from the battered Subaru as if he had hit the eject button, grabbed a gas pump nozzle and shoved it deep into the vehicle's filler hole. When he squeezed the pump's trigger ... fuel sloshed onto the ground! I could tell right off there was some sort of problem. The old feller, confounded, knelt and peered under his auto. "I'll be...," he mumbled, flabbergasted, and rubbed his grizzled chin. "There's no tank!"

He stood upright and removed the gas pump nozzle from the filler neck. From where I sat I could see daylight through the opening. The old geezer stooped and put his eye to the filler hole, peering into it like a lad intently watching a World Series ball game through a knothole or a youngster engrossed in peeking through a keyhole as an older sister undressed. "Yep," he nodded after a long while, "that confirms it. No tank."

Craig came out to check on the situation.

"I just bought it yesterday," the old farmer told him.

"I guess you got a good deal on it then," Craig deadpanned. "What does it run on? Air?"

The old farmer circled the Subaru twice, wondering if he'd been bamboozled. On his second go-around he discovered another gas flap. "Let's see what's behind door Number Two," he chuckled, and flipped open the cover. "Well, the good news is," he reported, "I can't see clear through this time."

The old codger pumped fuel into the second orifice, keeping a wary eye on the fuel-soaked ground as if this one too, might at any second, begin gushing like an out-of-control oil well.

Craig uncoiled a rubber garden hose and sprayed away the spilled gasoline. "Just in case old Farley comes by," he said. "Wouldn't want the old feller to quit smoking *that* way."

Craig didn't have any takers on our loaded touring bikes. "Guess we'll settle our tab and head out of Dodge," I said. We planned to spend the next couple of days in the Badlands Dinosaur Provincial Park — one of only a handful of Canadian sites to make the World Heritage list. (Another in Alberta is Head-Smashed-In Buffalo Jump, located near Fort Macleod — it's one of the world's oldest and best-preserved buffalo jumps known to exist. Indians used the Jump for more than 5,500 years to hunt bison by stampeding them over a cliff. I thought I'd like to work at the interpretive centre for a summer ... just so I could answer the phone, "Hello. Head-Smashed-In, may I help you?")

Recalling our 'Hussar Hunger,' we went for the gusto, stocking up on groceries. Satisfied we weren't going to starve anytime soon, we saddled up and spurred down the road to Duchess.

The prairies continued, flatter than a pancake. "Makes me hungry just looking at it," Sharon said. *I'd probably want some syrup to go with it,* I thought. *But then I'd get all sticky and want to take a bath....* A sea of blue flax, divided by a strip of black asphalt, waved in fields as far as the eye could see. White and yellow wild clover peppered the roadsides. Cattails poked brown tips from occasional man-made marshes. Sprinklers irrigated crops, pumping water from a canal system controlled by mini-locks.

In Duchess, Sharon spotted a sign for a meat shop. "Check if they have sliced turkey," she prompted. It didn't look like a deli to me, but I dutifully entered the shop.

A half-dozen brawny men sat around a table wrapping ground beef. Raw meat clung to their muscular forearms. Another fellow with a big knife trimmed an upside down hanging side of cow into giant steaks — nary a feather in sight.

"Um," I said with some hesitation, "you don't have turkey here, do you?"

They looked insulted.

"No poultry here, son," one replied.

"You're in Alberta beef country, boy," another bull-necked worker stated flatly.

A weak smile pursed my lips. Behooved, I thanked them, exited in some haste, and nearly smacked into the tailgate of a pickup parked in front. It sported a bumper sticker: SUPPORT THE BEEF INDUSTRY. RUN OVER A CHICKEN.

"No turkey?" Sharon asked on my empty-handed return.

"Nope! Not a one," I beefed. "And they don't play kd lang in there either."

Frying in the sun, slugging it out with a pugnacious headwind, we arrived at Dinosaur Corner feeling as dry as a hunk of old cowhide. Ranchers' brands emblazoned picnic tables. Make no mistake about it: we were in cattle country.

Toward Dinosaur Provincial Park, the prairie continued flat and brown. *Where are they hiding these so-called 'Badlands'?* I wondered. As we pedalled closer to Dinosaur Provincial Park, shallow ravines, arroyos, and coulees hinted of something different. Sandstone spires and pinnacles replaced the endless expanses of farmland we had cycled through for the past week.

The asphalt ended without warning. We reined to a stop at the precipice, and gaped into a vast cauldron of murky witches' brew, stunned into silence by the enormity of the spectacle spreading below us. An outrageous sunken bowl filled with daring wind and water carved stone formations — a wild west scene more dramatic than any John Wayne movie backdrop.

Mystified, breathless, and wide-eyed, we stared across the lip of the bowl. Small settlements and clumps of trees perched on the prairie's edge — all seeming about to fall face-first into the great abyss. Gazing down at the vast sunken treasure trove gouged deep within the magnitude of windswept prairie, my thoughts surprised me: It was the man-made structures amongst the incredible natural wonders that seemed foreign.

Beneath an indigo sky, I stood in awe, contemplating the tranquility, imagining a time when dinosaurs roamed there only 75 million years ago. Stark hoodoos, streaked with intermixed layers of chocolate browns, mustard yellows, burnt oranges, oxide reds, and coffee-with-cream tans, marched before us, holding tight their secrets of earth's past. It was as if time had stood still. I snapped a photo, locking a phase of geology into nevermore erosion.

Inspired, we lurched down a steep gravel road, bumping over a surface that would have made a washboard proud. We gripped our brake levers in hopes we didn't build up too much bone-shaking speed and become prematurely extinct ourselves. Besides, we wouldn't want to pass the mushroom shaped hoodoos, thousands of years in the making, too quickly!

Sand Piper Creek, our campground location, peeped into view. Not a sandpiper in sight. Sandflies and mosquitoes, however, buzzed without relent, attacking ears, eyes, and necks. Any exposed skin was fair game. Some of the more adventurous pilots even flew up our noses. "Maybe they should have named it Sand Fly Creek," I cried, slathering on copious amounts of insect repellent. Still, I swatted away clouds of biting pests. I was beginning to formulate my own theory as to the real reason why dinosaurs became extinct.

"This bug spray is like candy to them!" Sharon hollered.

"I'm a DEET man," I sang, slapping on more bug dope.

Sue, entertaining her own personal gnat groupies with a flashy little two-step, frowned. "Are we having fun yet?"

Forbidden Zone

> **"All the earth colours of the painter's palette are out there in the many miles of badlands. The light Naples yellow through ochres — orange and red and purple earth — even the soft earth greens."**
> ~ Georgia O'Keeffe

A clanging triangle signalled the announcement of a pancake breakfast. We had lucked out and landed in the park on Parks Day. Every activity was free, beginning with hotcakes.

"Hey, this is where I could shine," I said, joining the burgeoning line-up. "I wonder how many pancakes I can eat?" Too bad it wasn't a pancake eating contest.

While we waited for hot-off-the-griddle flapjacks, staff encouraged us to enter a draw for free T-shirts. *Why not?* I figured. *I'm out of clean clothes.* We dropped our completed forms into a draw box along with hundreds of others.

A park staff drew out a name: "Sharon Anderson."

"All right!" Sharon yelled, jumping up to collect her sparkling new and clean CELEBRATE PARKS DAY T-shirt.

When Sharon claimed her prize, I noticed they didn't ask her for identification — or even a ticket stub. *Hmmm,* I thought, *when they draw another name I'll jump up and shout 'All right!'* I could really use some clean clothes.

After breakfast, we grabbed our water bottles — the temperature already crispy, well over a hundred degrees Fahrenheit in the shade — and gamboled off on a self-guided hike.

After some distance, we stumbled across a sign that warned: YOU ARE ENTERING THE FORBIDDEN ZONE. The terrain was dry and barren, save for a couple of scattered cacti and sagebrush, and a few dinky patches of tawny yellowed grass tufts. The whole area resembled a moonscape — so stark and devoid of colour that it looked like dusty lunar craters rather than somewhere in southern Alberta.

We gained a vantage point, and gazed down at the Red Deer river. A protected species of cottonwood grew along the bank; sharp green leaves contrasted with the drab hard-baked earth browns and mottled yellows surrounding us. Two hours before noon and the temperature had reached meltdown. Poor Michael Jackson would have been reduced to nothing more than a steaming pile of mutagenic beige poop.

Relentless bugs. Searing sun. The main inhabitants were snakes and bloodsucking insects.

"Hmmm," I mumbled, squashing a pesky blackfly and shaking a drop of perspiration dangling from my nose. "No wonder old-timers called this the 'Bad Lands.' If the heat didn't get you the mozzies and blackflies did."

We managed to elude the Forbidden Zone, and sought relief from the all-that-is-solid-melts-into-thin-air temperatures by joining an air-conditioned lab tour.

Over 40 dinosaur species, some dating back 75 million years (as of Wednesday), have been unearthed in the area. Resting on a heavy-duty work bench beneath bright lamps and industrial-strength vacuum hoses was a Centrosaurus skull, 36 inches in length. (One of the most impressive bone-beds in the park is the Centrosaurus area. About the size of a football field, it contains approximately 20 to 60 bones per metre.)

"Before the 'well-horned lizard' can be exhibited," a paleontologist was explaining, "a year's worth of meticulous work needs to be completed. We chisel away any dirt and debris using a common dental pick and Pharmasave toothbrush."

Sharon whispered, "Sounds about as much fun as washing the Empire State building windows."

"Yeah," I grimaced. "With your tongue."

We left the dusty extinct beasts and joined a lecture on wriggling, live snakes. Luckily, we arrived late and had to sit in the back.

"Snakes are amazing creatures," a handler was saying. "How many times have you eaten today?" she asked. I began a quick tally. Before I had finished, she continued, "We have a snake in our zoo that hasn't eaten for two years!"

Sharon saw fit to joke about it. "Wasn't that right around the time that new zookeeper went missing?"

The lecture concluded with a draw for free T-shirts. Sue and I both won. Purely coincidental, of course.

Donning our new garb, we hopped on our bikes and pedalled a gravel loop through excavation sites. Sticks and string marked out various digs for examination. Glass enclosures covered some, keeping the site preserved as it was originally found with dinosaur bones sticking forth from the earth. A gentle breeze fanned our cheeks. The setting sun traversed chocolate hills, striking hoodoos and casting shadows of bygone Tyrannosaurus.

Oasis

"I know a shortcut. But it takes longer."
~ Kevin Kunderman

To beat the heat, we rose at 5:30 AM and headed back up the gravel road. It seemed straight up. "This is steeper than I remember," I said, puling like a schoolgirl, already initiating my new T-shirt to the rigors of bicycle touring.

On the plus side, my minuscule rate of travel supplied ample time to observe the surroundings. The rising sun streaked through coulees; oblique rays lit monstrous otherworldly formations. Eerie. Awesome. The bold landscape inspired a sense of wonder and awe in us all over again.

We attained the top and stopped to catch our breath. I pulled deep on my water bottle, drinking in one last view. The incredible landscape made it impossible not to think how bizarre the whole thing was, plunked as it was amidst otherwise featureless prairie. Something certainly had a sense of humour.

I shoved my water bottle back into its cage, and pedalled off into the surprising early morning heat. A tailwind swept us through the farming and ranching community of Brooks, then on to Kinbrook Island Provincial Park.

At Kinbrook we found Lake Newell, created in 1911 for irrigation purposes. Sharon and Sue plunged into the glossy water to cool themselves. "Warmer than the Bow River!" they yelped.

Must be shallow, I figured. *After all, how deep can it be? They just flooded flat prairie to create the lake.*

"If you think you're drowning," I called, "stand up!"

We camped nearby. Night passed quietly enough, but the morning sun's searing rays woke us early. I crawled out and groaned: we had missed setting our wee tent in the shade of a rather large tree by the merest whisker!

"Look at the bright side," Sharon said, squinting at the sun, "our string of early morning wake-ups is still intact."

"Terrific," I replied, bleary-eyed.

Leaving Kinbrook, we opted for an unpaved shortcut to Highway 36, in the mistaken belief that 30 kilometres on gravel would be faster and easier than backtracking 64 paved kilometres. Wrong. We'd been on worse gravel roads before, but not from choice. The stretch was rough; it rattled and shook us like a coin-operated bed at a cheap motel.

A herd of iron horses ran wild over the yellowed prairie grass, bucking hard, pumping oil. A wasteland of hardscrabble soil sat behind Lake Newell. *How had anything survived in the area before the irrigation project?*

I had little time to wonder; our own survival troubles were looming. Handling loaded touring bikes with narrow tires on loose gravel required an intricate balancing act. Wind gusts tossed us like rag dolls across the ball bearing surface — especially ultra-light, skinny as a stick of spaghetti, Sue.

Dusty, dehydrated, and darn near done in, we rejoined the paved Highway 36 at the crossroads to Rainier. The well-named Oasis Restaurant caught our attention. We wheeled into the parking lot for a well-deserved break and some rehydration.

"My knees ache like they've been clamped in a vise for a week," Sue complained, dismounting. Sue toured without front panniers. Her rear panniers were crammed well past capacity. Her rear rack was heavily utilized — festooned with sleeping bag, pad, tent, fishing rod and 5-pound box of tackle. But that's not all. A mound of clothes — larger than an average 3-year-old — topped the load. With all weight rearward, Sue's bike, like a hell-hound Cerberus, jumped on her at every opportunity.

A fierce gust suddenly erupted. It seemed to say: *I'll give you something to complain about!* The blast of wind hoisted Sue's bike off the ground like an aluminum feather, then hurled it down. A greasy chainwheel spiked Sue's calf. Four fang-shaped wounds appeared, dribbling blood and oozing oil.

I felt sorry for her. The poor girl had only a few days left before returning to work and she was a mess. The combination of relentless sun and fair skin had turned her face tomato-red. Her helmet strap had blocked the sun, creating a white strip beneath her chin and producing a perpetual ear-to-ear Cheshire grin. Her slender legs were sunburned and peeling, covered with bruises in various shades of purple and green. Her arms hadn't fared much better, red and blistered as they were. The backs of her hands sported oval burns where cycling gloves had left exposed skin. (How would she explain those?) She was a veritable walking commercial for the benefits of sunscreen. And her latest acquisition: calf perforations (so attractive in nylons) would complement her office look with a row of scabby dots. Not to mention she would return to work exhausted! Sue's fellow workers would wonder what kind of "holiday" her sadistic "friends" had dragged her on. I could hear her plaintive refrain: "Are we having fun yet?"

In Scandia, I received my chuckle for the day. I asked a fellow how the hamlet acquired its name. When he didn't know, a nearby 6-year-old came to his rescue. "From that rock over there," she said. Sure enough, marking the town's name, a large granite boulder had SCANDIA indelibly engraved onto its surface.

We arrived at the Bow River provincial campground, only to discover that the campground was an eyesore — and a smelly one at that! We continued on.

In Vauxhall, the municipal campground ridiculously saw fit to charge per tent — and there were no showers! Feeling taken advantage of (after all, our two tents' footprints were a fraction of one motorhome), we declined again.

Drowning our sorrows in ice cream at a nearby dairy bar we gazed out at the darkening sky in alarm. Grey clouds, saturnine and brooding, spit sporadic drops. By the time we returned outside, the weather had worsened — threatening to drown our sorrows in another manner. In a temporary lull, we made a break for it. About as inconspicuous as a tabby cat with canary feathers protruding from its mouth, we roamed back streets and alleyways, on the lookout for a suitable camp spot. A baseball field with its lush grass looked the most promising. It even sported outhouses!

It began to pour. "We can use the dugout for an emergency shelter," Sue decided. Throwing our bikes under the bleachers, we dove for cover. *Safe!*

Between downpours, Sharon stole out. She struck up a conversation with a field maintenance man and asked him if it would be all right to camp on the ball field. She hit a home run!

"Another first for our camping log book," Sharon said, relating the good news of her encounter.

Sitting on the bench in the dugout, like a trio of benched sluggers, we boiled up a giant pot of chili. After stuffing ourselves with the wonderful concoction, I suggested we set our tents at centre field. Alas, vigorous rain (not to mention my teammates) vetoed the idea. Instead, we pitched our tents inside the snug and dry players' shelter.

Flatter Than A No-Flat

"We know what happens to people who stay in the middle of the road. They get run down."
~ Aneurin Bevan

Our wake-up call was a couple of sluggers who came for early morning batting practice. Aluminum bats tinked long lob fly balls into centre field; I was glad Sue and Sharon had talked me out of setting my tent there. I might have been singing a different version of *Take Me Out to the Ball Game.*

Our day began with a shower of the welcome kind — a warm one at the public swimming pool. Happy and clean, our morning ride was smooth sailing despite a strong crosswind. Rolling fields of bright yellow sunflowers delighted us; mellow heads nodding in the breeze, as if bowing to their mighty sun god.

We rode from acres of sunflowers to fields of green-stalked corn. In Taber, the sweet corn capital of Alberta, we stopped at a park and refueled our tanks. Between bites, Sharon complained her rear tire felt a little on the low side. "It's only flat on the bottom," I kidded, grabbing my air pump and swinging into action. "Have you seen this?" I asked in alarm, pointing to a treadless bald spot. "Do you think we should replace it?" I wondered, erring for the first time in history on the cautious side.

"Ah, it's lasted this long," Sharon said (erring for the first time in history on the incautious side). "Surely it'll last two more days to Medicine Hat. We can get one there. Or we can phone Vicky and have her add one to our tab."

I added air to Sharon's tire and we departed town, assisted by a healthy tailwind (that alone should have alerted us that something was wrong). Sure enough, less than 15 kilometres later — on a lonesome stretch of highway between Taber and Purple Springs — Sharon's rear tire suffered a massive deflating episode.

The tire held a so-called 'no-flat' tube. Its end wasn't so much a bang as a strangulated, wheezing guttural croak. The 'no-flat' tube, stuffed to the gills with a green substance, battled valiantly to seal the gaping wound. Neon-green gook swirled out in astonishing looping circles, looking as if a million grasshopper guts were spewing on an out-of-control amusement park ride.

Sharon's bike fishtailed. I was certain she was headed overboard for a close encounter of the asphalt kind. But, instead of shipwrecking, the little mermaid battened down her rollicking vessel's hatches, reeled in her catch, and oared to a safe port on the road's sandy shoulder: rear tire a shredded mutiny, legs netted in algae-green slime.

"Can we fix it?" I asked, attempting humour.

"No," came her deadpan reply. "We can't."

A maroon Continental Mark IV, the size of a boat, drifted alongside and dropped anchor. A porthole opened. An elderly passenger peered out. "Do you need any help?"

Sharon elected to wait with the bikes and wipe herself up. Sue and I caught a ride back to Taber with the good Samaritans. They ferried us to a sports store where we received bad news.

"We only carry 27-inch tires," a clerk informed me.

"Great," I said, biting my lip. "Know where I can get a 700?"

"Lethbridge," came the earnest reply.

Considering Lethbridge was 50 kilometres away in the opposite direction, it didn't appear a viable solution. "Terrific," I said. "We're on bikes," I informed him. "Any other ideas?"

He shuffled off to query the manager. In the interim, I pulled a tire off an overhead nail and scrutinized the fine print on the sidewall: 700 x 28C. Perfect! Coincidence? Luck? Or the universe lending a helping hand once again?

"Sorry," the clerk apologized on his return. "No stock," he confirmed. "We only carry 27-inchers."

"Okay," I said. "I'll take this one until you get some 700s."

"A 27-inch won't fit," he advised correctly, not realizing I had found the one 700 in his entire stock of 27-inch tires. "It's 4 millimetres too big." He frowned. "Or small. I forget which."

"That's okay," I smirked. "We carry a spare foldable rim in our parts bag."

The helpful couple transported us to the edge of town. They pulled over and let us out. But they didn't intend to just abandon us on the side of the road. Oh, no. That wouldn't be rural hospitality. The man hopped out, intent on flagging down a vehicle that would give us a lift back to where Sharon waited.

Within moments, a battered primer-grey pickup rushed toward us, travelling a hundred-plus kilometres an hour. Our good Samaritan recognized the clunker as belonging to a pal of his. He flew into the middle of the road, flapping his arms like a deranged gregarious aquatic duck on quack cocaine.

"And I thought the muck on Sharon's legs was bad," I muttered, squeezing my eyes shut, believing his goose was cooked.

Fortunately for him, the brakes were the one thing still working on the junker. A brief scream of tires punctuated the afternoon air and the pickup scrunched to a juddery halt — mere inches in front of our nearly flattened friend. *"Whew!"* Sue breathed. Still in a bit of a shock, I opened my peepers.

The next thing I knew, Sue and I were bouncing along on a ratty coils-poking-through bench seat next to a crusty old potato farmer. The old tuber, face pockmarked like a field ready for seed, had eyes only for Sue. "Yep," he bragged, "I sell potatoes all over Alberta. Hell," he said, puffing his chest out, "I even sell them to Idaho!" The potato bug jabbed a thick thumb toward his thorax and declared, "Some folks around here call *me* the King of Potatoes."

"If you play your cards right," I whispered to Sue, "you could end up the Queen of Spuds."

Minutes later, the farmer stopped where Sharon still waited. We thanked the tater king for coming along at the right time. I slammed the jalopy's door and noticed that Sharon's legs were free of green goo. She was sitting cross-legged in the ditch, reading. Her bike, oiled and polished, rested upside-down on its handlebars, awaiting the new tire.

"What took you guys so long?" Sharon blinked, standing and marking the page of her book with a spare tire patch.

"We almost had to walk to Lethbridge."

"Oh. In that case, you made good time."

We installed the new tire. "Looks good!" I said, pumping it to the recommended pressure. "Too bad I can't say the same about your 'no-flat' tube."

Gas City

> **"Into every life a little rain must fall, but I think someone's mistaken me for Noah."**
> ~ Allison Raul

We reached Bow Island at 7 PM and stalked into a convenience store to buy buns for our leftover chili (always better the second day).

We cycled to Centennial Park and claimed a picnic table to reheat the ground beef, tomatoes, and kidney beans. Just as we prepared to chow down, our spirits were dampened. Literally. The park sprinkler system sprang to life, drenching us, our bikes, our stove, our food, and everything else on the table.

We hustled our bikes out of the line of fire. Sharon eventually had enough of the wet madness and dashed to the nearest sprinkler. She couldn't turn it off, but she managed to turn the nozzle away from us. We portaged our entire picnic table, complete with cooking gear and supper bowls, to dry land. In a new spot we sat triumphantly, picturing the faces of morning park workers who would discover a picnic table sitting in the middle of the field and a sprinkler watering the parking lot.

But our happy victory was short-lived. Another sprinkler head popped up and began watering us.

We spent an unrelaxed mealtime being chased around the field as various watering zones popped to life. It was as if someone was intent on giving us our daily shower along with our daily bread.

Tired of dodging man-made rain, we set our tents inside a nifty little gazebo at the far end of the field. "Ah," I sighed, finally a dry haven."

But I was wrong. Around midnight, sprinklers surrounding the gazebo turned on full blast. Water pounded the roof; water shot in through doorways; water sprayed in through window openings; water seeped in through invisible crevices. It even dripped down the stovepipe. Still half-asleep, Sharon muttered, "Now I know what golfers mean by 'water hazard.'"

In the morning, a new battery of sprinklers tormented us. At least it got us off to an early start. Maybe we'd miss some of the hot wind that had blown us across southern Alberta?

Nope. Not a chance. As usual, wind and heat gained intensity throughout the morning. We rolled to a weary pause in Seven Persons (the number of people inhabiting the place?) and, following the smell of fresh baked bread, crept into Grandma's Bakery. We zeroed in on cinnamon buns hot from the oven. *Six* of the sugary beauties set us back less than the usual cost of one in the city! Devouring the rolls faster than a teacher handing out study hall to unruly students, I returned for another half-dozen. They disappeared quicker than a bunny in a magic show. (Only piggy embarrassment stopped me from returning a third time.)

Pedalling against a hot wind, an hour later we were in Gas City (Medicine Hat's nickname because of its plentiful natural gas). It was Wednesday. We had plenty of time before Sue's return flight on Sunday. Vicky was scheduled to rendezvous with us Thursday for a ride to Cypress Hills.

We headed for Gas City campground, situated at the top of a hill. Why do they do that? At the end of a day's ride, that's the last thing cyclists want to see! We struggled upwards in the blistering heat, perspiration pouring off our faces.

After checking in we hit the showers. I'm sure we came perilously close to depleting the cold water supply. Eventually, we reluctantly pried ourselves away from humankind's best ever invention. We hadn't been so clean since our mothers' used to wash our toes in the baby bath tub!

Next on our list was the air-conditioned laundry room (humankind's second and third best inventions).

As we emerged from the humidity and temperature controlled room the outside afternoon air hit us with a force equalling the opening of a door on a blast furnace. Worse, gazillions of annoying blackflies and sandflies inhabited the campground. The pests flew up our noses and set upon the corners of our eyes. After relieving us of mandatory pints of blood — and souvenir chunks of flesh — they zoomed away to get their buddies. There was no end to the winged clouds.

"I vote we abandon 'Gnat City' campground," Sharon suggested. Flailing our arms, smacking our legs, we biked off to explore the city's network of bike trails.

The route led us to Caroline's Restaurant. We entered and sat in great relief. No bugs. No heat. No hard bicycle seats. We wolfed down platters of nachos and sucked up buckets of ice tea like three well watered little pigs. Near midnight, we vacated Caroline's restaurant. Maybe the gnats would be asleep?

The return route was through an unlit and heavily treed, pitch-black park. It was an adventure in blindfolded cycling. Sharon and Sue must have thought so too. Choruses of *Three Blind Mice* rang from the darkness around me.

Thunder Breeding Grounds

> **"I would rather be ashes than dust! I would rather that my spark burn out in a brilliant blaze than it be stifled by dry-rot. I would rather be a superb meteor, every atom of me in magnificent glow, than a sleepy and permanent planet."**
>
> ~ Jack London

Stifling air roused us — the sun already well on its way toward popping the top off the old thermometer.

What better way to spend an unbearable hot summer day than at a ball game in the sweltering sun? We sat in the broiling sun, watching a grueling sweat match while stewing in our own juices.

"They should've used the bullfight arena pricing scheme," I complained by the fourth inning. "Seats in the sun: five bucks. Seats in the shade: ten bucks." Sue figured she'd have to phone her workplace and say she wasn't coming in because she had evaporated. I wondered if anyone had ever used *that* as an excuse before?

Vicky, lucky as usual, arrived at 8 PM, just as the day cooled.

The following morning, Vicky struck any chance of sleeping in. She roused us early, eager to ride. Good thing. The forenoon was already heating up: another day in Hades was in the making.

We invented several new terpsichorean activities while packing, fending off vexatious insects. On several occasions we buzzed to an enclosed shelter for a sanity break. Those little devils were driving us buggy!

We exited the campground, and discovered why we hadn't seen any cyclists on Medicine Hat's roads. Broken glass was everywhere. The cyclists' nemesis reared its pointy head and poked fun at Sue. "Maybe it should be nicknamed 'Glass City,'" I stated flatly, watching her change her front tire.

We escaped Glass City by a sliver, and soon caught up with a cyclist from Germany. Dirk's plan was to ride his mountain bike to Ontario. His biggest burden? An overstuffed teddy bear strapped to his rear rack to accompany him on his interprovincial journey. "For company," he said. "It gets lonely out here by myself." (The movie *Cast Away* bounced to mind, where Tom Hanks converses with Wilson, a volleyball, for years.)

Dirk told us he was averaging around 170 kilometres per day — about double our Alberta daily distance. "What do you eat to travel distances like that?" I asked, expecting to hear the sordid details of some Ironman triathlete concoction.

"Smarties!" he answered enthusiastically.

The five of us cycled a few kilometres, chatting, exchanging war stories. But Dirk's tempo was a lot slower than our usual pace (he must have been spending 12 hours a day in the saddle!). Our philosophy was to crank out the kilometres at a good pace; slow enough to smell the roses, yet fast enough to get somewhere. We didn't relish sitting on our bikes *all* day.

Sue, Vicky, and Sharon must have thought the same. They turned it up a notch, leaving Dirk and me staring after their rapidly disappearing backsides. I'd make some sort of crack here, but that would be rude.

"Those girls ride like animals!" Dirk declared reverently.

"Don't I know it," I replied. I bid him goodbye and blasted off, trying to catch up with the brutes.

The ride to Cypress Hills was a grueling, hot, gradual, uphill slog through lonesome prairie. The only sound was the whir of our wheels and that of an odd grasshopper panicked into flight by our passage. (I hated when they landed with their little suction cup feet on my bare legs. It always gave me a start.) The landscape was 100 percent treeless. The only vegetation was a few tufts of sad brownish-yellow bunch grass and a smattering of bone-dry sagebrush liberally coated in moon-like greyish dust.

"I'd never make a cowboy," Sue lamented, flicking her tongue across her pearly whites. "Even my teeth feel dusty."

Cattle, utterly exposed to the pitiless sun, looked as miserable as we felt. Scorched, sunburnt, they stood there, expressionless, forlorn, chewing their cud. They did their best to elude the sun's searing rays by taking turns huddling in shadows cast by fence posts. "Ineffective," Sharon mused. "Looks like a 300-pound fat man attempting to hide from his wife behind a pool cue."

"Yeah," I drawled, eyeing their parched state. "If a farmer tried to siphon those titties, he'd get evaporated milk."

We crested a rise and stared in disbelief at a forest so green it practically dripped with emeralds. A sapphire blue lake glittered vibrantly in the harsh afternoon sunlight. The contrast to the burnt and stark prairie we had just traversed was like comparing Earth's silky tropics to the barren vermilion sands of Mars.

A cool, sporadic breeze nuzzled our hot brows. "Hard to believe," Sharon spouted, drinking in the remarkable change of scenery. "A few minutes ago we were surrounded with nothing but bald prairie — the sole scenic highlight a dehydrated cow."

Cypress Hills Provincial Park spans a portion of the southern Alberta-Saskatchewan border. Not only is Head-of-the-Mountain there, the highest elevation in Canada between the Rockies and Labrador, Cypress Hills also contains fossils of camels, dinosaurs, marine mollusks, and other exotic extinct mammals like sabre-toothed cats.

French fur traders had named the hills. Historians theorize they mistook the lodgepole pine for Jack pine — 'cypre' in Metis and French Canadian. They called it 'Montages de Cypres' or 'Jack Pine Mountains.' The English translated it — wretchedly as usual — into Cypress. (Somewhat ironically, despite a wide variety of trees growing in the area, Cypress has never been one of them.)

"I still think the original Native name was better," Sharon said. "Thunder Breeding Hills." First Nations people believe Cypress Hills to be a great spiritual grounds: the place where weather is born. And indeed it is. The area has a precipitous manner of spawning sudden thunderstorms. Sure enough, growling on the horizon, hoary, pit-bull-shaped clouds were snarling into anvil-topped thunderheads.

Cypress Hills, or Thunder Breeding Hills, has a native history dating back several thousand years. First Nations people consider it a wondrous spiritual place, but its abundant water, wildlife, and trees provided for their physical needs. Campsite remnants have been dated back 6,000 years (probably congealed marshmallows).

But, as they say, that's not all. Cypress Hills has the distinction of being the birthplace of the world's most famous police force. In 1873, Cypress Hills was the site of a bloody massacre. The story goes that one evening American wolf hunters had some of their horses go missing. During a search of the area they discovered a group of Assiniboine camped nearby, and assumed the Indians had stolen their nags. A bloody battle ensued. The slaughter killed many Indians and one white man. Likely, because of the one white man's death at the hands of red savages, Sir John A Macdonald — Dominion of Canada's first prime minister — enacted a bill establishing the North West Mounted Police. Today, the world over knows them as the Mounties, or the Royal Canadian Mounted Police. With their arrival, many whiskey trading ports, such as Fort Whoop Up, were abandoned.

In the town of Elkwater, I checked my altimeter. "Hey, we've climbed 2,090 vertical feet since Medicine Hat," I announced.

"That's the most uphill I've ever ridden in one day," Sue said, mopping her brow.

"How do you feel?" I asked.

"Like I need a stretcher," she groaned. "Every bone in my body aches." Not her best day apparently. It would come though. Her riding had improved remarkably since our Jasper-Banff tour a couple of years before.

"Better make it a wheelchair," I kidded. "That way we can bungee it behind our bikes and tow you back if necessary."

We trooped into a grocery store to buy a dozen wieners and some buns. "Why do wieners come 12 to a pack, and buns 8?" Vicky lamented.

I shrugged. "Buy 24."

Vicky thought that a good idea, bought two dozen of each, and added a pillow-sized bag of marshmallows to our purchases — just to round out our healthy eating habits. "Something for around the campfire."

We headed for the 700 site campground. It looked like a veritable metal village; the weekend motor vehicle crowd already occupied most sites. "Would you guys like a walk-in site?" the attendant asked as we rolled up to the check-in booth.

"Sounds great!" I said. "Where are they located?"

"Oh," he replied, trying to sound nonchalant, "they're about 14 kilometres from here."

"Fourteen kilometres!" Sue exploded.

"Uphill," he added quietly.

"Uphill!" Vicky cried in indignation. I thought she was about to smite the clueless guy with the marshmallow pillow. The last word a cyclist wants to hear after a tough ride is "uphill."

"I don't think so!" Sharon declared.

"They're really secluded and they —"

"We'll take your closest site to the lake in the drive-in sites," I wisely cut in.

We rode *down* to our beautiful lakeside site. "Is it just my imagination," Vicky asked, "or are there fewer campfires now that people have to pay for wood?"

"It's not your imagination," Sharon confirmed. "There's definitely fewer. Smaller, too." The Alberta government had recently implemented a user-pay firewood fee. The year before, the park system had reportedly spent a million bucks on campfire wood.

"I don't know what the big deal is," I said. "Most government money goes up in smoke anyway."

We set up our tents, bought an armload of overpriced firewood, and roasted wieners. We used the coals to toast marshmallows, but made a rather smallish dent in the pillow. I was unlucky. Mine caught fire, and oozed off the stick.

"What do you call that?" Vicky laughed.

"Cajun," I answered. (No doubt some hapless archeologist 6,000 years in the future would be unfortunate enough to discover the sticky remains.)

To work off our feast, we hiked Firerock Trail. The trail twisted upwards through a maze of poplars and pines. A meadow, filled with blue and yellow wildflowers, provided a splendid foreground to the sparkling lake.

The sun set. A full moon, the colour of burnished copper, rose steadily in the east and guided us back to camp. Twinkling celestial bodies dotted the milky way like a thousand glistening sequins. "My gosh!" Vicky sputtered, staring upwards in wonder. "This is better than the Space Sciences Centre! I can't imagine what it must be like on a moonless night," she said, and spontaneously burst into a chorus of *Starry, Starry Night.*

We weren't back in camp more than 20 minutes, stoking the fire with our remaining few sticks of wood, intent on cremating more marshmallows, when evening entertainment began in an adjacent site. Standing beside a raging conflagration, orange flames licking the night sky, a Johnny Cash imitator wailed out twangy country and western ballads. "They must have brought their own wood," Vicky decided, as we moseyed over to join the assembling crowd as the flames rose higher.

By 10 PM, a large contingent of campers thronged round the burning ring of fire, listening to the guitar man's bawdy renditions. Everyone joined in for the rousing choruses. "This is better than television!" Vicky declared.

Around midnight, the fire died down and the last of the rowdies roved off. We returned to our site — with all the hootin' and hollerin' beforehand there hadn't been much sense trying to sleep. I entered our tent and laid my sleepy head next to the partially eaten bag of marshmallows. "I hope I don't have that dream," I muttered.

Black Lace

"The harder I work, the luckier I get."
~ Samuel Goldwyn

Our streak of early morning wake-ups ended. Well, sort of. The cool mountain air let us sleep in comfort; other campers, tuckered from the late night sing along, slept blissfully. All was peaceful. Even the usually raucous crows had taken the morning off. But do you think I could sleep? No way. After tossing for half an hour, I gave up and stumbled out of the tent to greet the sunrise.

Sue was in her familiar pose atop a picnic table, waiting for us. "You couldn't sleep either?" I asked, stifling a yawn.

"Nope," she frowned. "It was too nerve wracking ... just lying there, waiting for something to explode." She gave me a tight-lipped little smile.

We roused Vicky by collapsing her tent. "Time to get up, Sleepy Head! What do you think this is? Vacation?"

Vicky crawled forth. We packed and rode to a beach concession to fill our water bottles for the return trip to Medicine Hat. While Sue, Vicky, and Sharon strolled the abandoned lakeshore,

I strode to a trash barrel to dispose our rubbish and jelled bag of marshmallows. Opening the lid, a surprise winked back at me: a racy pair of women's black undies. A twisted smile creased my features. Not wishing to pass up such fine luck, I liberated the risqué darlings and slunk over to my cycling partners' bikes. I tied the panties off one side of Miss Vicky's panniers — the side facing traffic of course.

When the three wanderers returned, I contained my mirth (barely). We cycled through Elkwater, past gawking tourists. Riding behind Vicky, chuckling, I pointed out Vicky's secret acquisition. Several young men gave me wide grins and thumbs-up (I wondered if anyone recognized the X-rated attire?). If Vicky was curious why she was garnering so many admiring glances, she didn't let on. I guess she was used to it.

Then we were out on the open road, taking turns in front to break the slight headwind. It wasn't until Sharon drafted behind Vicky that my naughty addition was discovered.

"Vicky, what *is* that you have stuck to your panniers?" Sharon asked in a perplexed tone.

"Huh?!" Vicky snorted. She reached around and tugged the undies free. Then she cycled up and pinched my bum. Hard!

"Hey!" I wailed in mock innocence. "Why do you suspect it was *me?"*

The return trip to Medicine Hat rolled off at an average speed of 32 kilometres per hour. Sue pasted herself in the slipstream between Sharon and Vicky and whisked along with the greatest of ease — her best day ever! Compared to our previous day's dogged uphill and wind five hour grind, it only took two hours to get back.

A fat-filled meal (one of the four food groups — the other three, of course, being salt, sugar, and caffeine) finished our robust feat of physical prowess. We headed straight for a burger joint and ordered two each with double everything. Along with cholesterol laden burgers and salty fries, Sue and Vicky ordered diet soft drinks.

"You don't think that's gonna save ya, do you?" I snickered, ordering a Jolt cola with all the sugar as regular cola and twice the caffeine. Nothing better than a caffeine overdose after a hot ride in the sun.

On our return to 'Glass City' campground along Medicine Hat's glass strewn streets, Vicky and I both suffered flats (three of our four Alberta flats occurred in Medicine Hat). Each time we found tiny slivers of offending brown glass. Perhaps beer bottle deposit fees were too low?

"Those little brown bottles cause hangovers for cyclists!" Vicky hissed as her tire assumed a horizontal position with the pavement.

"I'll time you!" I challenged.

She needed no further provocation. Vicky flew into action. Total time: 4 minutes. Flat.

"You're a pro!" I said, duly impressed as she replaced the valve cover, ready to roll once more. We made it to the campground without another deflating episode.

After setting up the tents and showering, we scuttled off to our favourite hang out, Caroline's Restaurant. We had a marvellous time inhaling mountains of nachos slathered in thick cheese, sour cream and spicy salsa. Chips were merely means of conveying the piles of sticky goodness into our gaping maws. Cheery conversation flowed amongst litres of ice tea.

"Hear about the Indian that drank 40 cups of tea?" I asked after downing an unknown number of glasses of the amber liquid. "They found him the next morning, drowned in his teepee."

Sharon excused herself — my bad jokes and all that iced tea. There was a momentary lull. Vicky and Sue cast dour looks my way. "Why the long faces, chums?" I enquired.

"You guys are so lucky!" Sue said, pouting. "You're going to have such a great time in Europe."

"And *we're* going to be slaving away at work," Vicky sulked.

I was being double-teamed and didn't even know it. Like a lamb before wolves, I joked, "You could join us in Spain for a week in February. We'll probably need some company by then."

Like blackbirds spying a shiny object, their eyes brightened.

"Yeah!" they crowed in unison. I knew immediately I was in big trouble. I flagellated myself. *See what happens when you open your big mouth before engaging your tiny brain?*

My brows knit together like a Granny intent on breaking the Guinness record for afghan-making. How was I going to explain this little turn of events to Sharon? For the past few weeks, Vicky had been dropping pregnant hints in an attempt to finagle an invite for herself to join us somewhere en route. Relishing our free-spirit status, we had resisted rising to the bait. After all, who knew where we'd be from one day to the next — let alone months in advance. The best bike trips were often affairs of spontaneity ... unchained from timetables, rigid routing, and written-in-stone schedules. "Plan to be spontaneous" was our motto.

Instead of admitting to Sharon that I'd fallen for the second-oldest ruse after tears, maybe I could keep my unplanned invitation a secret? I'd save my blunder as a delightful surprise, for that blustery day somewhere in Spain when Sharon was feeling a tad homesick for the old gang ... I'd casually slip it into conversation: "Wouldn't it be great," I'd say, "if Sue and Vicky joined us for a week or two?" *Yeah,* I decided. *That sounds like a great plan!*

Sharon returned. "Guess what!" Vicky spouted before Sharon even sat down. "We're meeting you in Spain!"

So much for secrets.

Sharon scowled at me. I blinked in horror. Feeling lower than a snake's bellybutton, I wanted to slither under the table and hide in a dark corner.

Fortunately, no sharp knives were present – and I doubted Sharon could inflict permanent damage with a nacho chip. Dodging a murder-one look, I puckered my lips and pretended to be *extremely* engrossed with a gob of cheese stuck to my fingernail.

The discussion turned to dates. February turned out not to be good for them. "Too busy at work." Same with January. And, naturally, they wanted to be home at Christmas.

Let's see ... that left the last week in November and the first three in December. They set a date. Sunday, November 20, in Lisbon.

Oh, my! Way too much reality for me! Our carefree agenda of happy wanderlust crashed around my feet. We were committed to a rendezvous! Not in February. Not in Spain. Not for a week or two. November 20. Three weeks. Portugal. Be there or be square. Me, oh my.

Screech

> **"Flying a plane is no different from riding a bicycle. It's just a lot harder to put baseball cards in the spokes."**
> ~ Captain Rex Kramer, movie *Airplane!*

By half past seven Sunday morning it was already too hot to stay in the old nylon sweat lodge. Extra sleep out of the question, we packed up and rode to the Medicine Hat airport.

There, we removed Sue's bike pedals, and turned her handlebars sideways. The plane's underbelly cargo hold was so small we even had to remove the bike's front wheel. And still, the baggage person had a tight squeeze getting the bicycle in (you know you're flying a small airline when the luggage handler and the pilot are one and the same).

A crackly speaker announced final boarding call (at least the voice wasn't the pilot's). The four musketeers clapped each other in hearty goodbye hugs. "See you in Portugal!" echoed throughout the empty terminal.

The screech of rubber on tarmac jolted me from my reminisces. We were in France. I gazed out from our cozy confines at a never-ending skyline of grey drizzle. "Hmmm," I muttered, wondering if we were going to make it to Lisbon in three weeks to meet our cycling buddies.

Suzanne's Secret 7-Up Apple Pie Crust Recipe

INGREDIENTS:
2 cups flour
1 pinch salt
1/2 teaspoon baking powder
2/3 cup Becel margarine
(Suzanne says the best Becel is from Québec
because they don't put any colour additives in it)
1/3 cup 7-Up

DIRECTIONS:

In a large mixing bowl combine flour, salt and baking powder. Cut in Becel margarine. Mix with a pastry blender until mixture resembles coarse crumbs. Sprinkle in 7-Up a little at a time, stirring with a fork until the dry ingredients are well moistened. Shape mixture into a ball and chill for half an hour. On a lightly floured surface roll out half of the pastry to about 1/8-inch thickness. Put into a 9-inch pie pan. Prick crust with a fork. Bake for a couple of minutes until lightly brown. Roll remaining pastry to 1/8-inch thickness for the pie's top and set aside until needed.

7-Up Apple Pie Recipe

INGREDIENTS:
4 tablespoons all-purpose flour
pinch of salt
3/4 cup sugar
1/2 teaspoon nutmeg
3/4 teaspoon cinnamon
1 tablespoon lemon juice
3 tablespoons 7-Up
6 cups of peeled and sliced tart apples (best
if stolen from neighbour's tree)
Secret 7-Up pastry (above, shhh)
2 tablespoons butter
1 tablespoon milk

DIRECTIONS:

In a large bowl combine flour, salt, sugar, nutmeg, cinnamon, lemon juice and 7-Up. Toss in apples and coat with mixture. Put apples into secret 7-Up pastry. Dot apples with butter. Place top pastry over filling. Trim edge. Pinch edge to seal. Cut a few 1-inch slits to allow steam to escape. Brush top with milk; Suzanne likes to sprinkle some sugar on top, too. Cover edges of crust with foil and bake at 425° Fahrenheit for 25 minutes. Remove foil and bake another 15 minutes or until lightly browned. Cool for a bit. Yield: 1 pie for your favourite cyclist!

About the Author

Neil met Sharon when he was living in Edmonton, Alberta. Sharon was an avid touring cyclist; Neil an affirmed petrol head with three cars.

After some introductory foibles, Neil and Sharon began going out in earnest (even though Sharon's good friends weren't overly enthralled that Sharon was going out with a non bike rider. How could anything like *that* last?) But Neil liked Sharon — she always laughed at his silly jokes — and once he made up his mind about something, he was like a pit bull on a postman....

In fact, the poor sod had fallen so hard that one Saturday he borrowed a friend's old clunker of a ten speed (it actually had only three usable gears — not that that mattered much since Neil didn't dare take his hands off the handlebars to shift anyway).

Sharon acquainted Neil with the local bike paths. My gosh! What tough work! Edmonton's bike trails are located in the North Saskatchewan's scenic river valley, meandering peacefully alongside the placid waterway. Or so Neil thought. Sharon, jokester that she is, took Neil from the west end of the city to its east end, and back, a distance of perhaps 40 kilometres. For Neil — who had never been on a bike much in his life — it seemed an *incredibly* long way.

The trails undulated, with some vigorous ups and fraught-with-peril downs. Neil became so worn out that on one steep downhill stretch he just let his bike roll headlong, going faster and faster, until he was careening recklessly out of control toward a sharp corner. (I think he believed that if he crashed, at least his jelly-legged, butt-numbing bike ride from Hades would be over.)

Fortunately, his days as a motorcycle rider saved his skin. Neil leaned perilously, but somehow made it around the corner. When he eventually made it back home, weary, wobbly, and darn near done in, smitten or not, Neil declared he would forever and nevermore go on any bike rides.

Little did he know ...